Exceptional Trading:
The Mind Game

Ruth Barrons Roosevelt

TRADERS PRESS®
PO BOX 6206
GREENVILLE, SC 29606

Books and Gifts for
Traders and Investors.

ISBN #0-934380-54-6

Published July 1999
by
Traders Press, Inc.®

Reprinted 2001

Editing, Layout and Cover Design by
***Teresa Darty Alligood,* Editor and Graphic Designer**

TRADERS PRESS®
PO BOX 6206
GREENVILLE, SC 29606

Books and Gifts for
Traders and Investors.

I dedicate this book to my clients
—past, present and future—
who discover the power
to overcome and excel
in trading and in living.

Biography

Ruth Barrons Roosevelt coaches traders around the world to trading excellence. She is exceptionally well qualified to offer such guidance to traders, as she herself has extensive trading experience and is to this day an active trader. Her experience covers multiple time frames, from position trading in virtually ever futures market, to active and intense intraday trading in currencies, T-bonds, and S&P futures. She has traded S&P's extensively and actively since inception of trading in 1984, down to and including 1 minute bars. Her trading experience also includes active trading of mutual funds.

She is a former Vice President of PRUDENTIAL SECURITIES and of THOMPSON MCKINNON. From 1981 to 1986 she headed the INTERNATIONAL MONEYLINE TRADING DESK at RUDOLF WOLF (New York). Before that she was a stock and futures broker at DREXEL BURNHAM LAMBERT where she broke records by opening 250 accounts in one month. A graduate of the UNIVERSITY OF MICHIGAN LAW SCHOOL, she is a member of the New York and California Bar Association. A frequent contributor to Technical Analysis of Stocks and Commodities, she writes articles on the psychology of successful trading. She is the coauthor of Living In Step (MCGRAW HILL, 1976). As founder and director of the WALL STREET HYPNOSIS CENTER, she works with Wall Street professionals to achieve their optimal effectiveness.

Ruth has appeared on numerous national and international television programs including: CBS, NBC, CNN, and WWOR EVENING NEWS, CNBC, NBC THE TODAY SHOW, GOOD MORNING AMERICAN, JAPAN PUBLIC TELEVISION, NIPPON TELEVISION, HUNGARIAN PUBLIC TELEVISION, FINLAND TELEVISION CHANNEL 3, and the DAVID LETTERMAN LATE NIGHT SHOW. She has been profiled for her work with traders in *Business Week, Barron's, The New York Times, New York Magazine, The Independent of London, The Toronto Star,* and many other publications.

Ruth Barrons Roosevelt, J.D.

165 William Street
New York, NY 10038
1-800-692-0080
fax: 212-732-3482
http://www.RuthRoosevelt.com

Preface

This book is written to give traders a winning edge. Winning eludes some 80 to 90 percent of people who trade.

Each year millions of dollars are spent creating and buying and selling trading systems. Hopeful traders seek the holy grail only to find that their latest acquisition doesn't work or they can't work it. Information flow is instant and vast. Computers calculate and grind out data 24 hours a day around the globe. Every conceivable edge is sought and provided. And still traders lose.

The rules for good trading are simple and understandable: Buy low, Sell high, or buy high and sell higher. Sell low and buy lower. Cut your losses. Let your profits run. Never overtrade. Act promptly on signals to enter and exit. Trade a proven winning system or strategy as it was designed to be traded; i.e., take every signal and stay the course. Control and balance fear and greed.

But traders don't follow the rules, not even the rules they commit to following. As the Book of Common Prayer says, "That which I would not do, that I do." The prayer goes on to say, "And there is no health in me." It's a simple human condition which becomes writ large in trading.

The good news is that some traders do win. They win consistently over time. Success leaves clues. This book examines the clues and shows traders seeking to win how to run their own minds the way winning traders do.

It's not enough to simply know how to think or what to think. It's important to do it. This book outlines proven techniques for making the necessary mind shifts that will enable a trader to create a mental winning edge. Trading is, after all, mind over markets, quick action, clear thinking, and an unclouded intent to win.

Table of Contents

- **Chapter Eight**
  UNCOUPLING YOUR EGO
  Egoless trading. Building boundaries between oneself and ones trading. The difference between walls, no boundaries and healthy boundaries. Becoming more than the trading.

- **Chapter Nine**
  REPROGRAMING THE
  SOFTWARE OF THE MIND
  Directing attention and focus. Using power questions. A new approach to affirmations. Positive worry. Taking control of self-talk. Rewriting your script. Using the trading trance for success. Self-hypnosis.

- **Chapter Ten**
  THE PHYSIOLOGY OF EXCELLENCE
  Physiology: the short cut to power trading. Posture. Breathing. Facial expression. Anchoring kinesthetically for calm and confidence. The quieting reflex. The relaxation response. The importance of exercise and nutrition.

- **Chapter Eleven**
  YOUR OFFICE
  The importance of environment. Taking control. Power suggestions for floor traders. Cleaning out clutter. Setting up for success. Screen and phone placement. Electromagnetic considerations. Air cleansing. Lighting. Sounds. Feng Shui. Privacy.

- **Chapter Twelve**
  THE CONFIDENT TRADER
  Trading in trust. Handling drawdowns. Turning failure into feedback. Using mistakes to grow. Developing consistency. Trading rules or guidelines. The evolution of better and better. Serenity Prayer

CHAPTER I

COMMITMENT TO TRADING EXCELLENCE

"Always bear in mind that your own resolution to success is more important than any other one thing."

—Abraham Lincoln

"Make no small plans...They have no magic to move men's blood."

—the architect and city planner of Chicago in 1913

About a dozen years ago one morning before the markets opened, I was leaning over one of my screens, immersed in studying charts with one of my assistants when I heard a voice standing over me saying, "My name is Michael McCarthy, and I want to be a technical trader." I looked up to see an attractive young blonde man holding a piece of paper by the corner, that turned out to be his resume. He went on, "My professor at NYU told me you were looking for an assistant, and I thought I'd get here before the others did."

My assistant jumped up and said, "Sit down." He was leaving New York City to move to Houston, Texas, and I suppose I'd made him feel guilty about leaving. This possible replacement looked like a Godsend to him. Michael was very clear about what he wanted. He wanted to be a successful technical trader. I had some requirements as well, so I asked him to sit down at another desk while the markets were opening and write down what he wanted on one side of a piece of paper, what he thought I wanted, and what he could do for me, on the other side. He was equally as clear about what he was able and willing to do for me as he was about the skills he himself wanted to develop.

Today, Michael is managing over $250,000,000 and has been ranked as the number one Market Timer by **Moni Research** for the past three years. The money that I have given him to manage has more than quadrupled in the space of a few years.

Exceptional trading requires a clear and purposeful commitment. It doesn't happen just by chance or with a half-hearted try it and see. Oh sure, you could win a few trades, but consistently profitable trading requires a different kind of engagement. You need to consciously commit yourself and your resources to developing a winning trading strategy, to installing a valid money management approach, and to achieving self-mastery as a trader. These are the three pillars on which successful trading resides.

Pillar number one is a proven strategy for making trading decisions as to whether and when to enter and exit the market. The strategy can be fundamental, technical, intuitive or a combination of the above, and it includes entry, reentry, and exiting with a profit and with a loss. Most unsuccessful traders think this is all they need as they search for the elusive Holy Grail of trading systems. In truth, however, a valid strategy is only the beginning.

The second pillar is a sound money management policy. It's important to risk only a small percentage of your capital on any one trade or idea. If you're right 99% of the time, but you risk everything on a single trade, you'll lose all your money on that 1% when you're wrong. Furthermore, if you risk fifty cents to make a dollar, you'll break even if you're only right 34% of the time. Money management is vital to successful trading, and is an area where many traders go wrong.

The third pillar is self-management. You need self-understanding and self-discipline as a trader so you can execute your trading strategy and money management policy in a timely and consistent fashion. Your market understanding plus your money management multiplied by self-mastery equals your results. Always remember that the you factor is your multiplier. Your trading will topple off the first two pillars without self-mastery, make no mistake about it. This book is dedicated to that essential third and multiplier effect of your trading.

Without all three of these trading elements in place your trading results are dependent on fickle luck, and that won't last. It may get you into trading, but it won't keep you there. You need to know what to do and do what you know, and you need to do it in a timely and consistent way because trading is based upon a series of probabilities. Those who are timid or rash when faced with probabilities sooner or later become a statistic in the casualties of trading.

TRADING OLYMPICS

The place to begin is with an unequivocal commitment to trading excellence. Consistently profitable trading is as possible and as rare as winning an Olympic medal. Nobody expects to go to the Olympics without an all out dedication and without training and practice. Trading requires an equally powerful dedication. It requires an engagement of capital, equipment, time, training, preparation, and the constant and unending development of interpersonal skills.

Tara Lapinski, the U.S. gold medal winner of the women's figure skating in 1998 Winter Olympics set her dream and commitment at a very early age. When she was two years old she stood atop a Tupperware container holding a fake bunch of flowers and wearing an imitation gold metal as she listened to the television playing the national anthem for the real American gold medal winner. She knew what she wanted at age 2 and realized it 13 years later at age 15. She didn't get there by just pretending: the dream was backed up by discipline. She supported her vision with hard work and total commitment—coaching, training, visualizing, day in and day out, year in and year out, in short an unending dedication by herself and her parents to take her to that level of physical and mental excellence that would one day win her an olympic gold medal.

It has always amazed me that many professional people—dentists, internists, surgeons, psychiatrists, engineers, or business people—who have spent years studying, training, learning and developing their profession or craft, in other words total immersion and commitment to excellence—display a very different attitude towards trading. They assume—and this amazes me—that trading is easy, that they can, because of who they are, excel at trading by just going out and buying a system, or researching a system, or following their intuition. Power trading takes more, much much more.

It further astounds me that some individuals think they can make a living trading off a $10,000 account. Usually they end up losing their $10,000 and their self-respect. Under capitalization, under preparation, under training are signs of an insufficient commitment.

Others may spend years developing a method only to find out that when they're ready to begin trading, they can't pull the trigger. They can't commit their capital to their strategy. I have spoken with many people caught in this trap, and yet they not only can't commit their capital to the actual process of trading, they can't invest in personal psychological coaching to take them out of their immobility. Because they are unwilling or unable to invest in their personal improvement, they condemn themselves to continue, day after day, with their noses pressed up against the glass, watching their systems make money while they do nothing and make nothing. Their commitment to trading is incomplete and extends only to developing a methodology which, of course, is insufficient.

Being successful at anything requires commitment, persistence, practice, and usually coaching. A colleague of mine is a mental coach for Olympic athletes. He works with athletes to help them with their mental preparation, mental rehearsal, and attitude adjustment alongside the physical coach who concentrates on the physical training. Like any athlete, Olympic athletes need practice, focus, subconscious skills, and the expectation of winning.

Olympic athletes have extraordinary mental discipline and control. They train their whole lives for one event. At that moment they can't be distracted by thoughts of failure or any other thoughts. You cannot train for the Olympics with a haphazard mental approach or with a lackadaisical attitude. Before my colleague takes on the mental coaching of an athlete, he asks a series of questions to determine the athlete's commitment to total success and the likelihood of success.

I have reworked these questions for traders who want to work with me. Because traders are in the World Money Arena, a winning trader needs the same level of commitment and coaching as an Olympic athlete. The following are the questions I ask of those traders whom I mentally coach. Consider each question and answer it honestly by writing in the space provided to determine your own level of commitment to trading success.

One. Are you willing to sacrifice other things to excel in trading?

____

Two. Do you really want to become an outstanding trader?

____

Three. Will you never let up or give up in your achievement of success?

____

Four. Are you willing to take personal responsibility for mistakes and work hard to correct them?

____

Five. Are you willing to give 100% effort in trading preparation?

____

Six. Are you willing to give 100% effort in actual trading?

____

Seven. Are you willing to fund your trading business with sufficient trading capital? Are you willing to invest sufficient capital in your own personal development, your strategic trading development, and the necessary trading tools and equipment?

Eight. Are you willing to stick with it even through drawdowns?

Nine. Do you feel more committed to improvement in your trading than anything else?

Ten. What do you want from your trading?

"Men are great only if they are determined to be so."
—Charles de Gaulle

What would greatness in trading be for you?

A CLEAR COMMITMENT BACKED BY ACTION AND MORE ACTION

"The world can only be grasped by action, not by contemplation...the hand is the cutting edge of the mind."
—Jacob Bronowski

A commitment is made by deciding to do something and deciding to do it despite any difficulty, against all odds, and following it up with action. It's always important after making a decision to take a concrete action and seal it with a plan of action.

If you say, "I'd like to be a consistently successful trader," or "I'd like to have a trading strategy that puts the odds in my favor and gives me an edge," that is not enough. It's no more useful than saying, "I'd like to have $100,000 trading capital." "I'd like to lose weight." "I'd like to stop smoking." This won't do it. It's simply a wish and becomes part of your wish list. No. A commitment is a determination to go for it, to do whatever it takes to succeed, and to cut yourself off from the alternatives, the excuses, the delays. A commitment means raising your standards to excellence and being willing to pay the price for that excellence.

"The moment one definitely commits oneself, then Providence moves, too."
—Johann Wolfgang Von Goethe

First, decide what you want. Second, take action. Third, pay attention to what is working and what is not working. Fourth, keep changing your approach until you get what you want. This is your prescription for success.

One of the presuppositions of **NLP (Neuro-Linquistic-Programing)** is that there is no such thing as failure. There is only feedback. As a trader, there is no need to fail. You simply take each setback as vital information that will help you to learn and adjust. You can use mistakes as your ladder to ultimate success. But to turn failure into feedback, you need to take full responsibility for what happens and be open and flexible enough to change what you're doing. In nature that mechanism that is most flexible survives the longest.

Despite what the systems mongers say, successful trading is not as easy as falling off a log or simply buying the next system that comes along.

Commitment to excellence in trading is one way to avoid falling into the 80%. Let me give you another formula for success in trading.

Find out what works.

Verify that it works.

Do it.

If what you are doing stops working, use the information to make adjustments and test it until you once again find out what works, verify that it works, and you can then do it.

Remember the famous comment of Thomas Edison when questioned why he didn't give up after failing so many times to make a light bulb. He pointed out that he hadn't failed but rather had identified those ways that would not work.

"I am not discouraged, because every wrong attempt discarded is another step forward."

—Thomas Edison

"Many of life's failures are people who did not realize how close they were to success when they gave up."

—Thomas Edison

Of course, in trading, your time and your money are very definitely finite factors. Both can run out. You need to run your trading as a business and make hard business decisions as you go along.

For some, trading is merely a hobby or a sport. This is okay, but you need to recognize it, and set your expectations accordingly. Do you want to make money or do you just want to watch the markets and play a little?

"If you don't know where you're going, you'll be lost when you get there."

—Yogi Berra

The legends of outstanding traders are replete with stories of repeated setbacks or wipeouts on the way to success. Failure can be defined as giving up on your goals. Super traders pick themselves up, dust themselves off, get another stake and proceed again, confident that the next time they will succeed.

Linda Bradford Raschke is one such trader. At the age of 22 she experienced a dramatic trading setback, and yet she remained confident she could make the money back. As she says in Jack Schwager's, *The New Market Wizards.* [1]

"I don't want to make light of this experience, because it was intimidating being faced with a mountain of debt at the age of twenty-two. In fact, I still had $10,000 in debt left over from college student loans. Fortunately, I was able to find another backer, and everything worked out. Overcoming that experience gave me the confidence that I could overcome anything that might happen in the future."

I met Linda Bradford Raschke at a **TAG Conference** where we were both speaking. We hit it off right away. She's a delightful person. I had read about her in Jack Schwager's book. Linda began her trading as a floor trader, first at the **Pacific Coast Stock Exchange** and later at the **Philadelphia Stock Exchange**. Now she trades from an office at home. I was pleased that she agreed to be interviewed for this book.

When I told her that the first chapter in my book was about commitment, her response was as follows:

Linda: "You can't want to be a successful trader and say, 'Oh yes, I'll make a commitment.' It has to be a commitment with feeling, with passion. You have to want to make that commitment so much that you don't need anybody to tell you to make that commitment. If you need somebody to tell you, 'Hey, you need to make a commitment,' you aren't there. If you tell yourself that kind of stuff, uh uh, you aren't there."

But commitment is easy if you love trading or any other activity. I asked Linda how her trading had changed over the years:

Linda: "When I started out I was on the trading floor, making markets. That's much different from sitting upstairs. I would say that I'm probably not as intense as I used to be about it. I used to put myself under a lot more stress while trading. I used to not be able to take a vacation. I think I went for ten years and always had a position on. Imagine ten years of your life always having sophisticated options positions in the market that needed adjusting. That's a lot."

Ruth: "Yes it is. Was it an attitude that you would always stay in the market because you couldn't make money if you weren't in there? Or what would keep you from just taking all the options positions off and going on a vacation?"

Linda: "Well, two things. It's like riding a tiger. It's not that easy to just get off! It's not that easy just to liquidate, and you're very much caught up in the game. Sometimes, even now, for a couple of days I'll have one small position on. It's meaningless, but it keeps me mentally in the game."

Ruth: "It's good to keep yourself in the game so you don't extract yourself from the process."

Linda: "Yes. Something's missing if I don't have any positions on. You know. Naked." (She laughs).

Ruth: "Sure I understand that. Once it was a 4th of July weekend, and it was going to be a long weekend and I felt like a plug had been pulled or something. It's a strange thing." And then I said, "Well, what is this?"

Commitment comes easily when you love trading. In fact, commitment is the natural outflow when you become involved with trading and your identity is intertwined with being a trader. I asked Michael McCarthy if he'd ever thought of quitting trading.

Michael: "Let me answer that in two parts. Quitting managing money, possibly. Quitting being in the securities business, the Wall Street thing, never. I'll do this until I'm dead. Happily. I'll be trading until I'm 90. It keeps me on the ball. This is my thing."

"Will I always have a money management business? Will I always have clients? Not necessarily. There's a great hassle with being a market timer. You have a lot of negatives. Funds don't want the money. You have regulatory issues, and you have to fill out a lot of paperwork for the regulatory agencics. And that does not aid my development. There are administrative issues that I could envision getting rid of for my peace of mind. I don't think I would because there are too many people who depend on me. If things got really unsavory, if the returns were still good in my opinion, but the clients didn't think they were good, and I was having regulatory issues, I might just say the negatives were outweighing the positives. I would go off and trade my own money. But I don't think I'd ever throw in the towel and say I'm going to go and be a doctor now. I don't think that would ever happen."

ESTABLISHING GOALS

It's easy to go on when you have a passion for trading, when you love what you do, and can do what you love. But in addition to loving it, you need a clear vision of where you're going and of the incredible rewards that trading holds. The past supports you with its myriad of learnings. Your envisioned future compels you towards it.

A survey was done many years ago at **Yale University**. Only 3% of the graduating class had written goals for their lives. Years later this 3% of graduates had made more money than the entire rest of the graduating class combined. Goals count because they're a target and they set the standard.

Get clear about your trading goals and what you're going to do to get there. Commit them to writing, and also write out what you're willing to do to get there. You need to decide what you want and whether you're willing to pay the price to get there.

Your goals become your guiding lights as well as your task master.

THE PRICE

"If A is success in life, then A equals x plus y plus z. Work is x; y is play; and z is keeping your mouth shut."

—Albert Einstein

"The only place where success comes before work is in the dictionary."

—Proverb

A goal is worthless if you're not willing to pay the price to get there. What is the price of becoming an exceptional trader?

First, there's a money price. You have to have risk capital and to be willing to put it at risk. You have to be willing to let it go. That doesn't mean you just pour your money down the rathole, or you throw your money at any idea that comes along, or that you put all your money behind a single idea. You need to have firm money management constraints and clearly defined rules for predetermined risk, but you can't clutch your money either. **Misers don't make good traders.**

Like any business you need to invest in it. That means you'll invest in computers and information sources, in learning how to trade, in an optimal place to trade. You'll also invest in yourself, in getting the necessary coaching to get yourself into the capacity for peak performance.

You need to invest your time. You need to do your homework, to be prepared. You need to give yourself the time to verify your methods. You need to give yourself the time to be able to focus your full attention while you trade. You need to dedicate the time for self-improvement, for personal growth.

There's also an energy cost. You need to come energized to your trading. You also need to rebuild your energy at the end of the trading day and week. Later in the book we'll talk about ways to do this.

WALT DISNEY STRATEGY

It was said that when Walt Disney went into a meeting, his business associates never knew whether he'd be playing the role of the dreamer, the realist, or the critic.

It is interesting to note that this highly successful man had the versatility to play all three roles. Each of the three roles was necessary to create his empire.

In his book *Strategies of Genius*, [2] Robert Dilts analyzes Walt Disney's strategy for success. The theory (and the reality) is that if a strategy works for one person, it can work for others, and so we analyze the strategies of successful people so that we can use them in our own lives. Let's take a look at Walt Disney's strategy.

THE DREAMER

First you become the dreamer. Allow yourself to dream and dream big. Far too many adults stint themselves in this aspect of creation or have stopped dreaming altogether. Allow yourself to relax with your posture symmetrical and gaze up at the ceiling as you ask yourself, *"What do I want to do?"* (The question is stated positively. You're not asking yourself what you want to stop doing, avoid doing or quit doing.) As you ask yourself this question, **take the attitude that anything is possible.** Do it now. Relax. Look up at the ceiling and answer the questions. Write down your answers.

***What** do you want to do and **what** do you want to do as a trader?*

___

___

Why do you want to do it? What is the overall and overriding purpose?

___

What are the payoffs? How will you know when you really have them? When can you expect to get them?

___

___

Where do you want trading to get you in the future?

___

___

Who do you want to be like in relationship to your trading?

___

THE REALIST

Now that you've done the dreaming about ***what*** you want, it's time to become the realist. The realist also takes the attitude that the dream is achievable, and from this point of view the realist asks questions about ***how*** all this can be implemented. Become the realist now. Assume a symmetrical posture leaning slightly forward and with your head and eyes looking straight ahead assuming the attitude that the dream is possible and achievable, ask yourself the questions. Write down your answers.

How specifically will your dream and your trading dream be implemented?

How will you know that you're on track with your goal?

How will the performance criteria be tested?

Will others be involved with your trading?

When will each phase be carried out? When will the overall goal be completed?

Where will each phase be carried out?

Why is each step necessary?

THE CRITIC

Now and only now is it time to become the critic. It's important that the critic stand back and let the dreamer and the realist do their work first. If the critic gets in there too soon, the dreaming and planning get hampered.

The critic looks at the dream and the plan and looks for areas where problems might arise. The attitude of the critic is a ***what if*** attitude—what if difficulties arise? The critic looks for what's missing and what might need to be changed. While the dreamer asks ***what***, and the realist asks ***how***, the critic asks ***why***?

Take the role of the critic now. Look down with your head down and tilted and your posture angular and ask yourself the questions. Write down your answers.

Why might someone object to this trading plan?

Who will the trading affect and who will make or break the effectiveness of the idea and what are their needs and payoffs?

____

____

Under what circumstances would you want to stop the trading and reevaluate?

____

____

What positive things do you get out of your current ways of doing things? How can you keep those things when you implement the new trading approach?

____

____

As a critic, you want to be a constructive critic, not destructive. It's useful to acknowledge what criteria have already been met before commenting on what's missing or needed. It is also useful to formulate criticisms as questions as much as possible.

Is the critic's basic criticism to the dream or to the plan? What is the positive intention behind the criticism? Turn the criticism into a question. Turn the question into a HOW question. Are you asking the question of the dreamer or the realist? Are you asking the question in such a way that the dreamer or the realist can understand it?

You can then go back and forth between dreamer, realist, and critic as you flesh out your dream and your plan.

BUILDING A CREDIBLE AND COMPELLING FUTURE

"If you limit your choices only to what seems possible or reasonable, you disconnect yourself from what you truly want, and all that is left is a compromise."
—Robert Fritz

"You have the power within you to attract to yourself all that you could ever want."
—Wayne W. Dyer

A dream and a plan have no power unless you believe it is possible for you to achieve them. For a dream to be a magnet you need to make it your future reality. If you don't think you can achieve a dream or goal, you'll be unwilling to lean into it, to take action, to correct the action, and to take more action. Things won't get done in the right way. You might find yourself taking broker's tips. Or buying system after system just to junk it. Or saying, "What the heck, I'll just buy/sell it and see what happens."

If deep down, you don't believe you can be a consistently profitable trader, you'll find yourself doing things in a self-defeating way and building small failures on top of each other. You'll take dangerous short cuts, or involve yourself deeply in pointless research. You'll find yourself losing self-esteem because you're not achieving your goals. Lots of traders don't set goals because they feel better with no goals than with failed goals. If you truly don't believe the full achievement of a dream is possible, it is merely a taunt and a source of frustration, a delusion.

One way to install a belief in your future is to write a one-page movie script of your life the way you want it to be. You set the scene, craft the words, and describe the emotions. It's a short slice of your life a year or so from now with your dream fulfilled. Then read the script every morning and every evening. Imagine it occurring. Let in the sights, the sounds, and the feelings. Soon you'll begin to believe it, and your actions will automatically support your vision.

[1] *The New Market Wizards*, Jack D. Schwager, Harper Business, 1992, ISBN 0-88730-587-3

[2] *Strategies of Genius,* Robert Dilts, Meta Publications, 1994, ISBN 0-916990-32-X

CHAPTER II

WINNERS AND LOSERS: A PSYCHOLOGICAL PORTRAIT

"If we keep making these mental errors, then you're leaving it to chance. When you leave it to chance, then all of a sudden you don't have any more luck."
—Pat Riley, Coach of Miami Heat

It's a cliche, and like most cliches, it's true. Too true. The vast majority of people lose money trading futures. The number of losers is ranked somewhere between 80% to 90%. Yet some people almost always make money trading futures—if you take the long view. What is the difference?

The difference that makes the difference is the mindset of the winning trader. It's a proven fact that psychological makeup is the major factor that makes or breaks a person as a trader. Learning to run your mind and your emotions is the single most important key to your trading results. Your own deep psychology is the multiplier of your trading profits and losses.

Trading is mind over markets. Good judgment and quick reaction to the information received. Most traders today are linked to the same information sources; it is how they respond to this information that separates winners from losers.

PROFILE OF A WINNING TRADER

A winning trader takes the time to find out how to trade profitably, then verifies that the strategy makes money over time, and finally without conflict and undue stress simply applies the stratagem. Because a winning trader has verified that his strategy works, he trusts it. He believes that money can and should be made in the markets. He believes in himself. He trusts himself to execute his strategy without a hitch. He trusts himself to respond to market action, knowing that he can handle anything that comes up. A winning trader believes the information that the market offers him and is willing to change his mind. A winning trader maintains discipline even through up and down periods. By believing in probabilities and lining them up, a winning trader seeks to rigorously exceed the odds. A winning trader has a clear, conflict free mind. He has a clear intention to trade and to make money trading. He trusts the trading process, and what's more, he loves the whole business of trading.

That's a rough thumbnail sketch. Now, let's break it down and look closely at some specific psychological attributes of winning traders.

WINNING TRADERS ARE OPTIMISTIC

Winning traders are optimistic about the future of their trading. They are confident about the next trade and the next trade and the next trade. They look forward to getting on with it. Their internal running commentary is encouraging. They paint positive pictures of their trading. They sort for opportunity, and since this is their focus, they find it.

Winning traders have a vision of future success. They look forward to an increasing equity curve. They anticipate doing wonderful things with that money.

Being optimistic about the future of their trading, they are able to look realistically at what is going on right now. Trading is viewed as a series of probabilities. They've stacked the probabilities in their favor, so no one trade has undue importance. In the words of **Tom Basso,** ***"Each new trade is but the first of the next 1,000 trades."***

Martin Seligman writes brilliantly about the role of optimism and pessimism in his book ***Learned Optimism.***[1] In the book he states that it's the way people think about the causes of their successes and failures that really matters. Your explanatory style is what makes the difference.

When a good thing happens to an optimist, the optimist says that it's *permanent, pervasive and personal.* When an optimist has a good trading day in one market, he will assume that this will continue in this and all markets and will consider the results to be due to personal skills. The optimist will say, "That's me alright. I'm a good trader, and I can continue to do this, here and in other markets as well."

When a good thing happens to a pessimist, he says that it's *temporary, specific, and not personal.* When a pessimist has a good trading day in one market, he will assume that it was just chance, that it won't happen again, and that it won't happen in other markets. The pessimist will say, "I got lucky. It probably won't happen again."

When a bad thing happens to a pessimist or optimist, the reverse explanation is utilized.

The optimist says it's just temporary, specific to that situation, and caused by external factors. When an optimist has a losing month trading a particular market, he will consider it to be only a temporary situation, peculiar to that market at that time, and due to causes outside himself. "I'm a good trader. This was due to X and that will change. The drawdown is temporary. I'll make it back soon."

The pessimist will say it's permanent, universal, and personal. After a losing month of trading, the pessimist will say, "I'm a terrible trader. It's impossible to make money in any market, and this losing streak will probably continue."

The same events are given different explanations. Permanent *vs. Temporary*. Universal *vs.* Specific. Personal *vs.* Impersonal. An optimist expects good things to continue, bad things to stop. A pessimist expects bad things to continue, and good things to stop.

An optimist views good things as pervasive and bad things as isolated events. A pessimist sees bad things as pervasive and good things as unique, specific events. The optimist believes that bad events have specific outside causes, while good events will enhance everything he does. The pessimist believes that bad events have universal causes and that good events are caused by specific extraneous factors. People who make universal explanations for their failures give up on everything when a failure strikes in one area. ***"People who make specific explanations may become helpless in that one part of their lives yet march stalwartly on in others,"*** writes Seligman.

The pessimist and optimist personalize events differently. The optimist interprets misfortune as externally caused and good fortune as internally caused; whereas the pessimist blames himself for causing the misfortune and interprets good fortune as due to outside forces. When unfortunate things occur, one can blame oneself (internalize) or one can blame other people or circumstances (externalize). People who blame themselves when they fail have diminished self-esteem as a consequence. They think they are worthless, untalented, and unlovable. People who blame external events maintain self-esteem when bad events strike.

Winning traders are optimistic about the broad scope of their trading. They are, however, extraordinarily realistic in interpreting current market action. Realistic in the present, they can easily take a hit because their personal esteem is intact and their future is promising.

WINNING TRADERS ARE GOOD RISKTAKERS

"The irony is that the person not taking risks feels the same amount of fear as the person who regularly takes risks."
—Peter McWilliams

"Don't play for safety—it's the most dangerous thing in the world."
—Hugh Walpol

Risk taking is an inherent part of the game for winning traders. They may even enjoy the element of risk. They may derive an element of enhanced aliveness through being on a truly uncertain edge. They love the high that comes with the uncertainty because that uncertainty spells the possibility of profit. They interpret the shots of adrenaline they get when taking a risk as excitement, and they use the excess energy to be alert and to focus totally in the now.

This does not mean they are reckless. Nor do they trade just for the joy of being in the game. Unlike gamblers who love the risk for the risk's sake, and see nothing but a sure thing, good traders are probability thinkers. **They continually make strategic use of the probabilities.** They consider the probabilities, weigh them, and when they are in their favor, they go for them. They understand that trading is a game of probabilities, and unlike some losing traders, they never expect to have an absolutely certain outcome. Because they realize each trade is only a probability, they always control the risk. Winning traders are risk managers. They welcome the uncertainty and take advantage of it.

WINNING TRADERS ARE DISCIPLINED

"In the last analysis our only freedom is the freedom to discipline ourselves."
—Bernard Baruch

Winning traders discipline themselves to do what needs to be done. They know their rules and they follow their rules. Their rules are their guidelines that keep them from losing their way. Unlike gamblers who randomly grab trades and routinely overtrade, winning traders have a plan and they work the plan. They predetermine their risk, and they cut out when that risk point is reached. They manage their money so that only a small percentage of their money is bet on any given idea.

A winning trader frequently asks three questions before entering a trade:

1. What can I make?
2. What is my risk?
3. Where am I wrong?

Winning traders are patient. They are willing to wait for the most opportune time to enter a trade, and they're willing to stay with the trade for as long as it's going their way or their method tells them to stay with it.

Discipline is one of those words that sounds like grade school, stern and awful, no fun at all. Discipline as a word has a bad rap. Disciplined traders, however, see discipline as a trading style that will enable them to get the results they want from their trading. Discipline in trading is doing what needs to be done to make money.

WINNING TRADERS ARE BACKED BY POWERFUL BELIEFS

Winning traders hold a set of empowering beliefs about themselves and the markets. At the center of these beliefs they hold certain values. These beliefs and values support them in their trading.

The beliefs and values are real and vivid to them. Winning traders hold beliefs, consciously or unconsciously, such as the following: Money can be made in the markets. An unlimited amount of money can be made in the markets. I have the ability to make money trading. I deserve the rewards of my trading. If I am committed, there is always a way to succeed. Mistakes are natural and inevitable, and I can learn from my mistakes and use those learnings as stepping-stones to greater success. If I lose, I can always make the money back. There is plenty in the universe and in the markets, and I can partake of it. Life and the markets provide rivers of opportunity that I can identify and take full advantage of. Money is good. I can use my money for good. We'll be looking at this more extensively in the next chapter.

WINNING TRADERS ARE CONFLICT-FREE

Winning traders are free of conflict. As my friend Mark Douglas repeatedly says, ***"Traders are comfortable in a state of not knowing, of only knowing what has already occurred and what is occurring, of only knowing the probabilities."*** They are comfortable with taking a calculated risk and waiting to see what happens. **They have no particular need to always be right. Their ego is not dependent upon being right.** They do not pit themselves or their ego against the market.

Their work ethic allows them the rewards of their trading. Their profits are not fraught with guilt. Money is good. Making money is even better. At the same time, losses are okay. Winning traders accept loss as part of the price of trading. They see loss as feedback, not failure. Loss is important information that can help them trade even better. They are comfortable within the process of both winning and losing. Both are expected and accepted.

Winning traders have a sense of deserving to create wealth for themselves and for others. They have a sense of abundance, of there being enough to go around. At no time do they think that because they win others will have to go without.

They love what they do, and choose it over any other professional pursuit. They would probably trade even if they had plenty of money already. Trading is where they want to be. They are totally comfortable in the market. They are also comfortable out of the market if they don't see anything to do. At ease in and out of the market, they wait their time.

WINNING TRADERS ARE OPEN-MINDED AND FLEXIBLE

"And ye shall know the truth and the truth shall make you free."
—Bible, St. John

Winning traders hold a clear mind and willingly receive the information that the market gives them. Their perceptual channels are clear. If they hold a scenario in their minds, they are willing to test it against the current facts. They are constantly asking, "What is the market doing right now? What is it showing me? What needs to happen for me to change my mind?"

They watch how the markets react to news. If a market can't go up on good news, something's wrong. If a market doesn't go down on bad news, there's something else going on. Winning traders want what the markets want. They have no vested interest in being right. **Their ego isn't attached to their current theory or position.** Their purpose is to make money, and they make money by responding to market action. They are able to take on information that might be against their position. They are able to stop and reverse when advisable.

I asked Linda Raschke what she thought was the difference that puts some traders into the 5% of winning traders. I asked her what was the distinguishing characteristic of a good trader.

> Linda: "I think it's just that you've got to admit that, you just have to accept, recognize, acknowledge that there are a lot of factors and variables out there that you can't control, and you can't predict, and once you acknowledge that—that you tried and could not foresee what was going to happen and nobody could, then you take the trade off or you get out of your position and you look for something else."
>
> "The people who don't seem to make it are the people who think they can find 'the way.' You have to accept the fact that you can just go in there. It's a good combination of just knowing your style. There's only so much you can do, and there are a lot of limitations. A lot of it just comes down to knowing yourself, having enough that you can accept what will work for you and what will not work for you. You need to accept that the grass isn't greener on the other side of the fence and just focus on a little niche."

"I think the people who can't make it try to do way too much, try to bite off far more than they can handle. They make the game so complicated and think that there's a way to figure out a particular thing. God knows, how many years I have spent, and there's always a new twist or variation that you haven't seen or it could have happened nine times out of ten, but the tenth time it's going to work a little differently and I think you have to be flexible. You have to be like a reed and bend with the wind. I think people that are tense or have a hard time compromising are going to run into trouble."

WINNING TRADERS MAKE POSITIVE ASSOCIATIONS TO THEIR TRADING

"If you are distressed by anything external, the pain is not due to the thing itself, but to the estimate of it; and this you have the power to revoke at any moment."
—Marcus Aurelius

Winning traders expect to win. When they see a signal, they associate to the potential for profit—even while they protect against loss. They never know whether a given trade will produce a large profit or a small loss, but with each trade they connect to the probability for profit.

They associate mistakes, errors and losing periods with opportunities to learn and improve. Their questions at such times are, "What can I learn from this? How can I make this better in the future?" They don't ask, "Why do I always lose?"

Winning traders associate trading with pleasure. The pain is only temporary on the way to greater pleasure. They set their intention. They intend to make money and to follow their winning methods as well as to constantly improve. Improving and making money is total pleasure. The rest is incidental.

WINNING TRADERS ARE PREPARED

Winning traders do their homework. They research their methods. They verify their methods. They stay up to date with current markets. When the opening bell rings, they are ready in terms of market preparation and self-preparation. Each trading day, each trading week, they are in a state of expectant readiness.

They prepare with whatever it takes to win. They acquire the necessary skills, information, and technology. They practice mental rehearsal. They resolve other life issues, or at least put them aside before trading. They keep themselves mentally and physically fit.

WINNING TRADERS ATTUNE THEIR TRADING STYLE AND METHODS TO THEIR OWN PERSONALITY

Winning traders trade in accordance with their personal strengths and skills. They accommodate to their own personality. They find ways to compensate or transform their weaknesses. They utilize their strengths.

A quick, intuitive person will probably not want to trade a long-term mechanical system off a weekly chart. Nor will a slow methodical person choose to trade intuitively off a one-minute chart.

A hesitant analytical person might have a computer enter the trades for him. A person who enjoys the action might team up with an analytical genius to advise and guide him while he himself makes the trading decisions.

Even while accommodating to their natural tendencies, winning traders are willing to stretch, to learn, to transform, and when necessary, to compensate.

WINNING TRADERS ARE CONFIDENT

Winning traders have a deep sense of self-worth that transcends their trading. Their self-esteem is not dependent upon the results of a trade. This is important. Winning traders feel good about themselves whether they have a winning or losing day, week, or month. Knowing that their self-esteem is intact regardless of the results of any given trading period, they are able to risk and survive any drawdown.

They know that whatever happens, they can make the money back. They can go into any market any time and create wealth. The markets are there for them, and they can always make enough money to meet their needs and wants. Being confident, they are in control of their future, and that future is promising.

Linda Raschke has tremendous confidence as a trader. I asked her how she developed this confidence.

> Linda: "You're a better expert than I am to go into it, but I'll just mention a couple of things. I was the first born child of four and oftentimes first born children get a lot of attention from the mother, and are given a great deal of encouragement. My mom was brought up by her mom who had never been allowed to do much of anything growing up. You can't ride a pony, you can't do this, you'll get your dress dirty, you have to have the proper manners, etc., etc. She swore when she was raising my mom that that would not happen to my mom. My mom was consequently encouraged to do absolutely everything. And so my mom has a

very adventuresome attitude in life. She was always vocal about preaching that if you put your mind to it, you can do anything. We were always brought up with that type of encouragement."

Ruth: "So that gave you the confidence. You approach trading just the way you would approach riding a horse or playing the piano."

Linda: "I started playing the piano when I was 5 years old. My mother started spending some time with me every day, and I got good really fast where you sit down to play and people are like, 'Oh that's wonderful! I can't believe she plays like that at 6 years old.' So you get a lot of positive feedback. I was good in school and so I grew up having a lot of positive feedback."

"I would get in a lot of scrapes when I was young because I was given too much freedom and I learned very quickly that you can take care of yourself. I graduated from high school when I was 16 and was pretty much out living on my own when I was 17. My mom got divorced, and I developed an 'I can do' attitude. Yes, I can put myself through school. Yes, I can do this. And I think that once you have overcome a major challenge in your life, once you have worked your way out of a major obstacle, you learn that you can solve any problem. Then it's just transferring that to the markets, the confidence of problem solving."

SELF-ASSESSMENT OF YOUR PERSONAL WINNING ATTRIBUTES

"They always say that time changes things, but you actually have to change them yourself."

—Andy Warhol

In what ways are you optimistic about your trading?

____

____

In what ways are you pessimistic about your trading?

____

____

What are some ways you can change your interpretation of trading events?

____

What kind of a risktaker are you? Are you too cautious, too casual, or too random?

____

How can you change?

On a scale of 1-10, how disciplined a trader are you?

How can you improve that?

What beliefs do you have that support you in your trading?

Do you have any beliefs that are holding you back?

How conflict-free are you?

What are some areas where you need some work?

How open are you to market information?

How positive are you in your trading expectations and interpretations?

Where can you make changes?

How prepared are you for each trading session?

In what ways does your trading style complement your personality? In what ways does your personality complement your trading style?

Does your self-esteem go up and down with your trading?

PROFILE OF A LOSING TRADER

By comparison, losing traders hold limiting beliefs about themselves and the market, are conflicted in their purpose to make money, are undisciplined, frequently unprepared, don't acknowledge their own weakness, misdirect their emotions, and do not seek to transform themselves.

LOSING TRADERS DON'T RECOGNIZE THE NEED FOR PERSONAL TRANSFORMATION

Jack Schwager asked Ed Seykota in his book *Market Wizards*[2], "What can a losing trader do to transform himself into a winning trader?" Ed answered, "A losing trader can do little to transform himself into a winning trader. A losing trader is not going to want to transform himself. That's the kind of thing winning traders do."

Bingo! That's where it all starts. Willingness to change. Recognition of the need to change. Sufficient humility to seek guidance.

Losers always insist that the problem is outside of themselves. "I have no psychological problems. I just need a better system, a better source of advice."

Losing traders tend to think that if they can just tough it out, they'll get better. They're not willing to admit that the source of the difficulty is their personality makeup. They're not willing to invest in themselves, in their own psychological growth.

Since losing traders generally don't acknowledge their own weakness or their own mistakes, it's close to impossible for them to change or to learn from past mistakes.

LOSING TRADERS PLAY THE BLAME GAME

Losing traders generally blame everything and everybody but themselves. It's the market, the system, the broker, the crooks on the floor, even the time of year. The real problem with blaming is that you miss what's really happening, so you can't fix it. The comfort of blaming is that it puts the failure outside yourself, so you feel better for a while. But the problem with that is that it also puts the control outside yourself, so you end up a victim.

LOSING TRADERS PLACE A PRIORITY ON PROTECTING THEIR EGO

"For many traders it's more important to be right than to make money, these traders will hold on to a loss until the pain of losing is greater than the pain of being wrong."
—Mark Douglas

Losing traders are so busy protecting their ego that they can't get around to making money. They're caught in an ironic double bind. The very thing that would enhance their self-esteem—making money—is put on hold so they can protect their fragile sense of self. I will ask a trader locked into a badly losing position, "Do you want to be right, or do you want to make money?" "Being right," I insist, "is taking the first loss." The first loss is the easiest loss. Unfortunately, the fragile ego cannot take the first loss, and often doesn't take the loss until, as Mark Douglas said, ***"...the pain of losing any more is greater than the pain of being wrong."***

"Anger is a short madness."
—Horace

Some losing traders spend a lot of energy being angry. Some even break their computers or their phones. Because they don't acknowledge their own role in the difficulty, because they can't own up to their own inadequacies, there's a lot of other people and things to get angry with. Anger covers up hurt. These traders are hurting because they want to win and they feel that the source of their losing is not within their control. They get angry at whatever they think is hurting them or whatever is a convenient substitute. Anger can be very depleting and it seldom leads to correction of the difficulty.

LOSING TRADERS HOLD LIMITING BELIEFS

Losing traders are severely hampered by limiting beliefs. These beliefs may not be conscious, but they do influence trading behavior. The limiting beliefs can be global—about markets, about money, about abundance; or they can be personal—about individual capability or worth.

Some examples of such limiting beliefs could be the following: The market is a dangerous place. It's impossible to make money in the futures market. You can't play with the big boys. The whole purpose of the guys on the floor is to take your money and rip you off. Trading is a war. You should have to work hard for your money. Money doesn't come without hard work. Money is evil. A rich man cannot enter into the kingdom of heaven. I can be spiritual, or I can be successful. Trading is gambling, and gambling is wrong. If I have money, I'm causing suffering for others in the world who are less fortunate. If I have too much money, I'll lose my friends. If I make a lot of money, my ex-wife will come after me. I don't deserve to be rich. I can't be better than my father. Everything I do ends up a failure. For some reason I'm doomed to lose in the end. My destiny is to be destitute.

Traders with any of these beliefs will end up losing or limiting their profitability once they start making money. Rarely will these traders realize that it is their own limiting beliefs that are causing their misfortune. Whenever you get into trouble trading, ask yourself, "What must I believe in order to be doing this?" We'll look at this more fully in the next chapter.

LOSING TRADERS ARE CONFLICTED

"The theory seems to be that as long as a man is a failure he is one of God's children, but as soon as he succeeds he is taken over by the Devil."
—H.L. Mencken

"Doublethink means the power of holding two contradictory beliefs in one's mind simultaneously, and accepting both of them."
—George Orwell

Limiting beliefs cause traders to be conflicted. On the one hand, they want to make money. On the other hand, it either can't be done or shouldn't be done. The losing trader gets tripped up when he begins to accumulate wealth because of an inner conflict. This inner conflict causes self-sabotage.

LOSING TRADERS ARE SUBVERTED BY NEGATIVE WORDS AND PICTURES

"What was once thought can never be unthought."
—Friedrich Durrenmatt

Losing traders often indulge in very negative self-talk. They speak in ways to themselves that they would never tolerate from an outside person. This verbal self-abuse only compounds their troubles and can become a self-fulfilling prophecy. These traders get trapped in a denigrating loop of negative self-talk, destructive behavior, damaged identity, more negative self-talk, more destructive behavior, and increased damaged identity, on and on in an endless cycle of destruction.

Losing traders often have negative pictures about trading. These pictures occur in a flash and may be out of awareness. Such a picture might be seeing the chart go in the opposite direction of their signal, or seeing their account depleted, or seeing themselves homeless. Naturally, they want to avoid this pain, but the picture operates like a magnet and they go towards it. If the signal says buy, but they imagine the chart going the other way, they'll delay putting on the trade until it's too late. If they're in a trade and it's going their way but they imagine losing their profits, they'll gulp their profits and jump out only to miss the trade of a lifetime.

LOSING TRADERS ARE UNDISCIPLINED

Losing traders frequently fail to have the discipline to rigorously and consistently work the probabilities of their trading methods and perceptions. They may overtrade. They may fail to trade. They may frequently enter trades a bit or a lot too late. They may fail to use stops or they may use CICs (cancel if close), and they may get stuck in a trade unable to take themselves out.

This lack of disciplined application of the probabilities takes a terrible toll on the trading results. Some traders may go along fine for a while and then blow up. Others abdicate a little bit each day. Very often these traders intend to follow their rules, but in the heat of trading they lose discipline. Their good intentions are deleted.

THE DOERS AND THE THINKERS

"We have left undone those things which we ought to have done; and we have done those things which we ought not to have done; and there is no health in us."

—The Book of Common Prayer

In my opinion there are two basic types of traders. Each has specific strengths, and each has specific vulnerabilities.

The first group I call the Thinkers. These are the analysis folk. They tend to be risk averse. They are not comfortable with risk, and so they try to avoid it. These people have barriers between their thinking and their doing.

The second group I call the Doers. These are the action folk. They are risktakers. Risk gives them a certain excitement, a sense of being truly alive. They actually enjoy being on the edge. These people are capable of acting before they think. They frequently act with insufficient prior analysis.

I often think that if I could match up my client base into pairs of thinker-doers, the clients could go swimmingly along. But the Thinkers don't trust the Doers with their precious analysis. And the Doers don't particularly trust the Thinkers' analysis, and besides they resist outside direction or limitation.

PROFILE OF A LOSING THINKER

"We have left undone those things which we ought to have done."
—The Book of Common Prayer

"He who desires but acts not, breeds pestilence."
—William Blake

First, let's look at a composite profile of losing Thinkers. The Thinkers' *modus vivendi* is thought. Their style of being is thinking rather than feeling or doing. Thinking is their protection. But it takes more than thought to be a successful trader. You have to do as well.

Thinkers very often are drawn into trading through systems analysis. They know their way around computers; and if they don't, they soon learn.

Thinkers love doing research and analysis. However, their problems start when the analysis is complete. First, they may have trouble bringing the analysis to a conclusion—there's always another aspect to research. Then when they do finally complete the analysis, they're often surprised to find out that they cannot trade. Their method gives them the signals, but they cannot put on the trades. They are trapped in the cliche of the paralysis of analysis.

After receiving a signal they may second-guess the system or they may decide to change the system. Sometimes they simply hesitate so long that the market has moved swiftly without them. They may end up chasing the market only to get scared and jump out, or worse still, find that the market has turned against them.

Losing Thinkers are totally uncomfortable with risk. They are fearful of losing money or of discrediting themselves. This fear causes them to have difficulty pulling the trigger to get into a trade. It causes them to grab profits too soon. It causes them to freeze in a trade and take huge losses.

Losing Thinkers find themselves constantly changing their system, or even changing systems. They are continually looking for a better way. Looking for a better way is all right, but the probabilities don't work in your favor if you keep shifting them or second-guessing them. I recommend to such traders that they create for themselves a rule that they can only institute changes at the beginning of a trading month. This gives them some kind of thoughtful discipline, and keeps them from being whipsawed in their methods.

Losing Thinkers often suffer from the need to be right. They want things to be correct. They often are perfectionists, holding themselves to an exacting standard of pristine perfection. They tend to look at things in small chunks. They demand precision. They tend to be rigid. With such a predisposition, how can they possibly be comfortable in the rough and tumble vagaries and uncertainties of the market place?

In short, Losing Thinkers just aren't players. Trading for them is not play. It's not fun. To be really good at something, to be outstanding, you have to love what you do. You have to have a passion for it. Loving what you do and doing what you love is the greatest blessing a person can have.

PROFILE OF A LOSING DOER

"...and we have done those things which we ought not to have done."
—The Book of Common Prayer

"Action without thought is like shooting without aim."
—American Proverb

"A man of action forced into a state of thought is unhappy until he can get out of it."
—John Galsworthy

Doers, on the other hand, love to play. They love trading. However, Doers have a different set of dangers and difficulties. Losing Doers often act before they think. They love the action for the action's sake. They also react quickly, and often they react mindlessly. These reactions can cause them to get whipsawed, can cause them to overtrade, and can cause them to dig a hole deeper once they're in it by adding to losing positions or by flailing out in many directions in an effort to make things better.

Losing Doers may have a valid trading plan, and they may have a proven methodology or system; but they tend to shift course during a trade or during the trading day and go off on tangents. Sometimes they may be totally disciplined trading in one pit, only to run over to another pit and throw on unresearched trades that will rob them of their entire week's hard earned winnings. They may even go along trading in a disciplined manner for weeks, and then suddenly go berserk. In one day or one week of wild trading they can give back all their profits.

Losing Doers have the attitude of let's try it and see what happens. They'll tend to play with their profits recklessly. When they're losing, they'll frantically try to get even.

Losing Doers, like Losing Thinkers, know fear. Losing Doers are thoroughly acquainted with greed as well. They may ratchet back and forth between the two emotional polarities. They tend to overtrade in quantity as well as frequency. If they get caught in a losing trade, they'll be inclined to add to it. If they see a strong opportunity, they'll frequently bet the farm. The trouble with betting the farm is that even if you're right 99% of the time, you'll lose your stake on the 1% when you're wrong.

Losing Doers often don't have a sound money management plan. They may not even have thought about money management. When they do have a money management policy, they're likely to violate it.

Losing Doers can get euphoric and lose sight of reality and lose their grasp on what is actually happening. Like gamblers, when they are euphoric, they tend to believe they're on to a sure thing. In such a condition, they tend to exaggerate the possibility of profit and disregard the possibility of loss.

Losing Doers are often gamblers. It's a fine line between trading and gambling. Each is based on chance. The problem with gambling (and trading) is when you haven't carefully calculated the odds or when the activity gets out of control and becomes compulsive.

Losing Doers may well have an inability to control the impulse to trade, and may continue to trade even when their trading capital is depleted. They may borrow or steal. Or they may simply keep filling their trading account with money they make at another job.

Pathological gambling is different from normal recreational gambling. And pathological trading is different from trading as a business.

Pathological traders and gamblers are looking for an intensity that eludes them in ordinary living. This sense of the action, this sense of being truly alive only when at risk has a tremendous draw for the losing Doer. The losing Doer trades excessively for the thrills. If you're one of these people, look elsewhere for your thrills. Go rock climbing, fly a plane, take up downhill ski racing, or any other dangerous and exciting sport. But, please, keep your thrills out of the trading arena. And, please, only trade with risk capital.

THE IRONY

Losing Thinkers dread the risk. They associate so much pain to the process of trading and being at risk that they are unable to trade effectively. Through countless and repetitive mismaneuvers, they actually create the pain they're trying to avoid.

Losing Doers love the risk. They associate so much pleasure to the process of trading just for trading's sake that they turn what could be a very profitable operation into a sick and losing situation.

Can you change your type? Of course not. But you can evolve to being a winning Thinker or a winning Doer. Or you could just form a partnership with a trader from the other type.

SELF-ASSESSMENT OF PROFILE TYPE

Are you a Doer or a Thinker?

____

How does being a Doer or Thinker enhance your trading?

____

How does being a Doer or Thinker jeopardize your trading?

____

What steps can you take to balance this proclivity?

____

Now let's look at how this all plays out in an infamous, cataclysmic trade made by an arrogant losing Doer.

ANATOMY OF A LOSING TRADE

"He that diggeth a pit shall fall into it."
—Bible, Ecclesiastes

"They have sown the wind and they shall reap the whirlwind."
— Bible, Hosea

"Who won't be ruled by the rudder must be ruled by the rock."
—Folk Proverb

Perhaps the most common cause of ultimate failure in trading is the inability to get out of a losing trade. Because the markets are continuous with no beginning or ending, traders have to take themselves out of each trade.

One of my gurus, a man by the name of David Johnston, taught me this lesson early on. He had worked for **Merrill Lynch** way back when it was called **Merrill Lynch Fenner and Beane**. Mr. Beane wanted to know why people lost and made money trading commodities. He set David to the task of finding out. What they did was to take all the commodity accounts and trades done at **Merrill Lynch** and list them by size of profit and loss. What they discovered was that the clients who made money took a lot of little losses and had some major big profits. The clients who lost money had lots of little profits and some very large losses.

We are told to cut our losses and let our profits run. It's common knowledge that this is the way to win. It's a cliche. Nevertheless, traders often don't do it.

I have seen traders stake their entire net worth and sometimes even more on one simple trade. I have seen brokers managing accounts risk their entire client base on one badly chosen investment that they won't get out of. In April of 1998, I heard of a man who had been short the S&P for more than three years. He kept rolling the position over afraid to take it off less the market suddenly sells off. Such traders become married to the idea, or even worse, they become one with the idea. They become the trade. Their identity, their very existence, is intertwined with the trade.

If they get away with it, they see themselves as a hero, and they're in danger of doing it a second time. The second time they probably won't get away with it. If they don't get away with it, they will not only have lost their capital, they will have broken off a chunk of their self-esteem and will often not have confidence to trade in the future.

Sometimes it doesn't even start with a strong conviction. The trader finds himself in a losing trade and loses the courage to get out. He freezes as the losses mount higher. To restore his ability to trade, I worked with one trader who had gotten into a currency trade that he held on to for a full year until he had lost over $150,000. The financial damage was terrible for him, but the psychic damage was even worse.

Losses are like dirty dishes in the sink. You're going to have to do them sooner or later. Why not get them out of the way immediately, so you don't have to live with them? It will clear up your mind and emotions and free you to look for a new trade.

I've seen it time and again. Traders take themselves out of the game by destroying their capital base or their confidence or both by clinging to a losing trade. Rather than get out of the losing trade and putting it behind them, they dig the hole deeper and deeper unable to admit they're wrong.

You've probably heard a losing trader say, "I can't get out now. I'm losing too much." Their misbegotten statement assumes that this trade is the best place for the money to be. Uncontrolled losses can grow like a cancer as the trader endures a living nightmare. If that trader had his hand on a hot stove, he wouldn't keep it there waiting for the stove to cool. The losses come up on him slowly like a frog in water slowly being boiled to death.

Often arrogance gets mixed up with denial and the refusal to take a loss. I spoke with Michael McCarthy about arrogance.

Michael: "Arrogance can destroy you."

Ruth: "Would you say it's the most dangerous emotion?"

Michael: "Oh yes, because you'll hold a position that goes against you."

Ruth: "Would you say that arrogance is more dangerous than fear?"

Michael: "Absolutely. Fear is there to protect you. If you're really scared, you will take out your position and go home. Arrogance is what keeps you in the market, and then you lose your money. You deserve to lose if you're arrogant because it's a bad thing. I think there's a big karma thing going on. If you're a nice guy and you're humble, you'll do well. You'll follow the rules."

In February 1995 the world was shocked to see the 233-year-old **Barings Bank**, the bank that had lent the United States the money for the **Louisiana Purchase**, brought down by a 28 year old trader named Nicholas Leeson.

This trader, like the others we spoke of, got into a trading situation and couldn't take himself out. Because he was able to utilize the credit of the bank, he ran a bad idea up to a 1.4 billion-dollar loss. And still he didn't get out. He did get out of the country, leaving behind a hand-written note saying, "I'm sorry." The British bank that had been profitable for centuries was purchased by a Dutch company for a mere $1.60.

Leeson started with a wager that the **Nikkei** index would remain stable at around 19,000 points. He sold an option straddle. By January 13 he was net long the **Nikkei** by 3,024 contracts. On January 17 the Kobe earthquake hit and the **Nikkei** began selling off, gradually at the beginning, and then more rapidly and extremely—first breaking 19,000, then 18,000, and finally breaking below 17,000 before all the positions were finally liquidated or transferred by those left to sort out the mess.

After the earthquake, Leeson had plenty of opportunity to get out of the position, plenty of opportunity to manage the position. He didn't. The market kept going down and down and down. He could have listened to the market and gone short. Instead he stayed long and added to the position. By January 20, he had 7,135 long contracts. By January 27 he was long 16,852 **Nikkei** contracts. By Friday, February 24, Leeson was long a total of 61,280 **Nikkei** futures contracts on three exchanges! In addition he was short a total of 25,900 Japanese government bond futures that were also losing!

What caused this phenomenally bad trading?

First, Leeson had a **dreadful ethical lapse**. He was dishonest with his firm. Furthermore, he violated the rules of the **Simex Exchange**.

His problems began in 1994 when he suffered a loss of $80,000,000 trading **Nikkei** options on **Simex**. He hid this loss in his firm's error account number 88888 at **Simex**. The firm was reportedly unaware of the loss in the error account. Leeson was sneaking and cheating. No doubt he was also frantically trying to make the money back so he could cover the hidden loss before it was discovered. He had made mistakes to the tune of $80,000,000, but he did not learn from the mistakes. He hid the learnings from himself just as he hid the losses from the firm. My guess is that he was in personal denial about the whole situation.

Rule 1502-D on the **Simex** states: "A person shall not own or control more than 1,000 contracts net long or net short in all contract months combined." Well, already by January 6 Leeson was net long 4,939 contracts on **Simex**. By February 24, he was net long 43,000 contracts on **Simex** alone. He was **not playing by the rules** of the exchange.

When asked about the size of his trades, he claimed they were for a mysterious, unnamed customer of the bank. He claimed to be short on another exchange. Both were lies devised to get away with the rule violation.

Rules of behavior were not for Leeson. He was in fact once charged with indecent exposure for dropping his pants down in front of a group of women. He then gave the women his phone number and address and dared them to turn him in. As good Singaporeans, they did. He was fined $140.

Leeson considered himself bigger than the rules of his firm and of the exchange and apparently of society itself. If he had any trading rules of his own—and my guess is that he did not—it would appear he had definitely abandoned them. He was well beyond trading within any reasonable normal trading disciplines.

Leeson was **undisciplined** to say the least. He was **out of control**. If he'd ever studied money management as a discipline—and my guess is that he'd never considered it, he certainly **did not practice sound money management**. Placing 63,000 futures contracts on a single idea just ain't money management. He bet more than the entire net worth of the bank on one idea. He was **overtrading** to say the least.

He did not use risk control. My guess is that he thought stops were something for sissies. Any good risk control would have taken him out of the trade when the market began sinking after the earthquake.

His risk-reward ratio was skewed. Instead of risking one unit to make two or three units, he was risking, risking, risking without any reward in sight.

He was **not a probabilities trader.** He was not calculating probabilities as he laid everything on this one bad idea. He could not have been viewing his trading as a series of probabilities. Everything was hinged on the idea that the **Nikkei** would go up and the JGB's would go down. Even this spread of long stock, short bonds was going against him.

You need to view each trade as nothing more than one point in a much bigger game. Leeson was making these two trades into one enormous game. He was plugging AGAINST the probabilities. **He was staking the existence of the bank on these two trading ideas.**

Leeson was **trading a scenario.** Scenarios tend to blind you to incoming contradictory information. Everything rested on the **Nikkei** going up when all evidence pointed to the contrary. He also was stuck on the scenario of Japanese interest rates going up, for he was short the JGB's to the tune of 25,900 futures contracts. The evidence on both positions pointed in the opposite direction. He did not see the glaring evidence, or if he did, he didn't believe it. **He was blinded.**

His perceptual channels were blocked. The market was giving him powerful and plentiful evidence that it, and he, were headed south. He ignored the information the market was handing him. He kept buying into a bear market. **He kept adding to a losing position.**

Leeson was trading from **blind emotion. Fear, greed,** and **hope** were in rampant ascendancy. Probably greed was first. Then came poor blind, passive, helpless hope. He hoped against hope the trade would go his way. Finally fear paralyzed him as well. He was stuck in the trade and could not take action to get out. He careened between fear, greed, and hope. Fear kept him from taking off the trade, from realizing his losses. Hope and greed kept making him add to it. His ego, his survival, indeed the survival of the bank was tied up in this trade. And it was going against him. He was throwing up in the men's room during his last week of trading. Finally, fear won the day. He fled Singapore and hid until he was arrested a week later in Germany.

It's a dangerous thing to get your **ego tied up in a trade.** Trading is an operating skill and not an ego achievement. **Arrogance** is a major sin in trading. It precludes alternatives. It leaves you no stop gap plan for being wrong. Leeson was a major arrogant.

No doubt he had **personalized the trade**. He wasn't just trading some objective probability out there. This trade had become Leeson himself. The trade, more probably, had become Leeson's manhood. You can't admit you're wrong. Giant out-sized egos have a hard time admitting fallibility. The ego gets propped up by a whole set of spurious bravado. Taking a hit means loss of self-esteem, and self-esteem is hooked in with survival. In a desperate way Leeson was striving to prove himself right.

Leeson simply **could not take the loss and face up to the consequences.** As the losses got larger, the possibility of realizing them became more and more terrifying. From his point of view the only way out was to add to the loss and hope the market would lift even a little distance. Since he was in this much trouble he might as well *go for broke.*

He didn't have a grasp of the fact that it was actual money he was trading. He was simply caught up in a game of numbers of contracts. Later in an interview on television he explained, ***"It wasn't as if there was real money there."***

He used **fraud to meet the margin** requirements. He falsely documented a letter saying funds had been posted to cover the margin calls. Many traders say you should never meet a margin call. Having a margin call means you're wrong. Get out and meet the call that way. Well, Leeson not only didn't liquidate to meet the call; he lied to pretend there was money there to meet the deficit.

Leeson was changing his game plan, his strategy, midtrade. Originally his trading strategy had been one of arbitrage. Shortly into the trade he abandoned the strategy of hedging. When queried about his huge speculative positions, he claimed to be short on another exchange, which, of course, he was not. His original position was a straddle. Now he had gone to outright speculation. No. Outright gambling.

It's said that those who think they are investing are speculating, and those who think they are speculating are gambling. Goodness knows what those who think they are gambling are doing! In the **Baring's** case Leeson was committing purposeful financial and career suicide. He *broke the bank.*

Leeson showed us how to lose. This was one massively bad trade, or rather two massively bad positions. He committed many cardinal trading errors—not taking a loss—adding to a losing trade—overtrading—not using money management—not looking at the evidence—not having risk control—blind emotional trading—not following the rules—not realizing real money was at stake—personalizing a trade—trading from ego—not using risk capital—doing unauthorized trades.

Leeson demonstrated for the world many of the traits of a losing trader. Despite all this, I am told that even as Leeson sat a prisoner in a jail in Germany, he was being offered new jobs as a trader. That to me proves that Leeson isn't the only one who doesn't understand the elements of good trading.

[1] *Learned Optimism*, Martin E.P. Seligman, Ph.D., Alfred A. Knopf, 1991.

[22] *Market Wizards*, Jack D. Schwager, New York Institute of Finance, 1989.

CHAPTER III

THE RELENTLESS AND COMPELLING POWER OF BELIEFS

"If ye have the faith as of a grain of mustard seed, ye shall say unto this mountain, 'Remove hence to yonder place;' and it shall remove; and nothing shall be impossible unto you."

—The Bible: Matthew 17:20

What you believe has a powerful impact upon how you trade and how you live.

Beliefs operate like giant filters for experience. What you believe totally affects your observations and interpretations. Quite often, if you don't believe it, you don't see it. Unlike the old saying, "I'll believe it when I see it," the truth is you'll see it when you believe it.

Beliefs not only filter our observations and perceptions; they filter our behavioral choices and affect our results. We believe. We interpret events and give them explanations. We delete evidence that goes against our belief. We act in accordance with our perceptions and interpretations. Actions produce results. Results reinforce interpretations and perceptions. Interpretations and perceptions reinforce beliefs. It's a reinforcing cycle that gets stronger each time it goes around. This is our reality, our model of the world.

My friend Joe wants to make lots of money trading. He wants it in the worst way. And that, unfortunately, is the way he goes about his trading. He spends thousands and thousands of dollars buying system after system that promises to yield enormous amounts of money quickly. He subscribes to hot-lines and faxes and newsletters that swear they have the inside secrets to wealth. Whenever he has losses, he changes brokers or shifts systems. None of this works for him. He has no staying power because he hasn't verified or tested any of his methods. In short, he doesn't believe in them long enough to persist, and perhaps he shouldn't.

Poor Joe spends thousands and thousands covering his losses. His wife accuses him of flushing money down the toilet. Fortunately, Joe makes lots of money at his other profession so he keeps the bill collectors—and his wife—at bay.

What must my friend Joe believe or not believe in order to behave this way? He obviously believes there's money to be made in the markets. He also believes that out there just over the horizon is a miracle method that will enable him to make all the money back and tons more. He believes that others outside himself hold the *Holy Grail* to profitable trading. He also believes whatever the latest purveyors of market wizardry tell him. Because he does not believe in the absolute necessity of self-discipline, restraint, testing verification, and systematically working with probabilities, he is doomed to repeat his trading history.

Joe has a large tolerance for present pain and an unwavering faith in the future. While this frequently works for him in other areas of his life, it does not work for him in his trading. Something needs to change. Joe needs a reality check with regard to his trading habits. He needs to pay attention to the feedback he is getting. Joe's a smart man, but sadly his beliefs are clouding his judgment.

Beliefs tend to be transparent, as transparent as the air around us. Because our beliefs color and create our reality, it's hard to see that it's a set of beliefs that underlie and support our reality. Again, the beliefs are the filters that select what information we let in and exclude. The beliefs effect our interpretation of events and the meaning we give to them. We then act upon these reference experiences and further confirm our original thought. A belief thus becomes a self-fulfilling prophecy that can cycle round and round.

It's a loop that goes belief—perception—cognition—action—results—conclusion—belief.

In order to do anything effectively and well, you need to believe three things:

1. It can be done.
2. I can do it.
3. I deserve to do it.

The opposite of this is:

1. It's hopeless.
2. I'm helpless.
3. I'm worthless.

If you have a problem with any one of these positive beliefs, it will tend to manifest itself in different ways in all areas of your life and, of course, trading. I have been amused with this in my own life. I have a very strong belief that if something can be done, I can do it, and, of course, I deserve to do it. Sounds great, doesn't it? But there's a corollary: it can't be done. Whenever I run into difficulty I'll get discouraged and say, "It can't be done." After a bad day of trading, I used to say, "These markets can't be traded!" Once I said to my son about my career as a psychological trading coach, "It can't be done." He said, "Mother, you've just spent the last six years proving it can be done." I had to laugh. He was right. Now, whenever I catch myself saying, "It can't be done," I simply laugh and say to myself, "There you go again!" Then I shift it around and I ask, "How can this be done? How can it be done even better?"

BELIEFS OF WINNING TRADERS

These three essential beliefs are at the core of successful trading and need to be internalized and sustained. They can be verbalized as follows:

1. Money can be made in the markets.
2. I can make money in the markets
3. I deserve to make money in the markets.

In addition to these three core beliefs, there are a host of other supportive trading beliefs that successful traders hold. For example, successful traders believe:

- Individual losses are unimportant.
- Each trade is but one of a series of probabilities.
- The probabilities of my trading favor me over time.
- Trading is a process, a process I can master.
- Trading is fun.
- I love trading.
- Drawdowns are temporary.
- It's essential to manage the risk.
- I always manage the risk.
- It's essential to manage the money (the bet size).
- Money management is at the core of my trading.
- You should never risk more than a small portion of your trading capital on any given trade or idea.

- Cut your losses. Let your profits run.
- It's important to have a method for sticking with winners and getting rid of losers.
- It's important to stick with a proven methodology.
- It's okay to improve or change or add to a methodology, but do it by design infrequently. Don't keep junking and changing systems with the wind.
- Following good trading principles is more important than individual losses or profits.
- You can go broke taking a profit.
- Money isn't as important as the trading process.
- It's important to be prepared before trading, to do your homework.
- It's important to verify any methodology.
- Get out or cut down when losing.
- Mistakes don't matter if you learn from them. Mistakes are okay, just fix them.
- You can learn from mistakes by acknowledging them.
- An opinion isn't worth much. It's more important to listen, watch, and feel the market.
- Watch how the markets react to the news.
- When you have a scenario in mind, it's important to be particularly alert to what is actually happening in the market.
- You can change your mind. Don't try to change the market.
- I want what the market wants.
- The market cannot harm you if you trust yourself to act appropriately under any market condition.
- The more you follow your rules, the more you trust yourself.
- The more you trust yourself, the more you can learn from the market.
- The more you follow your rules, the more consistent you'll be.
- Trade with the trend. If you trade counter-trend, be aware of the trend.
- Be aware of whether the market is trending or trading.
- I am a winner. I do the things that winners do.
- My trading is the safest place for my money to be.
- Money can be made and money can be kept.
- If you don't bet, you can't win.
- If you lose all your chips, you can't bet.
- If I lose money, I can always make it back.
- I can go into any market, anytime, and make money.
- I always expect the unexpected.
- It's important to be flexible.
- It's important to be open-minded, to be willing to take on information that is difficult to accept emotionally but which you recognize to be true.
- Ultimately the market is going to go where it's going to go.
- It's important to focus on the trading process rather than on the money.
- Focus on protecting money even as you expect success.

- The elements of good trading are cutting losses, cutting losses, cutting losses.
- One should never, never add to a losing trade.
- I'm optimistic about the future of my trading.
- Trading is a game.
- Trading is a game I rehearse and am good at.
- Mental rehearsal is important for success.
- It's important to choose a methodology that is compatible with your personality.
- It's important to get out of the market when you get hurt. Don't even think about it because your decisions will not be objective.
- One needs to get out of a losing trade and free up your mind for a new opportunity.
- If you stick around when the market is against you, sooner or later it will carry you out.
- Everybody gets what they want out of the market.
- I choose to make money in the market.
- I am responsible for my own decisions.
- I keep my own counsel.
- I am responsible for my own actions.
- I have market savvy, and I trust my intuition.
- I am patient and I wait for high probability trades.
- There is a time to act and a time to wait.
- I act on time and wait patiently for the correct time.
- The world is an abundant place.
- The market provides a river of recurring opportunities.
- I make money and give to causes I truly care about. The more I give, the more I make, and the more I make the more I give.
- Money is good.
- I am committed to my trading.
- I do whatever it takes to be a successful trader.
- I enjoy the fruits of my trading success.

When you get these good trading principles deep down inside you, you will automatically do what needs to be done in the course of your trading. These beliefs will set you on the appropriate course and empower your success.

Ask yourself, "What do **I** need to believe in order to succeed as a trader?"

____

____

I asked Linda Raschke what she believed about the markets.

Linda: "In regards to price behavior or what?"

Ruth: "In regards to anything."

Linda: "It's a broad question."

Ruth: "Yes. Just start with any angle."

Linda: "I believe that the markets show that there are identifiable patterns in the markets and these patterns will always exist. They are a function of crowd behavior, and so there will always be opportunity in the markets. That's a very strong belief."

Ruth: "Let's look at it from another angle. Do you believe that the market is a dangerous place or a place of great abundance? How do you look at it?"

Linda: "I don't look at it as a dangerous place, or I wouldn't be in it. Nor do I look at it as great abundance because I always perceive that we are responsible for our own abundance within. You make abundance with whatever is out there. I don't give the markets any distinguishing attributes. I wouldn't go so far as to identify some adjective with them. I'm much more detached from them."

Ruth: "You just see them as a neutral thing, a kind of place where you make your livelihood not that it's benevolent or dangerous or anything else."

Linda: "No. I wouldn't, I couldn't, say anything good or bad. I can do things like marvel at the wonder of price behavior at times. Sometimes I look at them with a little bit of awe. Not so much the markets but the beauty of the way things work out. There is just a very satisfying, classic beauty to the way prices behave. I guess I would attach more of an adjective to price behavior. I just marvel at the wondrous thing it does. But as for markets in general, I would say I'm just more detached from them."

At another point when we were talking, Linda said, "The strongest thing out there is believing you can do it. It's like the will. If the will is strong enough, the mind will find a way. And people are either lacking in it or have it. It's not always the belief, it's the will. But if you're driven, it's almost like an obsession, a strong desire."

BELIEFS OF LOSING TRADERS

"Evidence from actual trading results suggested that winning was not a chance matter at all, and that losing was systematic, behavioral, and predictable, among those who lost."

—*Winner Take All*, William R. Gallacher[1]

To understand what losing traders believe, all you'd need to do is reverse any of the above beliefs of winning traders. For example, starting from the top: Individual losses are significant. Each trade is vitally important. The probabilities of trading are that you lose over time. And so forth.

Looking at the three core beliefs there would be a lingering notion of hopeless, helpless, or worthless.

Take hopeless: It's impossible to make money trading futures, timing the market, or daytrading. After all, why do 90% of traders lose? How can you make money when the guys on the floor are such crooks? After you consider commissions, slippage, and the overhead of data feed and so forth, you're way negative of a zero-sum game: how can you possibly win?

Try helpless: I have a great system, but I can't pull the trigger. I don't have the temperament for trading. I need a good broker to tell me what to do. Sometimes I think I'm my own worst enemy trading. I can't make myself consistently use stops. I'm missing everything. I can't seem to get it right.

Consider worthless: Everytime I get my account up to a certain level, I give the money back. I make an ungodly amount of money and then I give it back. Every time I tell somebody how much money I'm making, I have a losing streak. There's something unseemly about making $60,000 a week. I'll lose my friends if I make too much money.

There are so many needy people in the world, who am I to make so much money? Trading is such a superficial activity: I'd much rather make a difference in the world.

In addition to the above attitudes—any one of which is enough to sink you—the following are some of the recurring beliefs I've observed in losing traders.

- The market has to go up/down because...
- If I lose, I'm wrong.
- I've got to be right. (I'll lose my self-respect if I'm wrong.)
- It's more important to be right than to make money.
- I've got to be perfect.
- I've got to develop a perfect trading system before I begin.
- They're out to get me.
- I don't have any psychological problems.
- Losing is a sign of failure.
- There's not enough to go around.
- If I make a lot of money, somebody else will be deprived.
- I can't afford to invest in myself/my trading.
- It's somebody else's fault I'm in trouble.
- It would be terrible to make a mistake.

- I am doomed to repeat past difficulties.
- I'm a macho trader. I'll do battle with anybody (the market) and win.

Ask yourself, "Do I hold any beliefs that are keeping me from my full potential as a trader?"

____

____

This business about winning and losing beliefs is not just an abstract matter. Behavior is actually organized around beliefs. Our beliefs motivate and mobilize our actions. Actions and inactions produce results. Ultimately, we win or we lose; and it can become a permanent state of affairs.

"As long as you can fit a behavior into someone's belief system, you can get him to do anything, or stop him from doing anything."

—Richard Bandler

IDENTIFYING BELIEFS

Since our trading and our lives are organized by our beliefs, it becomes important to know just what it is we do believe. Unfortunately, beliefs are often transparent. Each of us may be the last person to realize that we hold a particular belief. Some beliefs we know we hold, and we're so sure of them, we consider them facts or reality and don't realize they're simply an interpretation or presupposition.

How do we discover what we believe? Since beliefs mobilize and motivate our actions, we look to our actions.

The important question to ask is: ***"What must I believe in order to be doing this?"***

If you're not pulling the trigger on your trades, ask yourself, ***"What must I believe in order to hesitate in putting on a trade?"*** or, ***"What must I believe to totally avoid trading?"***

If you're overtrading, ask yourself, ***"What must I believe in order to overtrade?"***

If some days you follow your rules and other days you don't, ask yourself, ***"What do I believe when I follow my rules?"*** Compare it with, ***"What do I believe when I don't follow my rules?"***

If you keep gulping your profits and grabbing them too soon, ask yourself, ***"What must I believe when I rush the profit taking?"***

For each of your behaviors that serve you and don't serve you, explore the causes: ***"What must I believe in order to be doing this?"***

If you want to model the behavior of a winning trader, ask yourself, ***"What must this trader believe in order to trade like this?"***

Then ask yourself, ***"Do I hold any belief that might get in the way of my acting like this winning trader?"***

If you want to avoid doing what a certain losing trader is doing, ask yourself, ***"What must this trader believe in order to trade like this?"***

Then ask yourself, ***"Do I hold any belief that might cause me to do the same thing?"***

VALUES AT THE CORE OF BELIEFS

A belief is simply a generalization about ourselves or about life. Beliefs are usually organized around a value we hold. These values are criteria that are important to us, upon which our happiness depends. Some values are criteria we dearly want, and there are issues we desperately want to avoid.

The most direct route towards joy and peace of mind is to live in accordance with your highest values. Conversely, the quickest way to discontent and self-sabotage is to live in violation of your values.

Now, I'm not talking about what you think your values OUGHT to be: I'm talking about what your values ACTUALLY ARE! For example, a woman (or man) may feel that loyalty should be her highest value, but in point of fact love and intimacy are truly her most desired values. It could all work together, but if she's coupled with a self-righteous, self-absorbed, cold, indifferent person, she'll be unfulfilled and miserable doing obeisance to her false, obligatory—yet good—value of loyalty. A man could have adventure as his highest value, yet think security *should* be his highest value, so he stays unchallenged and unhappy in a methodical and routine job.

When a couple is unhappy together, usually one or both people in the pair are not having their highest criteria met. Since each doesn't understand that the other's values, which are different from their own, are crucial to the other, they don't make an effort to see that the other's values are met. For example, she might have beauty as her highest criteria, and he might have comfort. She decorates with pretty chairs that are not comfortable to him, or he insists on having ugly easy chairs that are offensive to her. If they understood each other's criteria, they could settle on beautiful, comfortable furniture. It's vital in relationships to understand your own and the other's prime values and communicate them so that accommodation can be made.

And just what does all this have to do with trading? A lot. If you are in an unhappy marriage or partnership, it's much harder to bring clear and purposeful motivations to trading.

We all hold different values. Also we hold different values at different times in our lives. The criteria that people hold important could include integrity, persistence, honesty, love, success, freedom, intimacy, security, adventure, power, passion, comfort, health, fame, contentment, creativity, fulfillment, beauty, peace of mind, fun, happiness, excellence, expression, wisdom, understanding, pleasure, independence, growth, spirituality, learning, or prudence.

How do you determine what a person's highest values are? These are some simple questions to ask: What about that is important to you? How is that important? What does that accomplish for you? What does that do for you? Of what value is that to you? You'll be able to notice high criteria because they will be repeated; they will be emphasized; they will be set apart.

You can ask yourself similar questions. What is most important to you in your life?

____

____

What is important to you in your relationships?

____

____

What is important to you in your career?

____

____

What is important to you in your physical being?

____

____

What is important to you in your mental and emotional being?

____

____

What is important to you in your spiritual being?

____

____

TRADING CRITERIA

What is important to you about trading?

____

____

As to your trading, you may have answered with some of the following values:

- Freedom
- Independence
- Wealth
- Success
- Security
- Excitement
- Challenge
- Involvement
- Learning
- Growth
- Future Possibility
- Making a Living
- Self-esteem
- Ego Enhancement
- ________________________
- ________________________
- ________________________
- ________________________

Now take those values and put them in order of importance to you.

1. ________________________
2. ________________________
3. ________________________
4. ________________________
5. ________________________
6. ________________________
7. ________________________
8. ________________________
9. ________________________
10. ________________________

Imagine how differently you would trade or your trading methodology would be if your tenth trading value was your first, and your first was your tenth.

Now ask yourself what do my values need to be in order to succeed here? And in what order of importance?

____

We've been looking at those values we desire and go towards. Equally important, however, are those negative values we avoid at all costs. Let's assume that what you want most is to make money trading. All well and good. But let's suppose that even more important to you is to avoid loss. Would you be able to make money? I doubt it, although I could be wrong.

In living there are many things we avoid. We tend to avoid rejection, failure, frustration, anger, loneliness, depression, failure, humiliation, guilt, shame, pain, sickness, mediocrity, fear, boredom, discontent, laziness, disorganization, distrust, treachery, and a host of other negative values. What do **you** most avoid in life?

____

____

Now ask yourself, what do you most avoid in your trading?

____

____

As to your trading, you may have answered with some of these negative criteria:

- Loss
- Insecurity
- Uncertainty
- Confusion
- Mediocrity
- Boredom
- Being Wrong
- Making Mistakes
- Humiliation
- Fear
- Self-delusion
- Ego Enhancement/Ego Denigration
- Euphoria
- Hope
- Remorse
- Panic
- ____________________
- ____________________
- ____________________
- ____________________

Now rank these in the order in which you would most like to avoid.

1. ____________________
2. ____________________
3. ____________________
4. ____________________
5. ____________________
6. ____________________
7. ____________________
8. ____________________
9. ____________________
10. ____________________

Ask yourself, *"How different would your trading be if your number one avoidance were your number ten and your number ten were your number one avoidance? How would your trading be different?"* ____________________

Now ask yourself, *"Are there any of these avoidance criteria that are getting in the way of your trading?"*

____

Put your towards values next to your away from values and explore whether or not either of these cancels the other out. For example, do you most seek success, but most desire to avoid failure? Could this need to avoid failure at all costs, cost you your success? Do you most want freedom but most want to avoid being wrong? Could this cost you your freedom? Do you most want wealth, but most seek to avoid uncertainty? Could this cost you your wealth?

Now each of these values, both towards and away from, are just words—big fat nominalizations. The question becomes what do we mean by success, wealth, security, or failure, loss, insecurity? For each of us the answer is different.

Take a moment to define the trading values you go towards, and as you do that make it easy to achieve that value. Don't make it so hard, for example, to achieve success that you'll spend your trading life discontent and discouraged because you never achieve it. Ask yourself, *"What has to happen in order for me to experience ___________?"* Remember, make it easy for you to experience your value.

1____________________

2____________________

3____________________

4____

5____

6____

7____

8____

9____

10____

Now take a moment to define those trading criteria you most wish to avoid. Just as you made it easy to achieve those criteria you wanted, now make it hard to experience those things you seek to avoid. For example, if you seek to avoid loss, don't define loss as a controlled, managed loss on a single trade but rather define it as far more extensive or out of control. Ask yourself, *"What has to happen for me to experience ____________?"* Remember, make it hard for you to experience what you at all costs want to avoid.

1____

2____

3____

4____

5____

6____

7____

8____

9____

10____

CHANGING BELIEFS

"We can believe what we choose. We are answerable for what we choose to believe."

—Cardinal Newman

We are electromagnetic beings organized by our beliefs and values. Our lives and each area of our lives are patterned around a cluster of ideas (beliefs and values).

Beliefs resist extinction and change. Usually this is good. Our lives have predictability and a theme. Beliefs give us coherency. We don't have to constantly be asking, what's important, what's true, what should be done. Our beliefs for the most part are transparent; they are just our interpretation of reality. We know that Summer follows Spring, that the sun will rise in the morning, that we are this kind of a person, and not that kind of a person. We define our reality and ourselves by stated and unstated definitions. It works: it's our short hand for being; our guidelines for doing. Our beliefs are in us like glue, the glue that holds us together and makes us our unique selves.

History is replete with examples of people willing to die to defend a belief they hold dear. Individuals and whole nations will willingly lay down their lives in support of what they believe. Our explanations of the world, of right and wrong, of who we are and should be, are intricately entwined with our beliefs.

The British philosopher **Bertrand Russell** went to jail on two occasions for championing certain causes, and yet when asked whether he was willing to die for his beliefs, he replied, ***"Of course not. After all, I may be wrong."***

Sometimes we find ourselves giving up on our dreams, falling short of our goals, alienating those we care about, and somehow just getting in our own way. As traders we may find ourselves overtrading, undertrading, not following our rules. Traders frequently complain about being their own worst enemy.

When this happens we need to look at our underlying beliefs. Remember beliefs are generalizations, conscious or unconscious, usually organized around a value. We have a value that's important to us to achieve or to avoid. A belief is a generalization we've made over time that helps us get what is important to us and avoid what we dislike or fear.

Can beliefs be changed? Of course they can. Think of some beliefs you had when you were younger that you no longer hold. You don't believe in Santa Claus or the Easter Bunny anymore. Perhaps you no longer believe in the religious dogma you were brought up with, or perhaps you do. Maybe you no longer believe in the American dream, or maybe you do. There are lots of beliefs that change as we experience life, and lots that don't.

Since beliefs motivate behavior, we need to look for the underlying belief that we hold when we don't like our behavior. In your trading, when you find yourself acting contrary to your purpose, ask yourself the discovery question: *"What must I believe in order to be doing/not doing this?"* If you're feeling strong emotions that don't support effective trading, ask yourself: *"What must I believe in order to be feeling this way?"* Think of something you do in your trading or a way that you feel that doesn't support your profitability, and ask yourself the discovery question. Write your answer below.

____

____

Now ask yourself, *"What is the worst thing I could say about my trading?"* Write down whatever first comes to your mind.

____

____

Whatever you just wrote down is your personal law about your trading. You'll want to reverse it.

ECOLOGY OF CHANGE OR LOOK BEFORE YOU LEAP

When you change a belief in your life you will begin to notice multiple changes in your life. When you change a belief in your trading, you will soon notice significant changes in your trading.

If you change a core belief that you hold, there will be major changes in your life, almost a domino effect. After all core beliefs organize a lot of a person's behavior. When you make a change in a core belief, you will correspondingly be making profound changes in your internal organization. If it's a peripheral belief, the changes will not be as significant.

Therefore it's important before changing a belief to explore whether or not any part of you has any objection to making the belief change. This is called checking the ecology.

One way to check the ecology of a change is to act **as if** it's some time in the future and you've already made the belief change. Pretend you already hold the new belief. Explore the positive effects of having made the change. Explore any negative effects of having made the change.

Come back to the present and go inside yourself and ask if any part of you objects to making this change of belief. If there are objections, you'll have to address the objections before you go about utilizing techniques for change.

There are several ways to go about changing a belief. Before you can replace a belief with a new one, you need to weaken the old belief first.

INTRODUCE DOUBT

"He who doubts from what he sees
Will ne're believe, do what you please
If the Sun and Moon should doubt
They'd immediately go out."
—William Blake

One way to change a belief is to simply **introduce doubt**. You can begin by doubting one small aspect of your belief. Once you have doubted one small aspect of it, the rest is open to question. This is what is done with the brain washing of prisoners of war. All they do is get the person to admit to one small, minor point of disagreement with their country's policy. Slowly they add to it, until, unwittingly, the prisoner of war has done a total about face, something he never would have done all in one step.

ASK QUESTIONS

Introduce questions. If you question anything enough, you'll begin to doubt it. Remember we never question a belief. That's the nature of belief. It's beyond question. When we believe something, we no longer question it in any way.

Questions can cast doubt. These are some good questions to ask yourself when a belief no longer serves you. Is there any part of this belief that is subject to question? How is this belief ludicrous? Was the person I learned this belief from worth modeling? What will it cost me if I don't let go of it?

Suppose someone had the belief, *"If I trade, I'll lose money."* Obviously this belief will not support successful trading. The person would either hesitate, cherry pick trades, or not trade at all. After all, who wants to lose money? Doubt could be elicited by asking a series of questions. *"Has there never been a time when I made money trading? Is it guaranteed that I'll lose money trading? How do I know the next trade will be a loser? And now start the positive. What if I can make money trading?"*

If the person holding the belief that trading equals losing money also suffered from a sense of unworthiness or a need to punish herself, she would go out and trade in such a way as to make the belief a self-fulfilling prophecy. She'd lose money! Lots of it. When she becomes aware of this demobilizing belief, she can begin to create doubt by asking herself: *"In what ways do I deserve a reward? In what ways do I deserve to make money? What valuable things can I do with the money I make?"*

USE AFFIRMATIONS

"Men willingly believe what they wish."
—Julius Caesar

"For what a man would like to be true, that he more readily believes."
—Francis Bacon

One powerful way to change a belief is through the **strategic use of affirmations**. An affirmation is a statement made in the present about the future as if it had already occurred in the past.

Well formedness conditions for affirmations are that they be stated in the present tense and be stated in positives. If you state it in the future, your unconscious will leave it out there in the future, and so it might never become a current reality. If you state something in the negative, the unconscious deletes the negative and hears only the unnegated word. If you say, "I don't fear loss." the unconscious hears, "I fear loss."

Notice that we're replacing one belief with another. To change a belief, you need to have something to put in its place, a new belief.

Try this exercise. Take the statement you wrote above about the worst thing you could say about your trading and reverse it.

____

This can become your new personal law of trading. Suppose you said, *"I don't follow my trading rules."* To have reversed it you would have said, *"I follow my trading rules."* Suppose you had said, *"I'm a terrible trader."* To reverse it you would have said, *"I'm a good trader."*

"I am always at a loss to know how much I should believe of my own stories."
—Washington Irving

There is a basic problem with simply reversing a belief. Everything in you knows better. It looks, sounds, and feels like a bald faced lie. Something you "know" to be untrue has little power to change you or the situation. There are several ways to get around this.

One way to handle the disbelief of the affirmation is to simply state the affirmation calmly. Then allow all the objections to come up. As the objections come up, exaggerate them to the point where the objections themselves seem untrue. Then calmly restate the affirmation and wait for some more objections. Handle these the same way. Keep doing this until you can state the affirmation without any negative response.

Another way to handle the natural disbelief is to turn the affirmation around into a question: *"In what ways do I follow my rules?" "In what ways am I a good trader?"* The mind assumes the truth of the question and goes on a search for the answer. You've dodged the baloney detector. Change your affirmation into a question.

An even better way to dodge the disbelief factor is to turn the affirmation into a process statement. Instead of saying, *"I follow my rules,"* a trader could say *"Each day I follow my rules with greater consistency."* Instead of saying, *"I'm a good trader,"* a trader could say, *"Every day in every way I'm becoming a better and better trader."*

The danger of reversing a perceived truth or even fact goes beyond simple disbelief: it could involve delusion. If you're undercapitalized, it does you no good to say you are fully capitalized. If you have no strategy with a winning edge, it is dangerous to pretend you do. Delusions have no place in effective trading. We need to know the truth, and the truth, if acted upon, can make us free.

We're talking here about limiting beliefs that are holding us back, not factual statements that are something we can wrestle with and overcome.

Take, for example, a person who is grossly overweight but has determined to become slender. Fat people often have an identity as a fat person—that this is who they are and who they always will be. It's simply who they are. This overweight person needs to change her identity before she can change her weight, or she'll just keep sabotaging the weight loss. It won't do any good to say, *"I am a slender person."* This, if believed, would be a delusion. More probably she simply wouldn't believe it, and the discrepancy would actually further enhance her belief in her identity as a fat person. She could, however, realistically say, *"Now I am becoming a slender person."*

Process statements work, particularly when you imagine the process-taking place over time. Take your personal law affirmation and turn it into a process statement.

VISUAL SUBMODALITY CHANGE OF BELIEFS

We think by making pictures, hearing sounds or talking to ourselves, and having feelings. We may think we just have ideas that are conceptually based, ideas that just come to us. Actually, however, in addition to cognition, we're busy seeing images—movies or still pictures—that flash, often unconsciously and fleetingly, into our mind. At the same time or sequentially we're hearing our own voice or someone else's voice talking to us, or we simply hear a sound that signifies something. These sights and sounds are accompanied by feelings.

The combination of the visual, auditory, and kinesthetic components make up thought. By taking each of these components separately and making changes, we can change our thoughts or beliefs.

One very strong way to change a belief is to alter the nuances (submodalities) of the visual component of the belief. For this exercise, we'll be working with a belief that underlies a trading behavior that you wish you didn't have. Use the limiting belief you wrote down above. Decide what belief you'd like to replace it with.

THE EXERCISE

1. Make an image of the old, limiting belief. It can be abstract, symbolic, or realistic.
2. Make an image of the new belief. It can be abstract, symbolic, or realistic.
3. Think of something you have doubt about. It's important that this something is unrelated to either the old or the new belief. Make an image of what you doubt.
4. Take the image of the old belief and the image of the doubt and put them side by side in your mind's eye. Now compare the submodalities of the two images. Which one is brighter? Which one is clearer, more focused? Is one fuzzy? Is one black and white and one in color? If both are in color, is one pastel and the other brighter colors? Are they still pictures, or are they movies, or is there one of each? If they're still pictures, are they framed or panoramic?
5. Give the old belief the submodalities of the image of doubt. Practice representing the old belief with the submodalities of doubt until you can only represent it this way.
6. Identify a belief that you have that you like. Make an image of it. Place it side by side in your mind's eye with the image of doubt. Contrast the two. Identify what submodalities makes the liked belief more certain.
7. Take the changed image of the old belief and focus on it. Imagine that old belief behind a door. Now slam the door on the old belief. Hear the door slam.
8. On the closed door put the image of the new belief.
9. Now move the door way out on the horizon so that it becomes just a tiny dot. Then bring it back giving the new belief all the impactful submodalities of the belief you like.
10. Do this several times to install the new belief.

For some of you it may have been very difficult to do this visualization exercise. Many people state that they can't or don't visualize. For these people, it just happens so fast that they're not aware of it. If you have trouble doing this, just stay with it for a while and pretend that you're doing it. Also, if you had trouble with the visualization process, you can try the following process based on a kinesthetic (or touch).

KINESTHETIC ANCHORING FOR BELIEF CHANGE

The other way we think is with emotions and sensations in our bodies. The following exercise is based on kinesthetic or physical touch accompanied with memory and future imagination of feelings.

THE EXERCISE

1. Think of the old belief you wish to replace. When you're in the full memory of that old belief, touch your thumb to your little finger of your left hand. Hold it for a while as you contemplate that old belief. Release the thumb and little finger.
2. Think of something you doubt very strongly. When you're fully into that experience, touch your thumb to your little finger of your right hand. Hold it for a while as you consider that which you doubt strongly. Release the thumb and little finger.
3. Touch the little finger to the thumb on your right hand and touch the little finger to the thumb on your left simultaneously and hold for a full minute. Release the touch on both hands.
4. Touch the little finger to the thumb on your left hand and notice how much weaker the old belief feels. Release the touch.
5. Think of a counter example to the old belief. (This would be something you did or felt that was quite contrary to the old belief.) When you're fully into the experience, touch your thumb to your ring finger on your left hand. Hold it for a while as you think of the counter example and then release the thumb and ring finger.
6. Think of the new belief that you want to replace the old belief. When you're fully into this experience, touch your left thumb to your left middle finger and hold for a while as you imagine the new belief. Release the touch.
7. Touch the thumb to the little finger and let go. Touch the thumb to the ring finger and let go. Touch the thumb to the middle finger and let go. Do this sequence several times.
8. Test: Touch the thumb to the little finger. You should immediately think of the new belief rather than the old belief.

Very often the beliefs we want to change aren't the ones that are limiting our behavior. It's important to get to the belief that is limiting your behavior. Once you've identified it, you can explore what belief you'd like to replace it with. Check the ecology to make sure no part of you objects to this change. Weaken the unwanted belief by introducing doubt through questioning and counter examples and exaggeration or by changing the way you represent it visually, auditorily, or kinesthetically. Then you can introduce the new belief using the exercises for belief change. Make sure your new belief is stated in positives and is also worded as a process rather than an accomplished fact.

[11] *Winner Take All*, William R. Gallacher, Mc Graw-Hill 1994

CHAPTER IV

EMOTIONS:

THE WELLSPRING OF TRADING SUCCESS AND FAILURE

"Nothing is more injurious to the character and to the intellect than the suppression of generous emotion."

—John Jay Chapman

Many traders have told me that they would prefer to trade with zero emotion—that if they could, they would feel neither fear nor euphoria. For these traders the essence of clear mindedness is the total absence of emotion.

Strangely enough, some of these same traders have told me that they want to employ their intuition in their trading. How, I ask them, could they access their intuition if they've blocked their feelings?

My answer to the traders who tell me they want to trade with no emotion of any kind is that it is impossible to be a human being and do anything of significance without feeling some emotion. The only way to trade without any emotion whatsoever is to program a computer to generate signals and to program the computer to call those signals to the floor. Even then, however, the trader would need to **feel** continuing trust, trust in the system and trust in the computer to allow the system to run.

"The traditional view is that emotions muck up thinking. The good thinker is supposed to be cool and detached and not influenced by emotion. The good thinker is supposed to be objective and to consider the facts in their own right and not for their relevance to his or her emotional needs... Yet any good decision must be emotional in the end. I place the emphasis on that phrase **in the end."**

—Edward De Bono

Emotions are ideas or thoughts connected to a physical sensation. People often deal with them as if they had no choice about them, no control over them. This chapter will show you that we do have control and that we can select and transform emotion even if we can't annihilate it.

Emotions are neither good nor bad. It depends on the context. Sometimes an emotion may be inappropriate for the current context or situation. Hyperconfidence may be good for giving a speech, but terribly dangerous in trading.

It is true that emotions often do run wild in trading and can create consequences equivalent to a train wreck in a trading account. However, to attempt to trade without any emotion whatsoever is to attempt the impossible. Emotions suppressed are emotions still, and as such have the power to effect behavior. Ironically, emotions suppressed have greater power than emotions appropriately recognized.

"There can be no transforming of darkness into light and of apathy into movement without emotion."

—Carl Jung

For many people emotions are like land mines, and they tiptoe through life trying to avoid uncomfortable feelings. Anytime a situation comes up that could be emotionally charged they back away. In order not to be rejected, they avoid reaching out to people. In order not to experience a feeling of failure, they avoid professional challenges. In short, they cut themselves off from huge areas of life in order not to risk feeling what they suspect might be an unpleasant emotion. In the process they miss much of what is valuable in life.

Other people miss fulfilling their potential and enjoying much of what life has to offer because they **are** captive to emotions that effectively block them from going forward. Feelings of fear, self-doubt, or inadequacy hold them back mercilessly.

We get into trouble with emotions when we get stuck in an emotion in a situation where it is not appropriate. We can avoid trouble by identifying the emotions. This way there's less chance of a buildup.

We need to have the choice to express our emotions. The situation determines whether it's appropriate or not to express our emotions. Our self-concept also effects how we express our emotions. Am I the kind of person who screams at a broker or money manager? Is it appropriate? Will it get me what I want?

What we will be exploring in this chapter are ways in which traders can acknowledge the emotions they're feeling, receive the information, and shift the emotion to something more helpful.

I asked Michael McCarthy how he handled emotions as a trader and as a money manager.

Michael: "I actually think my greatest asset is my mindset. I'm completely emotionally detached from myself as a person in relation to what's happening in the market. And there are a lot of people like that: soldiers in a war, doctors in an emergency room, fire fighters, and policemen. I think you're more effective by simply doing a very difficult job and being completely detached. The emotions are only going to drag you down."

"Think of a doctor who is operating on a little child who's been in a horrible accident. He needs to work really fast to save her life. It's to the child's detriment if the doctor sits there and cries and says, 'God, what a shame. She's so cute.'"

Ruth: "I would grant you that, but he's got to have a rush of adrenaline, a heightened sense of alertness because he's in an emergency. It's not just ho hum the kid has a cold."

Michael: "Yes, but keep in mind the doctor still has a great deal of emotion because he's decided to make his career saving people's lives. Eighty percent of his career is spent saving people's lives. He has a great deal of emotion, maybe even more emotion than the person who would sit there and cry. He dedicates his life to this. So the emotion is there, but it's not on the surface. It's not out there in front of him."

Ruth: "It's not being expressed."

Michael: "Yes, like me. I manage over a quarter of a billion dollars for thousands of people. I care about these people, no matter who they are, whether they have a small amount of money or a large amount, and I actually have a much softer spot for the smaller people. I feel like I'm a parent taking care of an infant because this innocent needs to be taken care of in a dangerous place. So there's a deep sense of emotion there, but if the market goes against me and I lose a percent—that's over two and one-half million dollars—if I were to say, 'Oh no! I'm doing such a disservice to these people. They work so hard for this money, how can I do this?' And all that. If that's how I feel, I'm going to be totally ineffective. At the same time when I make them thirty percent, I don't say I'm a genius either. You can't. You lose if you take that attitude. I just say, 'Okay great. It worked this year. We've got some nuts stored up in case winter hits. The dry season.' I look at it that way, like a squirrel gathering the nuts. I think you're much more effective if you take your—I call them upper emotions—and remove them. It's like having your emotions invest your money. That's really horrible. That brings people down."

Ruth: "Some of my traders say they experience a combination of anxiety and excitement, or a feeling of tightness. Everybody says they want to be totally detached, like a machine. But people aren't. But I like your analogy of the doctor. Tell me. What kind of emotions do you experience? Can you name them? And what do you feel when you're not in the market?"

Michael: "There are a couple of different scenarios. Let's say the market is going up a lot, and I'm not in. That does not bother me one bit. Not at all. I'm completely okay with that. The way I look at it is I'm not losing. That's my job. I'm here primarily to protect people's capital. The not losing takes precedence over the winning part. I think most people feel the worst when they're missing out."

Ruth: "What about when the market goes down and you're in?"

Michael: "Oh, I don't like that! I don't like that!"

Ruth: "Well, it happens."

Michael: "The only time that would get me bothered...if I lose a percent, I'm alright with that. But if I lose two or three percent in a day...and the only time that happens, knock on something, is once or twice in a year. I don't like that at all. If I lose my own money, that's okay. That's just part of the game. The only part I don't like is having clients call and yell at me for that. All they're doing is pushing emotions on me. That's cancer. So I push back."

Ruth: "Right. Does the fact that the clients are going to respond effect you?"

Michael: "Sometimes, especially with the number of clients I have right now. If I get one or two people complaining, that can stay with me for a while. My response to that is it throws me out of my efficiency zone. So I usually get rid of the client, and my rationale on that is that one or two clients are possibly being detrimental to the other 3,000, and I can't have that. I really believe that. These people can drag you down to failure."

Ruth: "That's what I advise in a situation like that. One or two rotten apples spoil the barrel."

Michael: "The tendency of most people in a different business would be to try to accommodate the squeaky wheel. It's so ridiculous that a client would make a complaining phone call like this, but the client is not doing well, and he calls up and yells at the money manager and wants him to make more money. All it's going to do, at best, if that client is really being heard is to make the manager nervous. Then he's really going to do badly."

"Again. It's like the doctor example. Take two patients about to go into surgery. One says, 'I hope you can save my life. I'm just so grateful. I have a loving family, and they really need me. We're all hoping you do well.' That person is probably going to get a great job. The other person says, 'You better save my life, or I'm going to sue you. When I'm dead my estate will sue you.' The doctor is going to slip with the knife."

Ruth: "It's very much like saying in golf. 'Don't hit it in the water.' The next thing you hear is a splash. The water hole acquires a magical attraction."

Michael: "Exactly. If you listen to those people, and it's easy to do, you run the risk of having them completely destroy what you so carefully crafted."

Ruth: "How would you advise somebody to get this detached state of mind where the 'upper emotions' are not on their sleeve?

Michael: "Try to think of other analogies. For example, if you're driving on the road going 80 miles an hour and you go into a dark tunnel with all the other cars, it doesn't help you at all to scream or to swerve or to hit the brakes. The best thing is to stay calm. And continue to drive efficiently. That's very hard to do, but when you're in a life or death situation it's a disservice to be emotional."

"Think of a plane crash. It doesn't help you to scream. You grab your life jacket and try to swim somewhere. If you have a cell phone, you call for help. Those sorts of things. Once you begin to understand just how detrimental emotions can be in certain situations, you stop getting emotional.

Ruth: "Basically, you're looking at trading as an emergency situation."

Michael: "Absolutely. No question. It is. You can die in a day. It's war. But it's fun."

Ruth: "It's fun. Let's speak to that. You really enjoy this heightened state of danger."

Michael: "That's how I take it but it's really not. What's the most I can lose in a day in mutual funds? On average 2-3 %. Maybe once every 5 years I'll lose 5% in a day. Maybe once in 20 years I'll lose 20% in a day. You're not losing all of it. You're not going to zero. If I lose 100%, the world's over."

Ruth: "Still, you're looking at it as an emergency situation."

Michael: "Yes. Maybe like an airline pilot. That guy knows with just a flip of a switch he can kill hundreds of people and himself. He has that power. And that keeps you awake. I think what I'm trying to point out is that my job is not that unique. It's similar to other situations."

Each trader handles emotions differently. I talked with Linda Raschke about how she handles emotions, and about how she stays in the present.

Linda: "I'm just used to doing it. I really do credit that I practiced the piano six hours every single day, not so much when I was younger, but definitely when I was in high school and college. I was practicing all the time, and it's sort of a single mindedness. You have to be able to concentrate, but concentrate in a detached way. You're not staring at every tick. You're not tense. You're concentrating in what is actually a very relaxed, aloof way. My mom always accuses me of being aloof. That's her word.

Ruth: "You have a detachment."

Linda: "Yes, a very detached way of being laid back."

Ruth: "I want to ask about emotions. What do you feel when you trade? Do you feel emotions when you're trading?"

Linda: "I really don't. I have such a thick skin. I had so many stressful situations on the trading floor, and I lost so much sleep in the eighties thinking why did I do that? Why didn't I have a little more patience? Why did I stick my nose in too soon? Why did I...waking up at 3:00 in the morning saying, 'God, I shouldn't have done that. How could I have been so stupid!' I went through that. I went through that for ten years."

Ruth: "And what was your answer? Why did I do that? How could I have been so stupid? You did the best you could at the time, of course."

Linda: "You know, I think about that. It was almost like I was more gutsy back then. I think I took a lot more risk back then than I do now. I don't think I'm quite as willing to take the same kind of risk that I did then, and I had a lot of volatility back then. I made huge amounts in one day. I can't believe so much money sometimes. But I also had days where I lost a lot of money too. Let's just say that over all..."

Ruth: "You made more than you lost."

Linda: "Oh well, sure. But you don't understand. It's the principle of the game. I could have made $1,000,000 and if you'd lose $80,000, it's still a huge, huge, huge loss even if you're still ahead by $920,000. It's the principle of the game, if that makes sense. It doesn't really matter if you've made $5,000,000 and you still have a bad day, the fact of the matter is you've still had a bad day."

Ruth: "The concern there is, am I going to have a bad day tomorrow?"

Linda: "No. No. No. You never think that. It's you didn't play the game well that day. You screwed up."

Ruth: "It doesn't effect your thoughts about tomorrow. You're always able to make that distinction. That's important."

Linda: "Absolutely. You know how I liken it? It's like cheating on a diet. You've been working hard, you've lost some weight, you're sizing, and you go to that wedding and intend to just have a strawberry or two and you end up eating chocolate cake, totally screwing up, and you come home that night and you say, 'Why did I just undo all that hard work? Why did I eat all that stuff? I feel terrible. Why did I just eat 3,000 calories?' It has nothing to do with tomorrow. You go right back on the diet tomorrow. You go back to the drawing board."

Ruth: "I can really relate to that."

Linda: "That's how it is when you make a mistake in trading, or you let a position get out of hand, or you don't exercise the patience, or you make a spontaneous trade you didn't plan on making, or you're thrown for a loop. It has no bearing on tomorrow or the week or the month or the year or anything like that, but the damage is done. It's just sometimes, you know, that it didn't have to happen that way. But on average you have to look at it like, okay, you're playing the game and I know I can play the game well, but it doesn't mean you play it great every day."

"On some days now I've gotten much better. I don't know if this is good or bad. I almost think it's bad. You know all those things they say—if you don't feel like trading that day, don't. Well, I don't always agree with that because it can get too easy to say, 'Oh, I'll let this trade go. Oh, I'll let this trade go.'"

"You have to force yourself to be on the battlefront. And, yes, it's true, you don't want to be trading multiple S&P contracts if you're going through a divorce and you've got a hangover, but the truth of the matter is this is a playing ground where we make our living and if you're not on that frontline, you're not making a living. So somehow you have to participate in some way; even if it's, okay, I may not be able to handle a lot of leverage or a lot of positions, but I'm still going to monitor the market and maybe I'll just trade a couple of gold contracts or something that you're not going to get in trouble on. You see what I'm saying? So you have to know I'm not going to really knock them dead maybe for whatever reasons, but you have to go in there and play somehow."

Ruth: "So you always go and trade. You just do it regardless of how you feel."

Linda: "Cause this is how you make your living. And I'm not one of those people that can sit there and trade three days on and two days off. I still have to be involved because that's what gives me my feel for the next day. It's like a continuum. If I'm away for a couple of days, I always feel when I come back to the market after a couple of days like I've been gone for a month. Even if you're not trading, it's still important, for me at least, to follow along with the patterns and follow along with the overall structure. The market is unfolding. And if you're not watching, you're missing clues to the puzzle, or pieces of the puzzle if you're absent from the game."

A NEW LOOK AT FEAR AND GREED

"Desire and force between them are responsible for all our actions; desire causes our voluntary acts, force our involuntary."
—Blaise Pascal

Fear and greed are so commonly referred to in trading that they've become cliches. As standard wisdom, they are still a fairly accurate portrayal of the dynamics of trading. Ugly words, but true—to a degree. And degrees of fear and greed are the essence of emotional management in trading.

The history of market action is the history of fear and greed writ large. Markets are moved by mass psychology, from the Dutch tulip mania to the crash of 1987 and the subsequent market recovery. The psychological patterns of blow-off, collapse, and recovery are well known by most professionals.

Fear and greed are as reliable in trading as rain and sunshine, night and day. They are an endemic part of trading, and as such they must be managed and moderated.

Futures charts and stock charts are classic portrayals of fear and greed. I particularly like looking at the black and white patterns of the candlestick charts. It's so graphic with the long and short black bars representing fear and withdrawal and the long and short white bars representing greed and advance. Of course, if there's a massive short interest, it could be the other way around. When the market is in a protracted trading range, fear and greed are in balance.

The two emotions of fear and greed are bimodal, that is, they are both held in the mind at the same time. You can feel both fear and greed at the same time. Fear motivates retreat.

Greed motivates attack. Since they are conflicting emotions, they will immobilize a person until one or the other dominates and overcomes the other. The law of dominant effect says that the strongest emotion always wins.

These emotions are primordial. They are housed in the deepest part of the brain, the limbic system. They take us back to the fight or flight mode of the earliest man out hunting. It doesn't matter how sophisticated your flow of information, how leading edge your technical indicators, at the moment of decision you are operating from your reptilian brain, and from your limbic system. You are flooded with emotions once used to fight lions and tigers. Your survival depends on it. Your are at the stress point. The fight or flight system has taken over.

Think of times in your own trading when fear took over. You may have grabbed a profit way too soon. You may have gotten frozen in a losing trade. You may have remained immobilized when a signal screamed buy.

Think of a time when greed took over. You may have jumped into the market anticipating a signal that never developed. You may have put on far too large a position for the size of your account. You may have begun trading a methodology way before you verified that it worked.

In any of these instances fear or greed predominated and was not balanced by the other emotion. Both emotions are necessary. Fear moves away from. Greed moves towards. Fear without greed does not move forward. Greed without fear throws caution to the winds. If you had only fear, you would have no reason at all to trade. If you had only greed, you would have no force to protect you against undue loss. History shows that in trading and investing, we need in some form both fear and greed. We need a balance between these two motivations.

Max Ansbacher is the president of **Ansbacher Investment Management** in New York, which has attracted more than ten million dollars under management in the two years since the firm commenced operations. Max is a regular guest on the Bloomberg cable television network where he discusses fundamental factors affecting the stock market, and frequently discusses option topics. Max has compiled an impressive track record over the past ten years trading. He exclusively sells out of the money S&P options according to a system that determines which ones are most overvalued. His formulation for calculating this is known as the Ansbacher Index.

I asked Max how he handled emotions as he traded.

Max: "We all have some emotion trading. I have not found my emotions have particularly intruded in my trading.

Ruth: "You have emotions but they don't intrude."

Max: "I hope they don't. I like to think they don't."

"Emotions are good too. When you get scared, maybe it's a good idea to act that way, to close down positions, trade fewer positions, take less risks."

"When you're doing well, the danger is you feel omnipotent or omniscient. You think you know what is going to happen. Then the risk is you put on too big a position, and if it goes against you, you can have a major loss."

Ruth: "How do you keep these emotions in bounds?"

Max: "I've developed rules over the years. The rules keep me from getting over exuberant and putting on too large a position."

"My stops are always in the market in a graduated sequence. I don't have as much fear as I used to."

"There are old traders. There are bold traders. There are no old, bold traders."

We need to moderate fear and greed. We certainly don't want them in their rawest, most virulent form. We need to honor them and at the same time trim them back. We need to transform fear to savvy caution and turn greed into realistic desire.

One way to moderate an emotion is to slide on a continuum to its opposite emotion. Do we go from fear to greed and back again? Only if they are the opposite of each other. The cliche holds that they are. They are not. They are two bimodal emotions held in the mind at the same time. Fear and greed are not the opposite of each other.

We can transform opposites. We can turn sharp to dull and dull to sharp. We can turn light to dark and dark to light. But we cannot turn sharp to dark or light to dull. Small does not become cold, and hot does not become large. To slide on a continuum away from extremes of fear and greed, we need to go towards the opposite of that emotion.

In effective trading we need to move along an analogue as we pull back from the extremes. We can begin by scaling fear back to healthy caution and scaling greed back to realistic desire. Then we can slide along the continuum towards each opposite until we get to our optimum-trading zone. This may be different for different traders. In order to move toward the opposite of an emotion we need to determine what that opposite is.

What, then, is the opposite of fear? Is it courage? It is true that in order to experience courage, we need to first experience fear. As **John Wayne** said, ***"Courage is being scared to death and saddling up anyway."***

I do not, however, think courage is the opposite of fear, because the opposite of courage is not fear, it's cowardice. However, fear can often masquerade as cowardice.

Some have said that the opposite of fear is love. Quite frankly, I think that's nonsense. We don't slide from fear to love anymore than we move from hot to dull. The opposite of love is hate.

Some say the opposite of fear is hope. This is getting closer, but I don't think so, because the opposite of hope is despair.

How do we move away from fear in trading? We move towards trust. In trading this would mean trusting your methodology, trusting the whole trading process, trusting that at the end of the day, the week, the month, or the year you will be profitable.

How much do you trust yourself in the trading process? Do you trust your methodology? If you don't, your fear may be well founded. It may be time to verify and/or find a method that you can trust.

Do you trust yourself to perceive clearly and act promptly on your perceptions? If you do not trust yourself, perhaps you should not. It may be time to make some changes in yourself, to get some coaching.

The elements of trust are confidence, faith, and optimism.

The **Oxford English Dictionary** has defined trust as confidence in or reliance on some quality or attribute of a person or a thing, or the truth of a statement. Trust is the confident expectation of something.

Confident expectation of ultimate success is a good place to trade as long as it's modified by a frequent visitation of caution.

The extreme opposite of fear, however, is not trust: the extreme opposite of fear is overconfidence. The path would be backwards from fear to caution to trust to confidence to overconfidence. If you slide from fear to unfounded overconfidence in your trading, you have set yourself up for a big fall.

Yes. We do need to have some form of fear in our trading. It serves a valuable function; but we need to moderate it to the most effective place on the analogue of the emotion. One extreme of fear would be panic: the other would be overconfidence or blinded arrogance. I like to trade with healthy caution and trust, moving back and forth between them.

This whole business of trading in your peak emotional zone is finding your best place along the analogues of these bimodal emotions, fear and greed, and trading from there.

What is the opposite of greed since it isn't fear?

First, let's look at greed itself. Greed is the inordinate wanting of something. Greed is needy. There is a nervous, almost panicky grasping in a greedy person. It is almost as if there is a black hole that devours and will not be filled. Think of the punch drunk trader going for it full tilt until the very greed demolishes the account and leaves the trader wanting even more. Or think of the greedy eater stuffing herself way beyond the point of satisfaction or satiation and still wanting more. Greed by its very nature cannot be filled.

Unadulterated greed cannot be satisfied, and it doesn't matter whether the greed is for food or money. The reason behind this is that the real longing is for something other than the thing a person is greedy about. All the money in the world will not satisfy a person whose real need is security. All the food in the world will not satisfy a person whose real need is love.

If you think money will satisfy your need for security, wait until you have it. It won't. You may start changing the numbers of the amount you need upward, or you may start looking around for other causes of insecurity. I coach traders to find security in the knowledge of their skills, in their awareness that they can always make enough money trading to meet their needs and wants.

For a month I went around asking people what they thought was the opposite of greed. Some said the opposite of greed was generosity. Others said it was spending. I asked myself what was the inverse of spending and generosity, and I came up with parsimony and stinginess. If parsimony and stinginess were the opposite of spending and generosity, then neither spending nor generosity were the opposite of greed.

Other people said the opposite of greed was self-denial or a vow of poverty. This probably is the extreme opposite of greed; just as arrogant overconfidence is the extreme opposite of fear. It would not be wise to trade from an attitude of unworthy self-denial or a commitment to the righteousness of poverty anymore than it would be wise to trade with an attitude of arrogant overconfidence.

In one of our long conversations, my sister, Marion Barrons, declared that the opposite of greed was contentment. My response was "Bingo!"

The **Oxford English Dictionary** defines greed as "Inordinate or insatiate longing, especially for wealth; covetous desire."

The opposite of inordinate or insatiate longing would be contentment. If you were totally content with the status of your account or your funds, there would be no need to risk making money. Total contentment could put you into neutral. It's not a bad place to be. It's just not going to put you into fighting form to trade. Why would I trade if I were totally content with my status?

To trade in an effective state of mind, you would need to move forward from self- denial and unworthiness right through contentment to a state of worthy desire, to a state of optimistic and reasonable anticipation of winning.

You would also need to move backwards from insatiate longing (greed) towards a healthy desire and a modulated anticipation of winning.

You slide along the scale from the extremes to a balanced position. You move from utter contentment or self-denial to an inspired desire but not all the way to a needy greedy motivation. You move back from all out greed to a rational and realistic hunger for profit but not so far back that you no longer want.

With fear you move backwards from all out terror to a confident and trusting anticipation of success and you move forward from over presumption and blind trust to a cautioned alertness to danger.

Properly balanced and moderated, you have an inspired desire to trade profitably and a confident anticipation of your ultimate success. You maintain a rational and realistic hunger for profits while you also maintain a cautioned alertness to danger. Desire and caution hold your hands while you trade.

All this is fine and good, but how do you change fear to caution and greed to desire?

SHIFTING EMOTIONS

The first step towards shifting emotions is recognizing what you are feeling and appreciating that that feeling is true and has a purpose. Traders may not want to have any emotions when they trade, but generally they readily admit to a vast array of emotions. In contrast to corporate people who will usually only admit to stress and ambition, or in a worst case scenario—burnout, traders will freely speak of remorse, panic, greed, euphoria, anxiety, excitement, frustration, anger, discouragement, glee, amazement, and so forth.

Some people are imprecise about what they're feeling. These people are aware of feeling "bad" or "good," but it doesn't go much beyond that. To understand what your emotions are telling you, and to have full emotional choice so you can begin to shift what you feel or express, you need to pay full attention to just what exactly it is you're experiencing so you can identify the specific emotion you're feeling.

I spoke with one trader who talked about the ego trip of making money—more on that in a coming chapter—and the pain of losing money. I asked him to be more precise about the pain. Did he feel fear, panic, anxiety, remorse, anger, guilt, discouragement, disappointment, frustration or some other emotion? He said, "Losing money is it's own emotion. Probably has all of those in there and something else as well." Probably does and the exact emotions one feels upon losing could be identified by paying attention and allowing for them knowing they will pass and can be transformed.

As you make friends with your emotions, you develop emotional choice. You can begin to experience a wider range of emotions. You can begin to understand what each of your emotions is communicating to you. You can begin to shift from one emotion to another.

EMOTIONS ARE MESSENGERS

It's important to know just what emotion you are feeling because emotions are messengers. You can think of an emotion as a wise, caring friend who is telling you something vital to your interests. It's important to listen and pay attention.

Just as physical symptoms tell you something about your body and your life, so too do emotions. Emotions are signals about what is going on in your life. Ongoing and chronic depression is a signal that a person needs to change something about herself or her life.

Often our response to an unpleasant emotion is to get rid of it. People turn to drinking, smoking, eating, Prozac and so forth to eliminate uncomfortable feelings. This does not resolve the underlying situation or give you the benefit of the message the emotion is giving you. Having an emotion about your emotion blocks you from learning from the initial feeling.

Rather than side stepping an emotion or trying to flatten it, it's important to pay attention, because pleasant or unpleasant, the emotion is a signal about some aspect of your life or activity. Each emotion has a **functional attribute**.

The positive emotions tell you that something's right, to pay attention to what you have, and to keep on doing what you're doing. Many people are afraid to allow themselves to feel the joyful emotions such as love, excitement, rejoicing, confidence, satisfaction, or gratitude because they're afraid they won't last, and they'll be disappointed.

To this I would say life's fleeting joys are wonderful highlights that lead the way to more. You tend to get more of what you pay attention to. You're also establishing memories that you can hook into later to make your future more rewarding. If your trading is going well, let yourself feel good about it, just don't lose discipline and don't lose clear vision of what the market is doing price wise. The positive memory will give you strength when the inevitable draw-downs occur.

One of my young trading assistants once told me that he had met the woman of his dreams who had everything he wanted in a woman. He went on to say that he was afraid to let himself care because he didn't want to get hurt. My response was to encourage him to go ahead and care and really enjoy the relationship. If it came to an end, we could handle it then; and we'd have a wonderful memory and emotion to anchor into and to transfer to other situations. Years later he told me it was the best advice he'd ever gotten. He had married the woman and was very happy. Even if it hadn't turned out well, he would still have had a resource in the positive feelings of the memory.

Positive emotions are messages that things are as we want them. To notice and invite and explore and develop positive emotions is to put yourself on the course of personal power.

Negative emotions are a call to action, a call to change something. As such they are a vital signal to your well being, and should not be ignored.

The functional attribute of regret or remorse is a signal that you could have done something differently in the past. It apprises you to do something different in the future. This is called learning from mistakes, and is an important part of trading.

The functional attribute of fear or anxiety is a warning that something in the future needs to be prepared for. In trading, if you've done your preparation, there's no need for fear. If the probabilities aren't in your favor, it's a signal to stop what you're doing and get a strategy that puts the probabilities on your side.

The functional attribute of guilt is notice that you have violated your own (or somebody else's) standards. You need to determine whose standards were violated. If it's somebody else's standards, decide whether you want those standards to be your own. If you violated your own standards, resolve not to do so in the future.

The functional attribute of anger is a message that somebody else is violating your standards and you need to do something to stop this in the future. If you're furious with slippage and speed of fills, you may need to get a new broker or communicate in such a way that corrects the situation.

The functional attribute of frustration is a sign that you haven't given up on your goal, and that you need to do something else to get you to your goal. Frustration is a good indicator: it means you need to keep exploring different solutions. You're on the path; you just haven't found the way—yet.

Each of these functional attributes is at the heart of emotional utilization. Once we accept the message our approach is signified. The emotion is worth having if we respond appropriately. Unfortunately, too often the negative emotions are felt and expressed but not responded to appropriately.

In their marvelous book, ***The Emotional Hostage***[1], Leslie Cameron-Bandler and Michael Lebeau show how to create a generative chain for employing and transforming emotions. Emotions are chained naturally. One emotion leads to another like links in a chain. Without consciously or unconsciously employing techniques to lift yourself out of a negative emotion, you could find yourself spiraling downward in a progression of more intense negative emotions.

The natural evolution for most people upon feeling a seriously negative emotion would be to link a set of ever intensifying negative emotions. For example, a person begins by feeling overwhelmed, which leads her to feeling inadequate, then she feels hopeless, and finally she becomes depressed.

Another example would be a trader having a losing trade and feeling disappointed, then imagining that he'll lose the next trade and the next, and feeling discouraged and then imagining losing all his trading capital and feeling fearful. If he's not careful, he can take it even further. He can imagine losing his wife and his house and ending up homeless. At this point his very survival is at stake. He's feeling terrorized and fighting for his life—just because of a losing trade!

Much better to build a generative chain that will take the functional attribute of the negative emotion and lead you to where you want to go. Here, in general, is how to do it.

First, recognize the emotion and identify just exactly what it is you are feeling. For example, are you feeling uncertain or are you feeling fearful? Are you feeling frustrated or are you feeling discouraged? If you're feeling frustrated, you're still in the game. If you're feeling discouraged, you may be on the verge of giving up.

Second, acknowledge and appreciate the emotion realizing that every emotion, no matter how negative, has a functional attribute. Pay attention to the functional attribute of the emotion you're feeling.

Third, get curious about what action needs to be taken.

Fourth, remember a time in the past when you effectively handled a similar situation. Replay it in your mind so you can build confidence.

Fifth, in your imagination go into the future and play out a successful conclusion to the situation.

Sixth, take action based upon the prior steps. This puts you in control. When you have a sense of control over your actions and your future, the negative emotions begin to dissipate.

Let's look at a version of ***The Emotional Hostage's*** generative chain for regret. Let's assume you encountered significant trading losses by overtrading, second guessing your system, not using a stop, or adding to a trading loss.

Generative Chain for Regret

1. Recognize you're feeling regretful
2. Feel respectful and appreciative toward your feeling of regret and realize it's a signal that you need to do something to ensure that you don't repeat the same mistake in the future.
3. With a feeling of curiosity, evaluate your mistake with respect to what you could have done to avoid making it.
4. Recall memories of mistakes you have made (past sources of regrets) that you corrected once you knew what to do. Use these examples as a basis for feeling reassured.
5. Imagine a future situation in which you do what you have identified should have been done in the situation you feel regretful about. Make this rich and vivid rehearsal of the future compelling enough that it fills you with confidence about your ability to actually fulfill that future.
6. Trade in accordance with your plan.

Let's assume you're anxious and fearful about your trading. The emotions flood you each time you trade. Here is a version of the ***Emotional Hostage's*** generative chain for anxiety.

Generative Chain for Anxiety

1. Recognize that you are feeling anxious.
2. Remember that feeling anxious is a signal to you that there is something in your future for which you need to better prepare, and feel respect and appreciation for that emotion as a vital signal.
3. With a feeling of curiosity, evaluate what you need to do to better prepare. This may involve gathering information to fill in your picture of the future, marshalling or acquiring certain skills, or establishing a positively stated outcome.
4. Recall examples from your past when you have done what you now need to do to meet this future challenge or threat, feeling reassured as you recall these memories of your capability.
5. Imagine yourself in the future preparing to meet the future challenge or threat, repeating this rehearsal until you feel confident about your ability to do what you need to do.
6. Move ahead with your trading, employing your rehearsed technique even as you remain alert to feedback.

THE STRUCTURE OF EMOTIONS

Each emotion has a different structure. Understanding the structure allows you to change an emotion and allows you to access all of your emotions.

Each emotion has two to four variables. Once you change one of the variables, you change the emotion.

The possible structural components of an emotion include time frame, modality, involvement, criteria, tempo, comparison, chunk size, and intensity.

Time Frame

Fear and anxiety are future oriented emotions. You're not afraid in the present; it's the future you're worried about. By pulling yourself back into the present, you can avoid fear.

It's really important to trade in the present, because that's all you have and all you know. The future is just conjecture and probabilities. The present is the only place of certainty—the past may or may not repeat. You don't want to trade yesterday's action today. That was then. This is now. If you stay in the present, you may experience a heightened alertness but you won't experience fear. Granted, it's hard to stay in the present when you're trading because something's always about to happen and you're alert for it, but it will help the fear factor if you can.

Regret and remorse are past oriented emotions. These emotions refer to something that occurred in the past or that you did or didn't do. By moving your attention to the future, and how you plan to make things different, you can eliminate the regret or remorse.

If you overtraded in terms of size or frequency and lost a great deal of money, you can take a lesson from that and begin to imagine yourself in the future with strict money management controls and using restraint so that you take only high probability trades. As you visualize a future of effective, disciplined trading, remorse can be replaced with hope or confidence.

Irritation and frustration are present oriented emotions. You can only feel these emotions in the present. By turning your attention to the past or the future you can remove the feeling.

If you're getting irritated with your broker, begin to talk about how you'd like things to go in the future. This will very quickly smooth over the irritation. If you're frustrated in developing a trading system, begin to think about methods that worked in the past or that might work in the future.

Modality

Our language shapes the modality of an emotion. These are words that describe the **necessity, possibility, and desirability** of something. They are verbal expressions revealing beliefs we have. When we say we "need" to or "must" do something, we are describing a belief in the necessity of doing it. When we say we "could," "can," or "might" do something, we are describing a belief in the possibility of doing it; whereas when we say "can't," we are describing a belief in the impossibility of doing something. Words such as "want," "will," "should," or "won't" describe the desirability or undesirability of doing something.

For many emotions the modality words are a key ingredient of the feeling. Change the modality and you change a key structure of the emotion.

Some examples are the following. Desperation or urgency would use the modal operator "need." Feelings of pressure overwhelm, or the modal operator "must" would imply obsession. "Should" implies a sense of obligation. "Should have" suggests you're guilty, regretful, or remorseful. "Could" implies hope or optimism. "Can" suggests able, adequate, confident, or capable. "Might" indicates vulnerability, apprehensiveness, or curiosity. "Might have been" or "could have been" suggest disappointment. If you were feeling helpless or inadequate, you would use the modal operator "can't." When you're despairing, resigned, or hopeless, you would say something "can't be done." When you're motivated, attracted, desirous or greedy, you would say "want." "Will" indicates tenacity, determination, or ambition.

As you read the following sentences, allow yourself to feel the difference of the emotion that is created by simply changing the modal operator. I *need* to make money trading. I *must* make money trading. I *should* make money trading. I *should have* made money trading. I *could* make money trading. I *can* make money trading. I *might* make money trading. I *might have* made money trading. I *can't* make money trading. Making money in the markets *can't be done.* I *want* to make money trading. I *will* make money trading.

You can reread the sentences using all of the modal operators in sequence but ending the sentence with an aspect of your trading that is either a weakness or important to you. For example, I *need* to follow my rules, etc. I *must* use stops. I *should* prepare for each trading day. I *should have* listened when the broker repeated the order. I *could* follow my intuition. I *can* trade profitably. And so forth.

It's clear that by shifting the modal operator, you shift an important aspect of the meaning of the sentence and alter the emotion.

Involvement

Involvement refers to **passive and active roles**. The feeling of hope is passive. The feeling of determination is active. When you have an outcome that you want, it might be passive or active. Raise the level of wanting to ambition and you become more actively involved. Reduce it to wishing and you have a passive involvement. We're not talking about the action here: we're talking about the feeling preceding the action. Winning traders are active in their emotional involvement.

There are active and passive roles with things we don't want. Self-pity is passive. Self-protection is active. A winning trader would be more involved with self-protection than self-pity.

Criteria

Criteria are the standards you are applying in a situation. Change the criteria, and you change the emotion. Suppose it's important for you to be right in a trade. You would have a high involvement in the outcome of a particular trade. Change the criteria to winning over time, and your emotional involvement in a particular trade diminishes.

There are criteria that we go **towards** and criteria that we go **away from**. Fear is an away from emotion, and greed is a towards emotion. **Some personalities will tend to be more towards in direction while others will tend to be more away from in direction.**

Whether you are predominantly towards or away from will definitely affect the way you trade. To determine which personality you are, ask yourself whether you think predominantly about the possibility of profit or the possibility of loss when you trade. Of course, you have to factor both considerations into your trading plan, but one will dominate your thoughts and thus your emotions and behaviors.

If you go predominantly away from loss you may have trouble pulling the trigger to get into a trade, you may hesitate longer than you should, and you may have trouble staying with a trade. If you go predominantly towards profit, you may jump the gun on a trade, you may overtrade, you may get stuck in a scenario trade, and you may not recognize when a trade is turning around.

Those who are strong away from traders need to think more about the criteria they want, and they need to create clear written positive outcome statements and visions for their trading. Those who are strong towards traders need to consider negative criteria, and they need to put written trading and money management rules into effect to protect themselves from danger.

Tempo

Different emotions have different tempos. The tempo, the speed with which you feel the emotion, will vary from emotion to emotion. The tempo may be fast, medium, or slow. Fast paced emotions would be excitement, anger, terror, restlessness, and impatience. Medium paced emotions could include determination, ambition, love, and curiosity. Slow paced emotions might include boredom, patience, depression, discouragement, and loneliness.

Emotions can also have an even or an uneven tempo. Calm has an even tempo. Anxiety has an uneven tempo. Anger is uneven. Patience is even. Calm and patient are slow and even in tempo. Anxiety and anger are fast and uneven.

By changing some aspect of the tempo, you can alter the emotion. Smooth out and slow down anxiety and you might get worried concern. This could be a better place from which to operate. Speed up patience and you become impatient. There are times when it's good to be patient and wait for something to develop: there are other times when it's important to get things moving so impatience will better serve you. Speed up discouragement and you get frustration, which will at least get you into action. Slow down furious and you get anger: slow down anger and you can create peeved.

Your tempo is something to pay attention to with regard to the trading style you employ. With a fast tempo, you probably wouldn't be comfortable with a buy and hold type strategy. With a slow tempo, you probably would not be effective as an S&P daytrader.

Matching/Mismatching and Comparison

When you match, you look at what's there, you look at what is the same. When you mismatch, you look at what's missing, and what is different. In feeling a liking for a person, you would probably be noticing what is there and what is similar to yourself. In disliking a person you would probably be noticing what's missing and what is different from yourself. In feeling satisfied, you would be noticing the ways in which circumstances have matched your needs or desires. In feeling dissatisfied, you would be noticing the ways in which circumstances have not fulfilled your needs or wants.

In trading you could mismatch to the losses or match to the wins. I have known people who create trading systems who can only mismatch to the 30% losses without ever matching to the 70% profits.

Some people are predominantly matchers. Others are naturally mismatchers. Either is fine, so long as you have a choice to match or mismatch depending on the situation. If something isn't working for you, notice whether you're matching or mismatching. Try doing the opposite.

We make comparisons all the time. We compare one day to another, one trade to another, one person to another. Comparing is part of our thinking mechanism. It's also a way that we create emotions. Comparing also involves a bit of matching and mismatching. It's the same. It's different. This is here. That is missing.

There are several ways we compare that contribute to emotions. We compare ourselves to another. We compare ourselves to ourselves. If we continually compare ourselves to another more accomplished or successful person, we will come up feeling inadequate or inferior or unable to do something.

If you continually compare your trading to that of a more masterful trader, you may feel feelings of inferiority. However, if you compare yourself and your trading to your past and assess what you've learned and how you progress, you'll feel a sense of accomplishment and improvement. Self-to-self comparisons generally evoke more useful and helpful emotions than self-to-other comparisons.

There's almost always going to be somebody doing better than you are. This is good because you can learn from them. It's important, however, if you make a comparison, not to let it make you feel inferior. You can always learn from them and others and yourself and improve. If you notice and compare your improvement to your past struggles, you'll be improving your self-esteem instead of damaging it.

Chunk Size

Are you looking at the big picture or the small details? If you're feeling overwhelmed (large chunk size), break what you're thinking about down into smaller chunks. If you're bored and feeling the tedium (small chunk size), move up the chunk size and look at the broader view of the thing. There are relatively few emotions that are built on a single chunk size.

You can experiment choosing the chunk size that's right for you in any particular situation or emotion. Experiment with chunk size and how it impacts your trading and such emotions as confidence, trust, understanding, and satisfaction. If you're feeling uncertain, anxious, or distrustful, expand and contract the chunk size and see what kind of difference that makes. Generally speaking, I think one trades best keeping the big picture (large chunk) in mind. However, there are times when you need to focus on the smaller chunk size, the important details.

Intensity

Intensity describes the strength of an emotion. Emotions have high, medium, and low intensities. Hysterical would be a high intensity whereas nervousness would be a lower intensity. In between the two extremes might be upset or dread.

It's quite easy to increase the intensity of an emotion by focusing on the situation and making the pictures in your mind bigger and brighter as you talk it up in your mind. You can take simple satisfaction and build it up to happy and move it further to thrilled and on to ecstatic.

You can increase the intensity of any emotion by exploring and developing the significance and the possibilities of a situation. You can take the reasonably cautious concern about the possibility of loss in trading and build it up in your mind until you're feeling intense anxiety and let that expand until you have crippling fear and you find yourself unable to enter a trade in a timely fashion or you freeze in an existing trade and fail to exit when you should.

You can also lower the intensity of an emotion. Many people do this automatically with powerful, positive emotions. If, for example, a person doesn't deep in their heart believe they deserve to be happy, that person will take ecstatic joy and move it down to merely happy and then on down to simple satisfaction.

On the negative side, one could reduce fury down to anger and then down to simple disapproval. Disapproval is generally easier to handle than all out fury. On the other hand, fury could be what is called for and therefore appropriate.

Whether you want to modify the extreme emotions or enjoy the full sweep of powerful emotions depends on your personality and style and the appropriateness of the emotion for the situation.

Remember the way to handle fear and greed is to reduce the intensity of the emotions and moderate them into new emotions.

PUTTING STRUCTURE TO WORK: AN EXERCISE

Think of a particular emotion that you feel with some regularity that gets in the way of your trading and doesn't serve you, or think of an emotion that you feel with regularity in some other aspect of your life that you wish you didn't feel. Name the exact emotion. Remember a specific time when you felt that emotion and relive it in your mind.

Are you looking toward the past or the future, or are you in the present? Try changing the time frame and see if that alters the emotion.

Go back into the emotion as you felt it before and notice what modal operators you're using such as can, should, want, and so forth. Alter the modal operator (change the helping word) and see if that makes a difference.

Get back into the original emotion and notice what criteria you're using. Try changing that. Does it have any effect on the emotion?

Get back in the experience of the original emotion and notice the tempo. Is it fast, slow, or medium? Is it even or uneven? Change that and notice the effect.

Resume feeling the source emotion and pay attention to whether you're noticing what's there or what's missing. Are you noticing what's the same or what's different? Are you comparing what to what? Try changing it and see if you experience a change.

Get back into the original emotion and check out the chunk size. Are you dealing with small pieces or the bigger picture? Try chunking up or down, and see if that makes a difference.

Get back into the beginning emotion and decide whether the intensity is high, medium, or low. Change that and feel the difference.

Decide which were the driving components, which changes had the greatest impact upon your feeling. Make a note of it, and the next time you start feeling the old emotion, make changes in the key components. By repeatedly doing this, it can become a habit; and your habitual emotional response will change.

You can also use this exercise to discover the key components of an emotion that you'd like to feel with some regularity such as courage, confidence, love, ambition, determination, and so forth. By using the driving structural elements, you can shift one emotion to another.

Also by using similarities of structural elements, you can shift one emotion to another. You can shift fear to excitement. Both emotions share a fast, uneven tempo and have a relatively high intensity and both are future oriented. That same shot of adrenaline can create thrill, fun, excitement, and heightened alertness, or fear, terror, panic, trepidation, and anxiety.

In summary, emotions are the natural God given feeling response we have to our thoughts and to the interpretations we make regarding events and experiences. Each emotion serves a valuable function and operates as a messenger from the unconscious to the conscious. It operates naturally from the most primitive part of our brain.

Our emotions make us beautifully, wonderfully alive and allow us the full range of human experience. Emotions are powerful assets and can be used to move us forward in support of the purpose of our lives. Emotions also keep us out of trouble and protect us. They give us power.

Emotions need to be appropriately utilized and expressed. Improperly utilized or expressed emotions can cripple us and cut us off from our full potential. Properly utilized and expressed, emotions are the key to living fully, healthfully, and effectively.

To boil it all down, there are three basic ways to create, transform, and direct emotions. Emotions are created by your physiology, your beliefs, and your focus.

The quickest and most direct way to change an emotion is to change your physiology. We'll be talking about this in a later chapter.

Another way to change emotions is to alter your beliefs. We covered this in the chapter on beliefs.

The third way to transform emotions is to direct the focus of your conscious thoughts. That is what we did in this chapter.

"Thinking can change emotions. It is not the logical part of thinking that changes emotions but the perceptual part. If we see something differently than we did before, our emotions may alter with the altered perception."

—Edward De Bono

[11] *"The Emotional Hostage,"* Leslie Cameron-Bandler, Michael Lebeau; FuturePace, Inc. ISBN 0-932573-03-7

CHAPTER V

RESOLVING CONFLICT

"Parts of the psyche detach themselves from consciousness and lead an autonomous life of their own."

—Carl Jung

"A part is not just a temporary emotional state or habitual thought patterns. Instead it is a discreet and autonomous mental system that has an idiosyncratic range of emotion, style of expression and set of abilities, intentions or functions."

—Richard Schwartz

John started each day with the full intention of trading his system. He'd spent three years developing the system for day trading the S&P's. The system gave 80 percent profitable entry signals. He'd paper traded the system for six months before he was ready to actually trade it. It made an enormous amount of money on paper.

The problem was the money was only on paper. Each day John would recommit to actually trading the system. His brokerage account was set up. He'd timed his speed dial making sure he had the fastest speed dial phone. He was set to go. But he just never put in a trade. He was still trading on paper.

At the end of each day John was sick. All his hard work meant nothing. He was still making enormous money on paper, but none in his account. Tension was building up inside him. He had begun to lose self-respect. No he'd begun to hate himself. Why couldn't he just pull the trigger? Tomorrow for sure he'd begin.

Tomorrow was the same thing all over again. Each day the tension became greater. John knew he'd have to get a grip on himself. For almost four years now he'd had expenses with no money coming in. He was sitting on the edge of a fortune, but he just couldn't make himself act. He couldn't understand it, and he couldn't stand it.

Roger kept fighting the market. He'd find himself pushing against the trend, canceling stops, adding to losing positions, and only taking them off at the end of the trading day. He knew he had to take them off because he didn't have enough margin to carry overnight. He kept refunding his account.

Roger had rules. He even had them written clearly. The rules said to take signals from the five-minute chart and to trade with the trend of the thirty-minute chart. He'd get into a position and start looking at the trend of the hourly, the daily, and the weekly charts. His rules called for strict stop placement. His rules did not allow for adding to any position, let alone a losing one. He'd set up a daily loss stop of $1500. If he lost $1500, he would stop trading for the day.

Roger would have a bad trading day where he would fling all his rules to the wind and end up losing serious money. He'd refund the account and trade appropriately for a few days, and then he'd do it again. The very same thing: cancel the stop, add to the position, ignore the trend, and fight the market all the way to the bitter close.

What do these two traders have in common? They both have an inner conflict that keeps them from trading their methodology as it was designed to be traded. They both have every conscious desire to trade their methods and abide by their rules and make money. They both, no matter how determined they are, fail to do what they have consciously decided to do. As the situation stands, they both are de facto incapable of acting on their rules.

"Complicated? Not really. (I'm) just a lot of simple selves."
—F. Scott Fitzgerald

We are all composed of many different parts. Parts get created as we grow and develop. This is true of everyone. We're not talking here about multiple personalities or psychological disorders. We're talking about ordinary people. Sometimes the parts don't agree or have conflicting purposes. This is when they get our attention.

Our very language depicts such conflict. "On the one hand, and on the other hand." "A part of me wants..." "Sometimes I feel like a..." "I'm of two minds about..."

Conflict between parts happens regularly in ordinary lives. It can be as simple as I want to lose weight but I want to eat the pizza. I want to stop smoking and I want a cigarette. I want to ask the woman for a date, and I don't want to risk rejection. I want to share my ideas, but I don't want to be criticized. I want to trade, but I don't want to lose money.

Parts get created around the roles we play in life, around our emotions, and around our attitudes. For example, I'm a trader, a psychological coach, a sales person, a writer, a researcher, an artist, a mother, a sister, a friend, and on and on. I also have a playful part, a creative part, a loving part, a nurturing part, a serious part, a worried part, an ambitious part, and a lazy part. As a trader I have a fearful part, a greedy part, a trusting part, and a cautious part.

The parts are there whether we acknowledge them or not. We may not like having a fearful part (or a jealous part or an angry part,) but that part is there and will make its presence known through our behavior. Sometimes it can be very puzzling. We think we want something, but we act in a way to prevent ourselves from getting what we consciously want. It's called self-sabotage.

John wants to trade, but he doesn't (can't) pull the trigger. Roger wants to follow his rules, but he periodically and repeatedly goes on a trading binge without any reference to his rules. There is an unacknowledged part in each of these traders that needs to be recognized, listened to, and given an appropriate place in the interior hierarchy of personal parts.

In working with parts it's important to start with the presupposition that no matter how we feel about the behavior of a part, there is a positive intention behind the behavior. We can begin by separating the behavior from the intention.

We must assume that the part of John that will not let him trade has a positive intention. We must also assume that the part of Roger that periodically violates his trading rules also has a positive intention. Neither of these parts intends to sabotage the trading and the trader, even though the behavior certainly does do that.

All behavior is a manifestation of a part. Sometimes that's the only way we know that the part exists. The part communicates to us through behavior. Behavior means actions, inactions, gestures, thoughts, words, or symptoms. Behavior is not the same as intention. Intention doesn't necessarily result in behavior, but all behavior is the result of intention.

A father continually criticizes his son's behavior. The son develops low self-esteem. The father's intention is to create a stronger and more effective son, but the behavior instead creates a self-questioning and insecure person.

A woman says she wants to get married, and yet she ends up alienating every serious romantic partner she has. We must assume that the part that drives away her partners has her best interest at heart even though it's intention may not be to get married. Consciously she wants to get married: unconsciously a part of her wants something else.

Remember that behavior is separate from intention. Together behavior and intention form the whole. The intention is always positive, even if you don't know what the intention is. In the case of the father, the intention was to create a stronger son. The behavior, however, created the opposite. The result of that behavior created the opposite of the intention.

And just as between people, the positive intentions of the parts of a person can miscommunicate and create the opposite effect. For example, a young student keeps saying to herself, "I'm not smart enough." The intention of the part is to **motivate** her to study harder. The effect of the statement, however, is to discourage her from even trying.

The intention of the part of the woman that alienated all serious romantic partners may well have been to **protect** herself from ever going through the pain her mother went through during a divorce.

You may not like the behavior of a part of you. You may even hate it. But before you can ever get the behavior to stop, you need to acknowledge the part and discover it's positive intention. Otherwise the behavior will persist because there's a positive purpose to motivate or protect you. Ignoring the part or pretending it doesn't exist will just make you a victim of the part.

Like the traders John and Roger, most of us just try to power our way through and beyond our negative behavior. However, if a part of us has a strong contradictory intention, simple will power is not enough. We need to come to terms with the part before we can change the behavior.

To resolve a conflict, we need to recognize that some part of us exists that has a contradictory agenda to what we consciously want. We need to acknowledge that part and communicate with it so that we can discover what its purpose (positive intention) is. Then we need to find a way to satisfy that purpose through some other means so that we can proceed to get what we consciously want.

In working with a trader like John, I would proceed something like this:

Ruth: "John, I know you want to trade your methodology. However, there's a part of you that does not want to actually trade. I'd like you to acknowledge the part that very strongly doesn't want to trade and get into that part and be that part wholly and completely right now."

John: "It doesn't make any sense. I need to trade. I want to trade. Why would a part of me not want to make money?"

Ruth: "I know. It doesn't make sense. The fact that you're not trading, however, tells us that there is a part of you that for some reason doesn't want to trade. I'd like you to just pretend right now to be the part of you that doesn't want to trade and has a valid reason for not wanting to trade. Close your eyes and pretend to be that part."

John: "Okay."

Ruth: "Are you in that part now?"

John: "Yes."

Ruth: "What's your name?"

John: "Stubborn."

Ruth: "Hi Stubborn. What do you want for John? What are you trying to accomplish?"

John: "All that comes up is the memory of a time four or five years ago that I got into a trade and froze up. The trade started to go against me. I got cold and sweaty and couldn't pick up the phone to get out of the trade. I lost $7,000 on that trade. After that I decided I better do some more research."

Ruth: "And the research has been done since then. As you think about that trade now, what is it about that trade that bothers you now?"

John: "I was out of control."

Ruth: "John was out of control. Staying with Stubborn, in this part that resists trading, is it your intention, Stubborn, to protect John from being out of control again?"

John: "That would be terrible."

Ruth: "Is there anything else you're trying to do for John?"

John: "Keep him from losing too much money."

Ruth: "You want to protect John from getting out of control again and you want to keep him from losing too much money. Is there anything else?"

John: "That's it. Isn't that enough?"

Ruth: "Yes. Thank you very much for communicating with us, Stubborn. We'll be talking with you again soon."

"Now, John, I'd like you to leave Stubborn for a while and go to your creative part, the part of you that can find new ways of doing things, that can find solutions to difficulties, and get into that part."

John: "Okay."

Ruth: "Does the creative part have a name?"

John: "Wizard."

Ruth: "Great. Wizard, I'd like you to come up with three to six alternative behaviors other than not trading that will protect John from losing control and from losing too much money. Some of these alternatives will come to consciousness and some will stay unconscious. Think of them now.

John: "Well, he could dedicate an amount of money to trading and just write it off and commit to not losing any more than that amount."

Ruth: "Good. How much?"

John: "Twenty thousand."

Ruth: "Good. What else can he do?"

John: "He can always put a stop in with the original order."

Ruth: "Good. Anything else come to mind?"

John: "He can mentally rehearse doing the trading right. He can rehearse doing it over and over until it becomes automatic."

Ruth: "Wonderful. Thank you, Wizard, for your ideas. Now I'd like to talk to Stubborn."

John: "Okay."

Ruth: "Stubborn, you heard the ideas that Wizard came up with to keep John from getting out of control and from losing too much money. Would you be willing to try any or all of these before going back to stopping the trading?"

John: "Well, if he'll really do that."

Ruth: "Let's try it and see."

"Now bring the parts Stubborn and Wizard back within yourself, John, and reintegrate them."

What I did in this transaction was to acknowledge the legitimacy of the part that was shutting down the trading. We set up a line of communication with the part, and we elicited its positive intention. Then we went to the creative part to find alternate ways of achieving the positive intention. After that we got the part to agree to at least try one or all of the alternate ways before reverting to the original behavior. We did not ask the part to fully abandon its original behavior. We did ask it to try something else first.

In any conflict situation within yourself, you can do the same thing.

EXERCISE FOR RESOLVING CONFLICT

1. Identify a behavior (internal or external) you don't like but that you do.

____

2. Separate the behavior from the intention.

____

3. Ask the part of you responsible for the behavior, what is it trying to do for you? What is its positive intention? Get into the part and answer.

____

4. Ask your creative part to come up with three to six alternate behaviors (some unconscious) that can satisfy the positive intention. Get into your creative part and answer.

____

5. Ask the part that does the behavior if it would be willing to try one or more of the alternate behaviors in lieu of the old unwanted behavior.

____

You can think of your inner parts as a family, your own internal family. As in a family, each part is distinct and separate even though a part of the whole. Each part needs to be respected and acknowledged and to be listened to, and each part needs to communicate its needs and wants. As in a family, there is an appropriate hierarchy. The baby does not decide on the family budget, but the baby does decide when she's hungry.

Often our parts work together effectively. Sometimes, as in any family, there is a conflict. We need to deal with the ecology of the whole inner family. If some part is not being acknowledged, and has an objection to an outcome or a goal, it can sabotage the whole enterprise. Sometimes the parts are quite alienated, and the only way to get through to a part is to work on an unconscious level. One way to do this is through visualization.

In working with a trader like Roger, I would proceed something like this.

Ruth: "Roger, I want you to begin to visualize the part of you that causes you to cancel stops and fight the market and add to a losing position. First, tell me in which of your two hands do you want to put that part?

Roger: "Here in my right hand."

Ruth: "Good. Now as you hold out your right hand, that part of you can begin to form. It's been a very powerful part of your trading, so powerful that you haven't been able to consciously understand it's useful purpose. Now as it begins to take shape there in your hand, tell me what you see.

As I begin this process of discovery, I'm apparently talking to Roger. However, I'm also communicating with this part that Roger hasn't been able to understand and has alienated by thinking bad thoughts about it. As I speak with Roger, I'm establishing rapport with this part by calling it powerful and assuming it has a positive intention.

Roger: "I see myself leaning forward looking at the trading screen."

Ruth: "Good. Really look at the details, at his expression, at his gestures. And when you can see that part really clearly, I'd like you to ask it what it's trying to do for you when you trade."

Roger: "It's trying to make the original plan work out."

Ruth: "The original plan or the original trade?"

Roger: "The original trade."

Ruth: "Great. Thank that part for communicating with you. And you can silently let it know you appreciate that it wants you to succeed."

As Roger does this, his physiology will alter letting me know that he has accepted the part and the part has responded positively.

Ruth: "Now keeping this part in your right hand, I'd like you to shift your gaze to your left hand. How would you describe this part, the opposite of the part that fights the market and cancels stops and adds to losing positions?"

Roger: "This is the part that creates and follows a proven system for trading."

Ruth: "Good. And as you look at your left hand, let that part take shape fully, and tell me what you see."

Roger: "I see myself trading, sitting back calmly following the rules."

Ruth: "And what is your purpose in following the rules?"

Roger "I want to make money."

Ruth: "That's certainly a helpful part to have around when you're trading. Thank that part for it's intentions."

"Now, Roger, you have one part that wants you to succeed in individual trades, and one part that wants to make money with your overall trading. Two quite positive intentions."

"And now I'd like you to fix your gaze in the middle between your two hands and as you do that allow your two hands to come together just as slowly or just as quickly as they want to, and as your hands move towards each other, they bring together the desire to have a trade work out and the desire to have all your trading make money. As the hands come slowly together so too do the part that wants all the trading to succeed and the part that wants a single trade to succeed. The hands are bringing the parts together in such a way that the two parts can benefit each other and learn from each other and blend in successful trading."

Roger: "The part that wants the trade to succeed will first have to take a couple of steps back so it can see more than one trade."

Ruth: "Absolutely. Ask it if it's willing to do that."

Roger: "He leaned back and got a bigger perspective."

Ruth: "Wonderful. And now with your gaze in the middle, allow those two parts, the part that wants to make money trading and the part that wants individual trades to work out to come together just as quickly as they're each willing to learn from and appreciate the other's purpose."

The hands come together forming an integration of the whole.

Ruth: "Great. Now bring the two hands together to your chest bringing this new blended part containing all that was of value in the two parts, a few trades working out, and all of the trading making money, into yourself, Roger, the trader."

Roger, himself, in this example, requested the first part, the part that tried to make an individual trade work out, to step back and get a broader perspective on trading. Fortunately, the part agreed. Because of this, I would end the exercise here. Otherwise, I would have gone on to the last step in the process, which would have been to generate alternate behaviors to satisfy the intentions of the first part.

While the intention to have a single trade work out is indeed positive, it is not beneficial to trading as a whole. The intention to have a single trade work out would have to be shifted to the intention of having a series of trades work out. Roger's "original plan" would have to be shifted to just exactly that—the plan as a whole—rather than just the individual trade.

EXERCISE: THE VISUAL BLEND

1. Identify a behavior that does not support you in your life or trading
2. Hold out one hand and visualize that part in your hand.
3. Ask the part what it wants to do for you.
4. Identify the part that is the opposite of the first part.
5. Hold out the other hand and visualize that part.
6. Ask that part what it wants to do for you.
7. With the two positive intentions in mind, fix your gaze in the middle, and slowly or quickly allow the two hands to come together joining together the benefits of both parts.
8. Keeping your hands together slowly bring this new blended part incorporating all that was of value in both your other parts towards your chest so that this new blended part fully joins with you and becomes a part of your thoughts, behaviors and feelings now and in the future.
9. Identify positive, alternative behaviors that can bring about the positive intentions of both of the former parts.

Conflict in trading can come from individual parts or it can come from conflicting beliefs or conflicting values that then attach themselves to parts. Most parts are organized around what is to that part an important belief or value. One way to discover if you have any part that conflicts with your trading success, is to simply ask yourself, **"Is there any part of me**

that doesn't want me to trade?" or, **"Is there any part of me that doesn't want me to make money trading?"** Ask those questions, and record your answers below.

____

____

You will need to come to terms with these parts before you can succeed in trading.

In the chapter, "The Relentless and Compelling Power of Beliefs," we talked about beliefs that don't support trading. You can refer back to that chapter and look for beliefs you hold that might be creating a conflict in your trading.

Some additional beliefs that can create conflict in trading are the following:

- Money is the root of all evil.
- A rich man cannot enter into the kingdom of heaven.
- It is easier for a camel to go through the eye of a needle than for a rich man to enter into the kingdom of heaven. (Note: The eye of a needle was a doorway in a wall that the camel had to crawl through.)
- Gambling (trading) is a sin.
- Life is a struggle.
- I have no right to be more successful than my father/mother.
- I'm not smart enough.
- If I make money, I'm taking it from somebody else and that's wrong.
- It's not right for one person to have more than other people.
- The market is dangerous.
- If I trade, I'll lose money.
- I can lose all my money trading.
- Something terrible will happen if I don't succeed as a trader. (And I'll probably fail.)
- It's important for every single trade to be a winner.
- If I lose on the current trade, my trading is in trouble.

In the case of John and Roger, there were clearly some conflicting beliefs. John believed he could make money trading, and at the same time he believed that if he traded he could "lose too much money." John also believed he had a method for trading that he could work, and simultaneously he believed that he was likely to get out of control if he traded. Roger believed that if he followed his rules he'd make money, and equally believed that by abandoning the rules on a given trade he could make it work out. One part of Roger clearly believed that his trading was a series of probable events and yet another part believed that each trade was so vitally important it amounted to his trading survival.

Ask yourself, **"Is there any part of me that believes something that conflicts with my trading?"** If you feel any conflict about your trading, ask yourself, **"What must I believe that's**

causing this conflict?" Write down any ideas that come to you.

If you hold any beliefs that conflict with your trading, it's important to replace those beliefs with supportive beliefs. Take any belief that you identified as causing a possible conflict with your trading, and change it to a belief than will enable your trading.

For example, if you said "Money is the root of all evil," you could say, "Money is a store of value that can be used for great good." If you said, "Life is a struggle," you could change that to "Life is an exciting challenge that I can master." If you said, "The market is dangerous," you could alter that to say, "The market is a neutral arena in which I can protect myself."

If you have two clearly conflicting beliefs such as John and Roger, you can seek to modify them into one overarching and supportive belief. John could say, "Money can be made over time in the market, and I can control the risk so the danger of excessive loss is minimal and temporary." He could also say, "By trading my methodology with consistency, I am in control of my trading behaviors." Roger could say, "By following my rules consistently on each and every trade, I put the probabilities in my favor over time and do the very best I can as a trader."

Write your new replacement belief(s) on the following lines.

You can use the techniques outlined in "The Relentless and Compelling Power of Beliefs" chapter to install your new beliefs.

We also talked about values in that same chapter. We talked about important criteria that you go towards and away from. Since parts organize around values, different parts can have different values that may conflict. If a part has a value that is not being met, that part will create behavior to get attention.

Just as in families trouble is created when the important criteria of one member is not honored or when two members have conflicting criteria, so too within a person the inner family of different parts can come into conflict. One of the parts may have an important criteria (towards or away) that is not being met. Two or more parts may have conflicting criteria.

Preserving capital and protecting it against loss was vitally important to one part of John. Another part of John wanted to create new wealth through taking risk. One part of John wanted to preserve the emotional status quo, while another part wanted to forge ahead and experience the possible turbulence of the unknown.

One part of Roger said it was important to work hard to make each trade work out at whatever cost to the general overall plan. Another part said it was more important to let the overall plan work out by following the rules and let the individual trades fall where they may.

As you separate the intention from the behavior of a part, you can identify the values that are underneath the intention. It's fully possible that these values are in conflict with the values held by other parts.

Sometimes the values are really not your own but belong to a parent or teacher or spouse or some part of society. These values can get installed in a nagging or recalcitrant or dominating and bossy part.

Look back at the values you listed in the chapter on beliefs and values, and look to see if any of the stated values are in conflict. It's possible to have conflicting criteria that could sabotage your trading. For example, if success is an important criterion to achieve, and failure is an important criterion to avoid, the avoidance of failure might take precedence over the achievement of success. It would appear that this is exactly what was happening in the cases of John and Roger.

If safety and security are high values, it might (but not necessarily) conflict with the necessary risk taking involved in trading. For some people security is a CD or a government bond or T-bill—and even then they might worry about the failure of the bank or the government. For others security is knowing that you can control the risk even as you trade the probabilities. For others security is simply knowing that you can always make enough money to meet your needs and wants.

If fun and adventure are important values, it might (but not necessarily) conflict with the steady execution of a mechanical system. I met one trader who had a successful system that made money, but he kept doing other things that lost money. I asked him why he didn't just trade the system. His answer was, "It's no fun. It's boring." My solution was to have a big serious account and let it be boring and to have a smaller fun account just for playing.

For some traders fun and adventure are just putting on a random trade and seeing what happens. For others it's overtrading and pushing the limits. For still other traders, fun and adventure is researching and trading their proven methodology. The word gamble came from the Old English gambol which means to sport or to play. Many successful traders have a high sense of adventure in relation to their trading: trading to them is total fun. They value fun and adventure and still trade with consistent discipline even while they're having fun. Too great a seriousness can easily get in the way of successful trading.

We want our ideas to be in alignment. We want our core values to support what we do, and we want what we do to support our values. If you have an important criterion that is in conflict with your value of trading successfully, there are a number of ways to resolve this conflict.

One way is to redefine the value so that it will no longer be in conflict. For example, if "being right" is a value that's causing problems with your trading, and you're defining being right as having a winning trade, you could change the definition. You could say instead, "Being right is taking every trade." If avoidance of failure is interfering with your ability to trade, you could create a new definition of failure. For example, you could say, "Failure is giving up on my goals."

Another way to work with important criteria that are getting in the way of profitable trading is to ask certain questions. Let's assume that you have security as a high value, and this value is keeping you from consistently trading a winning program.

You can apply the criteria of security to itself. You can say, for example, "How secure is it to not take a risk?" or, "How can I create security within the trading process?"

You can change the perspective. Ask yourself, "Whom do I know who also has security as a high value but does it differently from me?"

You can change the time frame. Act as if it's ten years from now and security is still important to you. How do you experience it now? How does security support your trading now?

You can look for counter examples. Has there ever been a situation in which you risked and felt secure?

You can reverse the presuppositions. In what ways could risk mean increased security?

The people who succeed at trading, the people who succeed consistently at any endeavor, are people who are conflict free about their endeavor. If any part of us has an objection to a chosen goal, sooner or later that part will make itself known through our behavior. The behavior—internal or external—will sabotage the enterprise.

You want to be clear about your desire to trade consistently and profitably. Any part of you that is not in alignment with that goal needs to be brought into alignment if you are to succeed in this dynamic and volatile arena. You can do this by paying close attention to the part that is in conflict, by listening to it's objections and satisfying them, by understanding it's intentions and finding new ways to fulfill them.

To fully succeed at anything, we need to be conflict free. All parts of our being need to be in alignment with our goal.

CHAPTER VI

CLARITY OF VISION AND MARKET ASSESSMENT

"Life is not an illogicality; yet it is a trap for logicians. It looks just a little more mathematical and regular than it is; its exactitude is obvious, but its inexactitude is hidden; its wildness lies in wait."

—G. K. Chesterton

"It's not so much that there's something strange about time. The thing that's strange is what's going on inside time. We will first understand how simple the universe is when we recognize how strange it is."

—Dr. John A. Wheeler

There is a story told in Douglas Adams' *Hitchhiker's Guide To The Galaxy*[1], of a massive supercomputer that was designed to give the ultimate answer, the final answer, that would clarify the issues of "God, life, the universe, and everything." The issues were so large that it took the supercomputer seven and a half million years to come up with the answer. Unfortunately, by the time the computer came up with the answer, everybody had forgotten the question. The answer—the ultimate answer—was 42. But nobody knew what the ultimate question was.

I sometimes wonder if with all our computing, all our elaborate theories of numbers and mathematics and chaos theory and every other technical and fundamental theory, if with all the mystery of the beauty of numbers and predictability calculations, we aren't just coming up with 42.

A friend of mine used to call technical trading the dumb school of trading. He would say, "Technical trading is simply saying, 'I dunno, it's going up.' Or 'I dunno, it's going down.' " Then he would add, "Ruth, you don't know anything about orange juice, or lumber, or corn, or copper. You might as well just go technical." Not bad advice, even if it was arrogantly male macho. (This same friend used to say that stops were so middle class!) I would add that it's even more important to go technical when you think you do know something. Ideas need to be checked against reality.

For purposes of this chapter, I am going to define reality as price action. Price is how we make or lose money. Anything else, fundamental or technical, is simply a possible indicator of where the price (reality) may or may not go.

Once I asked a floor trader what he thought of gold. He had a chart in his hand and he held it up for me. "That's what I think of gold," he said. The chart was in a clear down trend. I laughed and thought, of course, how obvious. It was the old story of stand up on the desk and throw the charts on the floor and see what you see. We get lost in the forest **because** of the trees. A checking of current and past price lets us know where we are.

Frequently, when one of my clients gets into trouble it will be because they are fighting the market. Either they don't believe what they see, or they don't believe that what they do see happening should be happening.

I asked Michael McCarthy what was his most practical tool for trading.

Michael: "Price behavior."

Ruth: "Can you expand on that?"

Michael: "It's a really good clue. If you just look at price, if you look at what the market does, and just follow that as opposed to trying to predict it, or trying to put some fancy indicator you can do without on top of it. The best thing to do is just to follow what the market has been doing. It may sound overly simplistic, and it is, but that is actually one of the most important tools. If you have a system that is based on price, and the market is going up, you'll have to get in at some point. If it's based on price for getting out, at some point you'll have to get out. A lot of people got buried by using an indicator. The indicator doesn't have to work, and the market can go down. So the bad thing with that is you have no money management."

Ruth: "Some people have so much stuff on their screens, they can hardly see the price."

Michael: "And so you've just masked your single most important clue. It's good to use simple indicators on price. MACD I think is great. If I had to give you one indicator to study, I'd say look at that one. That one's actually good for predictions."

"Look for divergences. If price is going up, and MACD is falling, it predicts a decline. And if MACD is below zero and rising especially like a double rising bottom, that predicts a market upswing. Those are great. They don't happen often, but they're very, very reliable. And, actually, if I had to do discretionary trading, that is what I would use. If I had to. It's really hard to quantify that into a system. Even when you test it out, it's not that great; but as far as a visual, it looks really good. A rising double bottom on the MACD and the stock market having a falling double bottom. You want it to diverge."

If reality is the price structure, then it becomes insanity to get out of touch or out of synch with price structure. And yet so many do just that.

Some people will cling to a stock that's sinking and sinking and sinking because they strongly believe in the future of the company. Others will stay short a stock that's soaring because they know that the company has yet to turn a profit, and they think it's ridiculous for the stock to be trading at elevated prices.

Did you ever hear yourself or another trader say something like, "I had a target of X price, but I didn't believe it." Or did you ever hear yourself or another trader say during market action, "I don't believe this." Let such statements be a red flag. It's there, and you better believe (accept) it.

If you're trading a methodology, you have to trust it. You have to believe your indicators. You've chosen them to give you probabilities. Don't ditch them midstream. Even more importantly, you have to give credence to price action. How can you possibly apply your methods to the market if you doubt either one of them? Trading is the suspension of disbelief. You need to accept both your methods and the price action and apply the one to the other.

We want to trade with a clean mind and a clear perception. We need to keep our perceptual channels open and unfettered. It's hard, of course, because fear and desire tend to distort what we observe. Perhaps even more dangerously our beliefs distort our minds and act as perceptual filters so we actually filter out what isn't in accordance with our beliefs. We're wearing perceptual filters and we may not even be aware of it. Often we're the last ones to recognize the beliefs we hold about ourselves or the market.

If you believe that a market is headed for the moon, you may filter out all indications to the contrary. If you believe a market is headed for a crash, any sell-off will look like the beginning of a disaster, any rise as simply an opportunity to get short.

A client of mine has a natural inclination towards optimism. His brand of optimism causes him to tend to predominantly think markets are bullish. Even on the worst down days, he'll tend to take more buys than sells. He knows he's going counter trend, but he seems compelled to buy. To protect himself from buying against the trend, he has placed a color-coded chart right by where he does his electronic trading. If his overall indicators are bearish, his chart will be red; and that is his red flag signaling that he's going against the trend. He has comprehended his bias, and color-coded his chart to alert him.

Another client, also an optimist, tends to think markets are going down. He made a lot of money during the '87 crash, and he keeps looking for it to happen again. When asked what he does for a living, he used to say, "I sell things." I put him into a hypnotic trance, and told him that markets go up as well as down, and that he would be sensitive and receptive to both bullish and bearish information. He called me the next day and said, "Ruth, I'm making so much money! You're a genius!" I laughed and said, "Saying 'markets go up as well as down' makes me a genius?"

TRADING WITH SCENARIOS

"The greatest obstacle to learning the truth is the belief that you already know it."
—Brian D. Biro

"It's what you learn after you know it all that counts."
—John Wooden

Sometimes traders get caught up in scenarios. The scenario is focused around a dominant idea or story. The subject matter can be technical or fundamental in nature. The theme dominates your thinking and colors your perceptions. This can be very dangerous, and it can also make you a fortune.

Scenarios are seductive. We are mesmerized by stories. Stories are entrancing, and we tend to suspend critical thinking while we listen to a story. We live our lives caught up in the unraveling of our personal stories. Sometimes our lives are a series of stories repeating the same theme. What is the story of your personal life? What is the story of your trading? Do certain plots tend to repeat themselves with simple variations of time, place, and people?

Do you listen to the stories told on **CNBC**, or in *Barron's*, or told by your broker, or trader friends, or even by the squawk box? Only to realize too late that the story had nothing to do with applying your methods to the market?

Ideas give meaning and direction to our lives. Wars and elections are fought over ideas. The idea could be a simple as the flat tax or as complex as justice or freedom. Marriages and divorces can occur or continue because of ideas. Love, convenience, duty, commitment, loyalty, or betrayal are all ideas creating and destroying marriages.

Ideas animate us and organize our lives. Businesses are built upon ideas. Fortunes are made—and lost—because of the power of ideas. A good idea has power. A bad idea also has tremendous power.

Stories and ideas can empower and guide our lives. What works in life, however, often does not work in trading. The staying power of a good idea that can get you through life's quagmires can bring you to ruin in trading if your timing is off. Rarely will an idea or story see you through to success—unless the idea is that your methodology works and you can succeed as a trader.

"The superior trader will never admit that it is possible to forecast perfectly. ... If he permits himself to have certainties, his mind becomes dull. Dull minds are not capable of quick movement. ... Over-confidence in your knowledge of the market may deprive you the grace necessary for success. One must have faith in his knowledge, but that faith is not adequate unless it is faith that permits doubt."

—Roy W. Longstreet

As traders we need to stay focused in the present. We need to willingly receive and act upon current information and price action. Unless you can do this, you need to be extremely wary of strong ideas and enticing stories.

I'm talking here about trading, not about investing. Because investing has a longer time frame, it's possible to sit and wait for the concept to develop. If your concept is sound, and intervening events don't alter it's validity, you could make a lot of money. Buy and hold has proven to be a sound strategy for many investors. The danger is that buy and hold also means never having to admit you're wrong. If your original premise was flawed or if time changes it's soundness, you may find that what you did was to buy and die.

Some people can trade scenarios successfully. George Soros is an example of an extremely successful scenario trader. He has high quality information sources. He also thinks clearly. He writes in *Soros on Soros*[2] that he bets heavily on a trade when he is convinced that an economic scenario is about to unfold. When he succeeds, it's widely publicized. The reaction of many is that that's the way to trade! What many of these people don't realize is that he is alert at the first sign that his scenario is not playing out as he anticipated, and he promptly removes himself from the market. He also takes some major hits.

In his writing, Soros talks of some of the problems of scenario trading. He says that when you are an actor (betting on a scenario), your observations are not pure. He also points out that facts are not always observations, and observations are not always facts. To further complicate the situation, observations can become facts. Facts change. Observations change. The actors or players change. The mix alters and changes the unfolding of financial events. As a scenario speculator, George **anticipates change and thus protects himself from the hazards of a rigid scenario.**

Not every scenario trader remains flexible in the face of an unfolding scenario. Some become dogmatic and fixed despite cascading evidence to the contrary. Again, the scenario can be fundamental or technical in content.

An example of technical scenario traders would be the Elliott Wave theorists who have remained fixated on an impending market crash ever since the market crash of 1987.

Believing this scenario some investors missed out on the subsequent market rise.

"Opinions have vested interests just as men have."
—Samuel Butler

More commonly the scenario is fundamental in nature. A friend of mine has several times lost huge amounts of money betting heavily that certain fundamentals were certain to have an impact on market prices. He'd do his research, and he would be convinced he was right.

In one instance, after intensive research, he had determined that the price of oil had to go down. There was a glut of oil. And **OPEC** was about to meet, and he, through his extensive contacts, knew that certain decisions were about to be made. Confident in his analysis, he began shorting crude oil. The price continued to rise, and he continued to short. The higher it went, the more he shorted. He had the courage of his convictions. The price of oil had to go down, but it kept going higher. He stood his ground, a brave hunter warrior. He was leveraged heavily, and he was losing heavily. Finally, he surrendered and unraveled his position. Two weeks later the oil market broke, but he was no longer there for the ride down.

This trader had two scenarios, one market related and one personal. Both scenarios were correct, yet still he lost. First, he was convinced that the price of oil was destined to collapse. Second, he believed he was a strong and courageous hunter-warrior-trader.

Trading, however, is not war. The courage this trader needed was to receive the information that price was giving him. It takes courage to receive feedback. It takes courage to say I'm wrong or I'm early and not yet right. It takes courage to set aside one's opinions in the face of market action. This trader utilized the wrong kind of courage and lost extensively when he could have won handily. He needed to work with the market not against it.

"Don't fight forces—use them."
—Buckminster Fuller

Think of the guided missile. It starts going towards a positive target, but only stays on target by getting negative feedback that it's off target. When the missile gets feedback, it corrects course, and sometimes overcorrects and gets more feedback. Ultimately the missile reaches its target by being responsive to feedback. As traders we need to be responsive to the feedback (market price) that we get.

There's a presupposition in **NLP (Neuro-Linguistic-Programming)** that says that there is no such thing as failure, there is only feedback. Had this trader seen the oil price as feedback, not threat of failure, he could have responded by getting out and waiting his time for the first sign of true market weakness. Unfortunately, his idea blinded him, and froze him in the increasingly uncomfortable position.

Scenario trading gives you a framework for viewing the market. Therein lies its power for good or ill, depending on the accuracy and timeliness of the scenario. I think it's much safer to view the market through the framework of your methodology, as long as that methodology is micro enough to encompass current action.

FOCUS

"We should treat our minds as innocent and ingenious children whose guardians we are—be careful of what objects and what subjects we thrust on their attention."

—Henry David Thoreau

"If the doors of perception were cleansed, everything would appear to man as it is, infinite."

—William Blake

What it all boils down to is focus. What are you focusing on? Are you looking for a preconceived notion? Are you looking for possibility for profit? Are you looking for the possibility of loss? Are you looking for the fit of your methodology to the market?

When you have something in mind, it directs your focus. Remember those times when you've bought a new car. Suddenly the road is filled with similar cars. If you think of the color red (or any other color,) you'll see it wherever you go. You'll notice it in the room you're in. You'll see stop lights, stop signs, tail lights, lipstick, nail polish, and so forth. Red will be everywhere.

What you focus on actually directs the quality of your life. Depressed people focus on past sad and terrible events. Their present focus is on what they don't like, and their future focus is on whatever they fear might happen. This guarantees the maintenance of their depression. Happy people tend to remember joyful and pleasant events and notice what is wonderful in the present. They anticipate what they want to happen in the future. This focus maintains their happiness.

The type of focus you tend towards in life will most probably carry over into your trading. However, in viewing the market it's important not to wear rose colored glasses or dark smoky glasses. You need to have as clear a view of the market reality as possible. Neither hoping for the best nor dreading the worst will work when it comes to market action.

Your self-talk and the questions you ask yourself will direct your focus. When you see a signal, do you say, "What if I lose?" Or do you say, "How much can I make?" The questions you ask will probably depend on whether you go away from loss or towards profit. The questions you ask may well determine whether you hesitate to take the trade or whether you jump in early or overtrade.

Depending on your methodology, some good questions to ask would include the following:

- What is the trend?
- Am I looking for buys or am I looking for sells?
- Is this a valid signal?
- What would I need to see to have a valid signal?
- What do my rules tell me to do?
- What does my method tell me to do?
- Am I following good trading principles?
- What is the market telling me now?
- What is the market showing me now?
- What does the market want?
- Where can I get in?
- What is my target?
- How much can I make?
- What is my risk?
- Where am I wrong?
- What would I think if I weren't in this trade?
- What are the probabilities?

Monitor your self-talk and the questions you ask. Be particularly sensitive to whether your talk and questions presuppose a bias. This will skew your vision of market action.

"In life, if you focus on possibilities, they become probabilities."
—Mona Lisa Schulz

It's important to remember that your focus acts like a magnet for what you focus on. We attract what we focus on. Focus on possibility for loss, and you won't want to trade. Focus only on possibility of profit and you may overtrade. If you fear loss, somehow you'll create it. It's best to concentrate your mind with an optimistic view of your future trading, even while you focus realistically and open-mindedly in the present.

If you trade a system, it's best to focus on the demands and the probabilities of that system rather than the suggestions or probabilities of any other system or indicator. I spoke with Michael McCarthy, who is a systems trader, about his focus, and about systems trading.

TWO TRADERS TALK ABOUT TRADING

Michael: "I think I'm one of the few people who listens to those boring rules that everyone keeps chattering away about. They're so redundant, you almost resent them. Money management. Go with the trend. Follow your system. People must be so sick of hearing that one. It's true. I listen to those basic things, and I don't know any other person who follows the rules all the time. I have systems that make sense to me, that I like, that I feel comfortable with. On a level they are my armor, my clothing. They protect me. They tell me what to do."

"There are systems out there that work, but I would never do them, because I don't like the way they do it. They say get a system you're comfortable with, that fits your personality. I don't think that can be stressed enough, because I don't think people realize how many systems are out there. There are thousands you can buy, and I'd say there are probably 10 that are good, that really work, that you could buy out of the back of the magazine. And you can find them. So you find the one that's going to make sense to you."

"If the day to day activity is uncomfortable for you, you won't follow it. If a system makes 100% a year with a 25% drawdown, and that just wrenches you, you won't follow it entirely. You'll stay for a while, hit the drawdown and then stop. You'll never stay long enough to see the pot of gold. It's classic: a winning system with a losing trader equals failure."

Ruth: "How do you make your trading decisions? You follow a system. But how do you decide what system to use?"

Michael: "I only have a few systems per market. That's a little more of an art than a science. You print out your records. Draw an equity graph. Did it beat buy and hold? Did it match it or beat it? What were my worst drawdowns, and how often did they occur? How much lower were they than buy and hold? Since I manage money for other people, I also take note of flat periods because people get angry if they're flat for a few months. They want it to go up."

Ruth: "You're in a sea of human emotions with your clients."

Michael: "Yes, and I really like to limit my contact with their emotional side. Let me rephrase it. They get antsy."

Ruth: "What do you say to those people who say systems don't work?"

Michael: "We need people like that. If everyone believed systems work, it would be too easy. So I encourage that kind of thinking. It saves effort. I tell them dollar cost averaging works, buy and hold works. It saves you an argument. You might as well talk about politics or religion. It's just going to get heated up and nobody changes their mind in the end anyhow. No point in having an unproductive conversation."

Ruth: "There are people who use their discretion and make money."

Michael: "Yes there are people who do that. God bless them. I'm not like that. I can't look at a market and decide the future. I can more and more as I get older, though. You pick up stuff. But if I had to do something discretionary, I would think of myself as a very good sailor but you're making me sail in the middle of the night. I would be just as ineffective as a novice."

Ruth: "Or you don't have any charts."

Michael: "Yes, and I wouldn't feel comfortable. These discretionary traders only trust themselves. They just cannot for the life of them hand it all over to a computer. And I see that. I understand that point of view. I just have the opposite view. Because with a computer, I can at least test back thirty, forty years. I'm looking for disastrous trades where it blew up. That's why I go back so far. People say that I go back too far."

Ruth: "They say that because they say it's no longer relevant."

Michael: "And that's fine but it takes five seconds to do the test. And I think it's irresponsible not to do the test from all the information that's out there. Sometimes you will find that a good system will blow up. You look at that period and say what happened?"

Ruth: "How would you know that a system was blowing up? At what point would you say that? Would you decide in advance?"

Michael: "It's a hard question to answer and a very good question to ask. Especially if it's worked well for you in the past. It's the same thing as taking a look at whether or not you're getting old. Let's say you're talking about your spouse. You know that when you first got married, you were in your twenties and vibrant. But then as you get older and things start to slow down. Then you notice that they start forgetting things. You start to notice that they're going to the doctor more often. Or you start to notice that one of the shelves in the medicine cabinet is full of medicine whereas it used to be toothpaste and toothbrushes. If you start to see those signs, you know that someone is getting older."

Ruth: "So when a system starts to have a lot of losses in a row, you say the system is getting sick."

Michael: "I wouldn't put it that way. I would say it's acting out of character. For example, let's say for the first time the system missed a really, really big move. And you didn't have a rule in there that would have kicked you in. The condition wasn't set in there and now it's moving, moving, moving away from you and that's never happened before. Or you start losing a ton of money, and you don't have an exit. You see that the price behavior of the market has changed where it has found a glitch. It's found a loophole in your system rules. When that happens, then I'd say, 'Pull the alarm. The boat has sprung a leak.' And this has never happened to me, but then I would say I didn't do the system right. I didn't take into consideration this characteristic. Then I would go back to the drawing board and start testing more. I wouldn't just make a rule to fill that gap, but I would certainly give myself a hard work assignment and say I had defined my program inaccurately. I would be the first person to say something is wrong. My father taught me: if you're wrong, say it right away. It minimizes the damage. I don't permit embarrassment. It's unproductive."

Ruth: "So do you say I'll trade this system until something like this happens? Or do you say this system works and I'll stay with it?"

Michael: "I never say always. Everything is relative."

Ruth: "You're always researching anyway, so when you find something better, you would make that change. Do you change your systems?"

Michael: "I've had the same one for five years. I only recently changed it, and that wasn't in response to the system. It was in response to the mutual funds not accepting my frequency of trading. My original system works great. What I had to do was take into consideration other factors. I kept the same characteristics of the system; it just trades half as much. I was able to identify which trades were unproductive. I think every system is probably going to have that twenty-eighty rule you find in life. Eighty percent of your money comes from twenty percent of your trades as well as eighty percent of your money comes from twenty percent of your clients. I make the same money but trade less. I just knocked out trades that had a low probability for profit."

Ruth: "How would you say you're different from other traders?"

Michael: "I think I'm one of the few people that really follow a system. I think a lot of people don't, even though they say they do. I think a lot of people doubt themselves. They think something's different this time. Or this system isn't taking this particular moment into consideration. You think you haven't researched the system that fits the criteria that it should. Either it doesn't fit your personality or you know you fudged something. You don't tell anybody about it but you know."

Ruth: "If you don't remember it consciously you have an unconscious memory of it."

Michael: "Yes, that's going to come out in your behavior. You know there's a glitch here. I'm scared to be on the wrong side of my system. The only time I'll be upset, my emotions will kick in, is if I'm in the market and my system is on a sell. I'm afraid to **not** follow it because I know the probabilities are against me."

Ruth: "How would that happen?"

Michael: "The only times that would happen is when you have to exchange the funds before the close, and the market could settle against you after the close. Or if you have an administrative error, which we've never had (knock on wood,) where you couldn't get the call in."

Ruth: "It happened to a friend of mine. The market closed early because of a snow storm, but he was down in Florida; and when he called in, the mutual fund had gone home early."

Ruth: "What you're saying is you really have enormous faith in your system, and you wouldn't want to be any other way. You have this one system, and you trust it. Some people have more than one system and they don't know which one to believe."

Michael: "I have a friend who has multiple systems for different markets. What I would do is split my money up into pieces and trade the first piece on the gold system and the second piece on the S&P, and the third on the international system and so forth. What they do is they get a gold system signal, and if they like it, they put all their money on that. Then when they get another signal, they don't take it because they've spent all their money. That's not system trading. That's just throwing darts. You're just kidding yourself. That's discretionary trading. That may work for some people. They look at their technicals as indicators, not systems. But they're probably deficient in the peace of mind category."

Each trader is so beautifully and wonderfully different. I spoke with Linda Raschke about her focus and her trading methods.

Ruth: "How do you keep your mind clear while you're trading? How do you keep a clear point of view? In other words, how do you keep your perspective on the market?"

Linda: "Well, the best way is to look at the markets while they're closed. Then you're really not influenced by the price action. I think you can be most objective when the markets aren't trading and you can be most objective when you don't have positions on. And I think you can be most objective, at least myself, when I don't read anything, when I don't read letters or opinions. I don't listen to **CNBC**. I don't read the *Wall St. Journal*. I don't read *Barron's*. I don't pay attention to any of that kind of stuff. It doesn't work for me. Some people are information gatherers, and it works for them, but it doesn't work for me. So I keep it fairly pure. That's what works for me."

" If you have a game plan, you know before the markets open. That is the best way to keep the emotions out of it. I have to say that experience is everything. I think that I can look at them objectively or more detached because I've been doing it for so long. It's like, been there, done that, seen that. Okay. I don't know how I would feel if I were a new trader just starting to learn about the markets. I would imagine that it would be fairly overwhelming."

Ruth: "Well, you were at one point a new trader, and you approached it from a certain way."

Linda: "I was also twenty-one years old. It was right out of school; I had nothing to lose, and everything was a big adventure. And I didn't have to worry about paying the rent or financial responsibilities. I had a good friend who was a trader. Actually what I was doing initially with equity options was more of an arbitrage. So because there was inefficiency in the market at the time, I could do the arbitrage. And that takes a great deal of pressure off you from having to make directional calls."

Ruth: "And yet, of course, you're making directional calls now."

Linda: "Yes. And actually when you're on the floor you're making directional calls every microsecond, because when you're putting on a spread, it's which side are you going to put on first, so you do have exposure. It's just that it's taken off fairly quickly, but there's always exposure for a couple minutes."

Ruth: "You've said that part of the way you keep your vision clear is by just being there every single day and partaking."

Linda: "Oh yeah. Oh yeah. Because you're always waiting. You don't know when it's going to come. But the market is going to let you know. It will give you a clue. It will give you a sign. And it's not going to happen always when you're looking for it. But you just have to be patient and sure enough you'll see a big gap down and maybe a heavy volume spike and reversal. And it's finally had it's flush. Or finally it's shook off the baggage that it needed to. But if you miss observing it do that, then you won't have the confidence that the trend has turned."

Ruth: "Sure, so that takes us back to where I wanted to start. We were speaking about intuition. Now you don't like facts and figures and statistics and you want to be in it. So how much of your trading is intuitively based?"

Linda: "Well, keep in mind I do a huge amount of testing and quantitative research all the time just to get the probabilities—to find out if there's an edge or a meaning to one of those little puzzle pieces I was telling you about. If a market gaps up big but closes in the lower end of its range, what are the implications for follow through the next day? And you can get the confidence from testing the numbers."

"I feel like intuition for me is a summation of experience. I don't think that a person can just start off and expect to have intuition. There is none. And I think that people don't always recognize that. They think that some people have something special that somebody else doesn't and that's what makes them a good trader. And that's not true. I never had any special gift more than anybody else did. If anything, I've seen people who have better gifts in the market place than myself. I've seen people that have been able to learn faster or recognize patterns faster, a lot faster than it took me. It took me a number of years to get through my thick skull there might be a better way of doing this. But I really feel that it's all the experience of witnessing things happen over and over and over again."

"That's all intuition is. It's not ESP. It's not a sixth sense. Somehow you're picking up a clue in the market place but you may not be able to identify where it's coming from at the time, usually because there is a tangible clue given at the time. But sometimes I can't put my finger on it. It might just be the way something trades. But I bet if you did work on it, you could quantify it. You could say, "Well, it made the low first and then it came up and took out the opening price and it did it in a very open manner."

Ruth: "You probably saw something even if you weren't conscious of it. You saw it, and you may not be aware of what it was, but you saw it."

Linda: "It's just the way the price is acting. It's very much a tape reading type of thing. But tape reading again is an experience thing. Somebody can't expect to watch the market for two months and be a good tape reader. It's just that I've watched the price action for a long time, and I can say there were markers along the way where I felt a veil had been lifted, and I could see the light a little bit better, if that makes any sense. It probably took me about three years of trading on the floor, making hundreds of trades day after day before I felt like that first veil was lifted."

"But even so I can remember a feeling when I was off the floor, I'd been a floor trader for seven years and I'd certainly done a lot of technical analysis. I'd done my charting—I kept put-call ratios, advance decline etc.—but I can remember I was off floor; and I was trading out of my house; and all I had was a Quotron—we didn't have charting software in those days, intraday charts. I was just watching the prices and I can remember sitting there thinking to myself, I wish I knew what I was doing. I wish I felt like I had a better handle on being able to forecast the market or have a better handle on what the bigger picture is."

"At the time I was trading S&P's and I think I was having a wonderful, wonderful year. I think I had had something like forty winning weeks in a row. It was like all of a sudden I lost my way a little bit. The market started getting into a very strong trend. A very strong bull trend was going through, and I remember the feeling of being sort of clueless. There were no resistance levels. I didn't have a benchmark anymore for monitoring support or resistance. There was no resistance, and there was just this sort of trend climbing upwards, and I knew not to sell it, but I didn't know what to do with it. I really wasn't participating on the upside but just doing a small scalp. I can remember that distinctly. It must have been in 1988."

Ruth: "Do you ever trade a system?"

Linda: "I have used them in the past in my CTA programs. Now I use systems as indicators. You have to make the mechanical system into so much of the game, that you might as well hire somebody else to do the signals for you. You've got to make it into a game. You've got to monitor your performance versus the system's performance. Did you get more slippage this month or less slippage on your executions? What kind of deterioration are you experiencing in the system? You do all these types of things to make that into a game. Can you out perform your benchmark against the system? That type of thing."

Ruth: "What is your most practical tool for trading?"

Linda: "My most practical tool? You mean like an indicator?"

Ruth: "Yes, something you use, something you see that guides you."

Linda: "Well, the most practical thing for me is having a conceptual idea of what that market should do that day. Some way to conceptualize, not look at a concrete chart but think about what should this market be doing. Should we be testing the high we made yesterday? Should we be having a morning correction and then resuming the trend? And that's why I always do the buy days and the sell short days. Maybe it's a sell short day, but we should only approach it from a scalp. So for me, it's having a conceptual idea of what the market should do that day."

Ruth: "And you work this out the night before?"

Linda: "Yes, it really only takes me one minute to do it. It's terribly simple. I don't sit there and look at hourly charts. I can look at the dailies in two minutes and say okay now I'm going to look to buy a morning sell off, or I'm going to look to sell a test of yesterday's high, or we just had a big move the day before and so today should be a consolidation day and we're going to chop back and forth, so if the market sells off, I can buy it and if it rallies back up, I can sell it. In other words, I can pretty much be a counter trend trader."

Ruth: "Do you ever think I'll stop trading in maybe ten years and do nothing but horses?

Linda: "Oh God, no. I'll be trading these markets until the day I die. I'll be watching them. Because it's so much a part of my universe. I mean the patterns, the charts. I just love studying charts. Even if I didn't have positions on, I'd still be looking at the charts. It's not some sense that I have to do it every day, it's just like something's missing if I don't. Like the person who's grown up watching television every day, and then their TV is taken away. I have to say this. The markets and the price action is my connection to the world. It's what is going on out there because I don't watch TV. I don't watch the news. I don't read newspapers. I will not read newspapers. I won't listen to news on the radio. I abhor all that."

Ruth: "So how does Monica Lewinski show up on your charts?"

Linda: "It shows that she's really irrelevant. Anything that's relevant and pertinent will show up in the markets. That's how you're finding out about it. I'll be watching the bonds or the currencies or the meats. That's my way of finding out about things."

TRADING METAPHORS

"Via metaphors we organize not only our thoughts but also our emotions, responses, and our actions."

—L. Michael Hall, Ph.D

The metaphors you consciously or unconsciously choose to represent the trading process can effect your market perception and your response to that perception. A metaphor is a comparison of one thing to another. The word metaphor comes from the Greek word, meta-pherein; it literally refers to bearing (carrying) something over to something else. By bringing something over to another thing (meta-phor), we set a metaphorical frame. This then gives us a very specific way for thinking and acting. It offers a coherent account of things and thus makes meaning.

By equating one thing with another, we have changed the meaning and thus it effects our perceptions. On some unconscious level, we assume the truth of the metaphor. The unconscious mind is very literal. In essence, we become the metaphor and live it out with all it's biases and presumptions.

If I see myself as a worm, or a snake (I don't!), that will effect my perceptions of my relationships. If I see myself as a femme fatale or a ray of sunshine (Do I?), that too will effect my view of my relationships. If I see love as madness, I will approach it much differently than if I view it as a collaborative work of art.

Life's a smorgasbord of opportunities. Life's a struggle. Life's a bitch and then you die. Life's a ball, a dance, and a bowl of cherries. Chose any one of these metaphors for life, and you change your perception of life's possibilities and offerings.

The same thing would be true of your selection of metaphors for trading. Think for a moment about what you liken trading to. What are your metaphors for trading? Write them down briefly.

Metaphors are symbolic ways of thinking. They have a mythical power. They liken one thing to another, and cause us to assume, quite unconsciously, that what is true of one part of the equation is true of the other. If we addressed this consciously, we would probably say it wasn't so, but as a metaphor it becomes assumed.

The metaphors you use can either bring you beneficial power or cause nagging limitation. A limiting metaphor can be toxic to your self-image, your life, and your trading, while an enabling metaphor can work wonders for you. Metaphors are subtle, and have a profound impact upon your perception.

A metaphor is a symbolic representation of a belief, and, like a belief, it is not generally consciously chosen. Like a belief, a metaphor can act as a filter for information. In short, it colors your thinking. A metaphor becomes a frame of reference, and as such it becomes an attractor in a self-organizing system. Metaphors work by eliciting and creating models (or paradigms) which we then apply to various referents.

Typical metaphors for trading involve sports and warfare. Trading is seen as a contest between two competing forces. One side wins. One side loses.

Combat metaphors for trading are part of the idiom. For a long time, knowing I was woman in a predominantly male field, I didn't question warlike metaphors. And I still say, if it works for you, use it. However, many of my clients have had greater success after shifting their metaphors.

Warlike metaphors are ubiquitous in trading parlance and literature. How often have you heard traders talking about trading as a battle? About getting "killed" in the market? The trouble is that warfare is extreme, and requires you to bring up all you've got. In war you squander your resources. It's a matter of survival. It's an all or nothing business, and involves ambush, pillage, rape, wounding, life and death, victory and defeat. If you go out each day to do battle with the market, chances are you'll be exhausted at the end of the day or week. Even more serious than exhaustion, is the possibility that it could cause you to lose money due to over or undertrading as you attack and retreat.

If you are at war, you have an enemy. Who is your enemy? The market? The other traders? The locals on the floor? Your broker? Is the enemy nameless and faceless? Or is the enemy yourself?

Books have been written urging traders to take a samurai warrior's approach to trading. The samurai warrior has a lot going for him, but he's still a warrior. Such a metaphor presupposes that trading is war. One author went so far as to urge the trader to approach trading in the same way a samurai warrior approaches battle: release your fears, enter an egoless state, make peace with any future outcome—because you are willing to die. *Willing to die?* Isn't that conceding the possibility of a total wipeout?

As a woman, I'm more of a nurturer gatherer than a warrior. To me trading is like harvesting. The planting has been done, the crops have grown, and now is the time to harvest. I encourage the traders with whom I work to shift their metaphors from those of life and death struggle and contest to something more cooperative and less intense. At the minimum I suggest they think of the market as a neutral arena in which they can make a living. It works for them. They become more comfortable in the market, less fearful and less overly aggressive.

You can think of the market as a continually flowing river of opportunities. You can view it as an ocean of abundance complete with tides and waves that you can ride, and you know the low tide will always be followed by the high tide and vice versa. Furthermore, the ocean doesn't care whether you go to it with a bucket or a teaspoon.

You can also try thinking of the market as a friend or a business partner. If the market is your partner, you can work together. Your partner will tell you what's happening. You can want what the market wants. You're in a win-win situation.

You can think of the market as a dance partner. You're dancing with the market. The market is Fred Astaire and you're Ginger Rogers. Together you respond to the beat of the music. You let the market do the leading.

If you like sport's metaphors, it's a good idea to think of trading as a sport you're good at. Think of it as sport, a game, fun. Don't think of it as a serious, heavy competition—unless that works for you.

I personally like to think of trading as sailing. In sailing you work with the forces of nature: the wind, the tides, the current. You have a destination and you use nature's power to get you where you want to go. You have charts to guide you, and you constantly adjust to nature's forces, sometimes running before the wind, sometimes pointing into it, sometimes tacking. You're always in partnership with nature. If a storm comes up, you put down your anchor and your sails and wait out the storm. You always have confidence that you can get back to your safe harbor, your port, and your destination. And you enjoy the day, the journey, and the variables.

In sports remember that each point does not win or lose the game. Each game involves a series of events. And in most sports each game is a part of a larger series of games. Basketball, baseball, football, golf, or tennis, when played by successful athletes is played by athletes who expect to win. Remember winners expect to win. Losers expect to lose.

The successful athlete visualizes his successful performance before he begins. The golfer visualizes a tight target and imagines the ball arching up gracefully landing near the target. She sees the ball rolling into the cup even as she hears the sound of the ball hitting the cup. The baseball player keeps his eye on the ball even as he anticipates swinging and knocking the ball out of the park. In trading you keep your eye on the market, your focus on price action and your methods, even as you imagine your own success.

I spoke with Michael McCarthy about the metaphors he used when thinking about trading. He had said that when trading you're doing battle in a certain way.

Ruth: "Who are you doing battle with?"

Michael: "The market."

Ruth: "When you're trading, do you think you're trading against other people? That you're taking money from other people to make it for your people?"

Michael: "No. You could make an argument for that, but I don't think that way."

Ruth: "But you don't think like that."

Michael: "No. I don't think some stranger has my money now." On the battle thing, I don't take an adversary attitude to the market. I don't say it's my enemy. It's somewhere between a thing I have a relationship with and a friend. I like the market."

Ruth: "You see the market as a friend."

Michael: "Not so much a friend but a person that I'm in a relationship with. Good things will happen and bad things will happen, but we're always going to be here. And I'm always going to be trying to make it as positive every day as possible. I want to be in on the up days, and I want to be out on the down days."

"The sailing thing is an even easier analogy to get. You love the ocean, you love the water and all the beautiful things about it, but you don't want to be out there during a storm. If you die, if you fall off the boat...those are very negative things. So you just want to make sure that the environment is safe. That's kind of an easy way to sum up what I do."

Ruth: "You want the environment to be safe, and then you play. So that's the metaphor you're looking at.

Michael: "Yes."

Ruth: "It will have its dangerous times and it's safe times."

Michael: "It works as an analogy with any kind of weather thing. You want to go swimming in your outdoor pool and go hiking, but you only want to do it in nice weather. If you do it during a blizzard, it's not going to be very nice. Time and place sort of thing."

What metaphors would assist **you** with your trading? Write down a few and explore what it's like to trade using the new metaphors.

LEFT BRAIN ERRORS

There was an article in *Scientific American*[3] entitled "The Split Brain Revisited" that examines the different effects of the left and right brain hemispheres upon thinking. One very telling passage warns us of the dangers to perception of left brain analyzing. The following is an excerpt from that article.

> "George L Wolford of Dartmouth has lent even more support to this view of the left hemisphere. In a simple test that requires a person to guess whether a light is going to appear on the top or bottom of a computer screen, humans perform inventively. The experimenter manipulates the stimulus so that the light appears on the top 80 percent of the time but in a random sequence. While it quickly becomes evident that the top button is being illuminated more often, people invariably try to figure out the entire pattern or sequence—and they deeply believe they can. Yet by adopting this strategy, they are correct only 68 percent of the time. If they always pressed the top button, they would be correct 80 percent of the time."
>
> "Rats and other animals, on the other hand, are more likely to 'learn to maximize' and to press only the top button. It turns out the right hemisphere behaves in the same way; it does not try to interpret its experience and find deeper meaning. It continues to live only in the thin moment of the present—and to be correct 80 percent of the time. But the left, when asked to explain why it is attempting to figure the whole sequence, always comes up with a theory, no matter how outlandish."

It has been my observation of traders that very often the right-brained traders do have an easier time perceiving and acting upon current market action. The analyzers tend to get lost in theory, and distort current information, and even if they don't distort, they may miss the moment. We need, perhaps, to use the left brain to make the plan and the right brain to carry it out.

THE INFLUENCE OF THE PAST

Sometimes past market action or past personal trading experiences influence the way you view the current market. Have you ever found yourself expecting the market to do today what it did yesterday? Have you ever expected this trade in this market to go the way of the last trade in this market?

It's quite human nature to expect a repetition. Every day I go out running. During changeable weather, I used to find myself wearing shorts one day if the day before had been too hot for the sweat clothes I was wearing. That day I find myself cold in my running shorts, so the next day I wear the sweat suit, and so forth back and forth. One day I realized I was dressing to yesterday's weather, and yesterday's weather during a changing season is no more reliable than is yesterday's market action today. With my realization I laughed and said I was no different from the traders who trade yesterday's market today. All I needed to do was go out on the fire escape *today* to feel the weather *today,* just as a trader needs to sense the market *now,* not in the past nor in the imagined future.

The trouble is we learn to think in patterns. Once we've thought in a pattern, we tend to think again in that pattern. The more we think with that pattern, the more automatic it is. The pattern gets etched deeper and deeper. The mind is extremely economical, and is inclined to run on the same tracks.

Edward De Bono outlines this process in his book, *The Mechanism of Mind*.[4] He likens the surface memory of the mind to ordinary table jelly. If you spoon hot water unto the jelly, it will make a hollow. The next spoonful will tend to follow the same hollow, and so forth until it becomes the automatic formation and path.

THE FOLLOWING ARE EXCERPTS QUOTES TO GIVE YOU THE SHAPE AND ESSENCE OF HIS ANALYSIS:

> "What happens to patterns put on to the memory-surface is largely determined by the traces left on the surface by previous patterns. The memory-surface is no more than a system which allows past information to interact with present information in a self-organizing, self-selecting and self-maximizing fashion."
>
> "What does this flow represent? In the first place, the interpretation and recording of the incoming information...The main point is that there is flow, and that the flow is dictated by the contours of the surface."
>
> "This implies that patterns which are linked up to one central pattern will establish that central pattern very firmly."
>
> "It is almost impossible to establish a new pattern which is closely related to an old pattern. The new pattern is assimilated by the old pattern and does not become established as a separate pattern."
>
> "Once the channels and depressions have become sculpted into the surface, then it becomes difficult to alter them, since any new patterns tend to follow the old contours and to reinforce them rather than alter them."
>
> "This implies that a chain of successive connected images will always lead back to the original image, no matter how far it is extended."

"This may represent a unifying theme or organizational pattern that develops to link up otherwise separate patterns. The interesting thing is that this channel becomes more firmly established than what it is linking up."

"Since each memory is processed by the preceding memories, the actual sequence of presentation may make a very great difference to the pattern that is established, even though the individual patterns presented may be the same."

"The memory-surface just selects out which ever part of the pattern is most familiar and reacts to this. This is the selecting property of a memory-surface."

I find DeBono's theory of the prepatterning of the mind a little scary. If our past perceptions tyrannize our current perception, it becomes all the more important to keep our observations simple. The market's going up. The market's going down. The market's going nowhere.

If DeBono's theory be true, then we need to be extremely diligent in looking at our charts, so that we can see the new and the fresh, so that we can see newborn diverging patterns. Remember, the mind is economical. It wants to understand, analyze, differentiate, and interpret with the least amount of effort. This is good in that we don't have to reinterpret Christmas, Spring, loyalty, betrayal, who we are, or what we want each time we confront it. Maybe we don't want to have fresh eyes each time we look at the market, but it is vital to keep our perceptions as close to reality (price action) as we possibly can.

That takes us back to Douglas Adams's story of the supercomputer that took seven and one-half million years to come up with the amazing answer to the meaning of life—42. Only to discover that nobody remembered the question to the answer. There they had it after so many years, the ultimate answer. Wonderful! With such an important answer, they knew they needed to find the question, so they held a contest to see who could come up with the question to the answer. Many profound questions were offered, but the winning question, the ultimate question, to the ultimate answer of 42 was this: How many roads must a man (or a woman) walk down?

Does that remind you of your trading?

[1] Adams, Douglas, *Hitchiker's guide to the Galaxy,* Balantine Books, 1980.

[2] Soros, George, *Soros on Soros: Staying Ahead of the Curve,* John Wiley & Sons, 1995.

[3] Gazzaniga, Michael S, *The Split Brain Revisited,* Scientific American, July 1998.

[4] De Bono, Edward , *The Mechanism of Mind,* Penguin Books, 1969.

CHAPTER VII

IMAGINATION VERSUS WILL POWER

"Now is always beginning."
—Thomas Hornsby Fevril

As a professional hypnotist, I work not only with traders but also with people who want to quit smoking, lose weight, overcome phobias, and reach goals.

One thing I have learned is to never ask *why* a person does something, but to rather ask *how*. Why just gets people bogged down in a lot of rationalizations, buries them in their pain, and keeps them doing the thing they don't want to do. Instead I ask how. How gives me a clue as to ways to reverse what they're doing.

"How is it you were never able to stop smoking?"

"Well, I just say to myself, 'It would be so nice to have a cigarette.'"

"How is it you keep putting on weight?"

"Well, I wake up in the middle of the night and feel ravenous for something to eat. It's as if there's a black hole inside me. I start thinking about what I'd like to eat. If there's nothing in the apartment, I'll get out of bed and go down to the all night deli. When I wake up in the morning, I start the day thinking about where I'm going to eat that day and what I'm going to eat."

"How do you keep yourself from trading your winning system?"

"Well, I think to myself, 'What if I lose?'"

"How do you decide to violate your rules and add to a losing position when you're already under water?"

"Well, I'm pretty sure it will turn around, and I can fight my way back to even."

Each of these people has given me the blueprint for the problem. Each of these people thinks that the problem lies in insufficient will power. Each day they resolve to do better the next day. Each day they repeat the behavior. I know, but they don't realize, that will power alone will never take them out of their problem.

I will then ask each of these people the following question: "If your will power and your imagination were in conflict, which would win?" The answers vary. The truth, however, is **imagination is infinitely more powerful than will power.** Imagination overcomes will power hands down every time.

Coué, a hypnotist and international leader in the uses of autosuggestion, developed an insight about imagination way back in the early 1900's. He wrote, ***"When the will and the imagination are in conflict, it is always the imagination that wins."*** And he added, ***"In the conflict between will and imagination, the force of the imagination is in direct ratio to the square of the will."***

What is he saying? No matter how determined you are to do certain things, if your imagination doesn't support your resolute commitment, you're in trouble. And the more determined you are, the worse it will be.

The smoker will continue to smoke. The overweight person will continue to overeat. The one trader still won't pull the trigger. The other trader will still overtrade in a losing position.

Why? The smoker is imagining how great it would be to have a cigarette. The overweight person is imagining all kinds of delicious food (the rich hot fudge sundae with the creamy vanilla ice cream and the whipped cream and the salted nuts). The one trader is imagining how awful it would be to take a loss. With solid determination and yet with a vivid imagination, all the king's horses and all the king's men couldn't get him to put on a trade. The other trader is imagining the market turning around and a way out of the mess. Why shouldn't he just add a few more here?

You can square the determination of each of these persons when it's opposed by the imagination, and know that that's the degree to which they will fail.

There is a way out, however. You can use your will power to direct your imagination. The smoker can imagine being healthy, poised, and comfortable as a nonsmoker. The overweight person can imagine being fit and trim and looking great in some new clothes. The trader who can't pull the trigger can imagine the trade going his way. (What if I win?) The trader who doesn't follow her rules and adds to a losing position can imagine getting out of the trade and finding a better opportunity to make money. Or she could imagine what would happen if the market keeps going against her.

Coué taught thousands of people to use autosuggestion. His famous prescribed autosuggestion for physical or mental ills was, "Day by day, in every respect, I'm getting better and better." Or, as it became translated to English, "Every day in every way I'm getting better and better." As a trader you can translate it to, "Every day in every way I'm becoming a better and better trader." And imagine the ways in which you can become a better trader.

For it to work, however, you need to align your imagination with your affirmation. It won't work to will yourself to be a better trader even as you imagine the markets going against you or yourself getting out of control and consequently losing all your money.

Coué developed four laws or proposals that govern his concept of autosuggestion. The laws definitely apply to trading. The rules are:

1. Imagination can be directed.
2. When the will and imagination are in conflict, it is always the imagination that wins.
3. When will and imagination are in agreement, one does not add to the other, but one is multiplied by the other.
4. In the conflict between will and imagination, the force of the imagination is in direct ratio to the square of the will.

What is he saying? Basically he's saying that if your will power and your imagination are working together, there will be a multiplier effect in enabling you to do what you want. If your will power and imagination are in disagreement, not only will your imagination win, but also there will be a squared effect on your determination in keeping you from what you want.

"Imagination is more important than knowledge."
—Albert Einstein

If you want to follow a system that you have verified is profitable over time, and you imagine it making money for you, and you set your intention to follow it, there will be a multiplier effect on your ability to replicate that system in the market. However, if you determine to follow the system by trading it, yet you imagine it losing money for you, you will not be able to consistently apply that system in your trading; and the degree to which you commit to following it will simply square your inability to do so because your imagination is working against your will power.

What do we learn from this? We need to put our imagination and will power on the same team. How do we do this? We use our will power to direct our imagination in the same direction that we will. Sounds simple enough. Unfortunately, it isn't always so simple.

Consider a balance beam. If you lay a four by four-inch balance beam on the floor, and ask people to walk from one end to the other, it's easy. Most people will instinctively focus their vision and attention on the far end of the beam and walk confidently and casually until they reach their target.

But put that beam thirty or forty feet into the air with no net underneath and the task has changed immeasurably. The goal becomes not falling rather than walking to the end. It's the same physical act, but the consequences are vastly different. Fear and danger enter the equation. It's difficult not to imagine falling.

Consider the difference between paper trading and real time money trading. You have the same probabilities, but you have different consequences. This is for real, and you could make or lose real money. Do you imagine making money or losing money? Depending on how you run your imagination—towards profit or away from loss—may effect whether you overtrade or undertrade or even not trade at all.

Sometimes it's hard not to imagine losing when real money is on the line. Let a little pessimism slip in, and before you know it, you're imagining the worst despite the probabilities. You let one loss lead you to imagine a second loss and a third. You let circumstances control your thoughts instead of the other way around.

Consider the golfer who lets the first few holes or even the first swing control his thoughts. If he does well, he takes on a relaxed, confident and focused frame of mind. But if he doesn't do well in the beginning, his concentration is shattered. He allows himself to be the victim of the first few holes rather than managing his mind and using it to influence subsequent events and the rest of the game.

I see this often with traders. They become superstitious about the first trade or the first few trades of the day. They let the first few losing trades bring them bad luck for the rest of the day. Instead they could say, "I'm glad I got that out of the way." And start to look for winning trades. I tell myself, "If the morning is difficult, the afternoon will be sweet." Some traders start the day with a win or a few wins, and they begin to imagine giving up their profits. They often stop trading just before the really big win comes along. Fortunately, we have free will and with that we can direct our imagination and make positive interpretations of events. The bad trade is out of the way. An even bigger winner is just ahead.

The golfer can imagine his ball flying true to the pin, or veering into the woods. He can choose whether to think about making a putt or just getting it close. The trader can imagine the rest of the day going well, or she can feel jinxed.

"The formula for bitterness: working for one thing but expecting something else!"
—Danny Cox

THE POWER OF QUESTIONS

Imagination can be skittish, a really wild child. And yet we can use our conscious mind to direct the imagination in support of our goals. How do we do this? One way is with the proper use of questions. **Questions are vital because they direct the focus of the mind.**

What we focus on creates the quality of our lives. If we focus on troubles, that's all we'll see. We'll miss the good things that are happening. On the other hand, if we only focus on the good things that are happening or have happened, we may miss the warnings and the lessons that life gives us.

Each of us has one or more core questions we ask ourselves repeatedly. And it usually has to do with a value we hold or a fear we have. Our basic personality type will often determine what questions we ask.

I used to get up every morning and ask myself what I had to do to survive. Not bad in that it assumes that I could do something and survive. However, it was treacherous in that it assumed I wouldn't survive unless I did something. There have been many periods in my life when I lived by pulling metaphorical rabbits out of my hat.

A friend of mine used to wake up every morning and ask himself, "How can I make money today?" Guess what? He made a lot of money. Each day he had a moneymaking idea for the day. Of course, major projects take more than a day so he couldn't utilize all his ideas, but many of the best ones did get put into action.

Others may ask questions such as "What do they think of me? Do they respect me? Do they love me?" Such questions put the power in other people's estimation. Such questions can create personal insecurity around others.

Others may question whether their actions and circumstances are good enough. These people often have unrealistically high standards of perfection, and so constantly come up feeling cheated or inadequate.

In his book, **Awaken the Giant Within,**[1] Anthony Robbins tells a true story that illustrates the vital importance of the questions a person asks.

"They needed no reason. They came simply because he was of Jewish descent. The Nazis stormed into his home, arresting him and his entire family. Soon they were herded like cattle, packed into a train, and then sent to the infamous death camp Auschwitz. His most disturbing nightmares could never have prepared him for seeing his family shot before his very eyes. How could he live through the horror of seeing his child's clothing on another because his son was now dead as the result of a 'shower'?"

"Somehow he continued. One day he looked at the nightmare around him and confronted an inescapable truth: if he stayed there even one more day, he would surely die. He made a *decision* that he must escape and that escape must happen immediately! He knew not how, he simply knew he must. For weeks he'd asked the other prisoners, 'How can we escape this horrible place?' The answers he received seemed always to be the same: 'Don't be a fool,' they said, 'there is no escape! Asking such questions will only torture your soul. Just work hard and pray you survive.' But he couldn't accept this—*he wouldn't accept it.* He became obsessed with escape, and even when his answers didn't make any sense, he kept asking over and over again, 'How can I do it? There must be a way. How can I get out of here healthy, alive *today?*'"

"It is said that if you ask, you shall receive. And for some reason, on this day he got his answer. Perhaps it was the intensity with which he asked his question, or maybe it was his sense of certainty that 'now is the time.' Or possibly it was just the impact of continually focusing on the answer to one burning question. For whatever reason, the giant power of the human mind and spirit awakened in this man. The answer came to him through an unlikely source: the sickening smell of decaying human flesh. There, only a few feet from his work, he saw a huge pile of bodies that had been shoveled into the back of a truck—men, women, and children who had been gassed. The gold fillings had been pulled from their teeth; everything that they owned—any jewelry—even their clothing, had been taken. Instead of asking, 'How could the Nazis be so despicable, so destructive? How could God make something so evil? Why has God done this to me?' Stanislaw Lec asked a different question. He asked, **'How can I use this to escape?'** And instantly he got his answer."

"As the end of the day neared and the work party headed back into the barracks, Lec ducked behind the truck. In a heartbeat, he ripped off his clothes and dove naked into the pile of bodies while no one was looking. He pretended that he was dead, remaining totally still even though later he was almost crushed as more and more bodies were heaped on top of him."

"The fetid smell of rotting flesh, the rigid remains of the dead surrounded him everywhere. He waited and waited, hoping that no one would notice the one living body in that pile of death, hoping that sooner or later the truck would drive off."

"Finally, he heard the sound of the engine starting. He felt the truck shudder. And in that moment, he felt a stirring of hope as he lay among the dead. Eventually, he felt the truck lurch to a stop, and then it dropped its ghastly cargo—dozens of the dead and one man pretending to be one of them—in a giant open grave outside the camp. Lec remained there for hours until nightfall. When he finally felt certain no one was there, he extracted himself from the mountain of cadavers, and he ran naked forty-five miles to freedom."

This man had courage and a determination to live. He also asked the right questions. Had he simply asked, "Why does God allow this?" he would not have found his way to escape. His burning, "How can I get out of here?" provided his way to escape.

Questions are vital because they predetermine your focus. The questions you ask direct your imagination, and the imagination rules. Had Lec imagined dying like the rest of his family, that is probably what would have happened. Instead he assumed that he could get out of there, and asked "How?"

Questions are incredible tools of communication with yourself and with others. The purpose of a question is to directionalize thinking. The whole point of questions is to direct your own thinking or the thinking of another person. Pay attention to the questions you ask yourself when you trade. Some questions support the trading process. Others impair the trading process.

Some traders have trouble taking trades because they're asking themselves the wrong questions. Questions such as, "What if I lose?" will do a pretty good job at creating trading hesitation. Another question that causes traders difficulty in taking trades is, "Is this signal going to be a 'good' one?" The question causes the trader to cherry pick his signals and often ends up missing important winning trades. A much better question would simply be, "Is this a valid signal?"

The question, "What if I give up my profits?" can cause you to exit too soon or to fail to continue trading when the trading's going well. "What if this losing streak continues?" can cause you to quit trading a methodology just before it kicks in.

"How can I make this trade work out?" is also an undermining question to the trading process. The trade is not working out: get out and go on to the next one.

There are many different types or forms of questions. Let's look at them, and see how they work.

1. **Open Ended Questions**
   What do you want from your trading?
   What additional resources do you need to improve your trading?

2. **Menu Questions**
   Do you most need to improve your strategy for entries and exits; or do you need to develop better money management guidelines; or do you need to work on your own self mastery? The downside of a menu question is that you may be leading inappropriately.

3. **Outcome Sequitur Questions**
   What is the outcome of the outcome? What will the consistent application of your trading system do for you? What will profitable trading do for you? These questions keep chunking upwards. *What will that do for you? And what will that do for you?*

4. **Metamodel Questions**
   These questions chunk down to specifics asking who, what, when, how, with more specificity. *How specifically will you use this additional filter in your trading? When specifically will you utilize discretion in following your system?*

5. **Lateral Questions**
   You say you don't have confidence when you trade: do you have anything like confidence?

6. **Either/Or Questions**
   Will you continue to be depressed about your trading, or will you make some constructive changes? Will you continue to overtrade, or will you once and for all commit to your guidelines?

7. **Contrast Questions**
   How is one thing different from the other? What is the difference that makes the difference? What is the difference that makes the difference between confident trading and overconfident trading?

8. **Counter Example Questions**
   Has there ever been a time when you were not stressed out trading? Has there ever been a time when you were confident trading?

9. **Comparative Questions**
   What is better? What is worse? Is it safer to use a mental stop or to actually place it in the market?

10. **Meta Questions**
    How do you feel about how you feel about your trading? What do you think of yourself when you skip a trade? What would you say to a friend if they were overtrading as you are?

If you have any trading problems, try some of these forms of questions to get your thinking organized and solution oriented.

One question I like to get the imagination going in the right way begins "*Can you imagine?*" *Can you imagine trading your system as it was designed to be traded? Can you imagine ending each trading day with confidence for the next day? Can you imagine being consistently profitable over time? Can you imagine trading with a calm, alert curiosity? Can you imagine trusting yourself to do the right thing at the right time? Can you imagine trading with a willingness to assume the risk, and a focus on the potential benefits of trading?* To decide whether or not you can imagine something, you need to imagine it first. And imagination is the fuel in the tank that gets you going.

Questions alone, of course, are not enough. They have to be the right questions. Whole lives and whole societies and whole eras can be impoverished or unenlightened because of the failure to ask the right questions. When you think about your life, ask yourself, "Am I asking the right questions?" When you think about your trading, ask yourself, "Am I asking the right questions?" A good question to ask yourself in any situation is, "What is the best question to ask right now?"

POSITIVE WORRY

"A man may dwell so long upon a thought that it may take him prisoner."
—Marquis of Halifax

There are times when we all fret over something—and it either comes to pass or it doesn't. The problem with an anxious concern about future events goes beyond the fact that it ruins the quality of our present. **Worry often brings to pass the very thing we're worried about.**

How do we get ourselves into a state of worry? Surely we don't decide to think about all the possible things that could go wrong, and explore them, and visualize them, and let ourselves feel terrible about them. No. Worry just slips in. It starts with two magic words: **What if...?**

What if I lose?
What if I give up my profits?
What if the system doesn't any longer work?
What if I lose my margin money and can't continue trading?
What if it can't be done?
What if I'm wrong?
What if this drawdown continues?
What if the market turns around and I'm out of the trade?
What if I lose my job as a trader?
What if my spouse leaves me because I'm losing?
What if I lose my touch, my market savvy?
What if my fear is warning me about a market turn?

And you're off and running with the scenario depicted by what if. You imagine it fully and completely. You build upon it until it expands and feels very real. Naturally such a scenario creates a fabric of emotional distress. Thought mixed with emotion burns itself into the brain. This in turn enables us to magnetize the thought and we somehow bring to pass the very thing we don't want. Worry can be a self-fulfilling prophecy.

A person doesn't sit down and say, "Now I'm going to imagine all the things that could possibly go wrong with my trading and visualize the consequences. Then I'll feel bad and burn the thought into my psyche." It just slips in innocently enough before it creates it's own havoc.

Of course, it is true that we need to consider the possible negatives that are out there. If there were no chance of loss, we wouldn't need a stop. If there were no chance of loss, the game would be over because everybody can't win all of the time. There is a vast difference, however, between considering possible future alternatives and fixating on the worst possible outcome.

But it's natural to worry. It just creeps in. Trading is so fraught with uncertainties that it creates fertile soil for the seeds of worry. How do we counteract it? We counteract it with positive worry.

As soon as you hear yourself saying a negative what if, shift it with what if the opposite.

What if I lose? ***What if I win?***
What if I give up my profits? ***What if my profits keep growing?***
What if the system doesn't any longer work? ***What if my system continues to win over time?***
What if I lose my margin money and can't continue trading? ***What if my account grows? What if I can create extra trading capital?***
What if it can't be done? ***What if it can be done?***
What if I'm wrong? ***What if I'm right?***
What if this drawdown continues? ***What if this is the end of the drawdown?***
What if the market turns around and I'm out of the trade? ***What if I get out of the trade and save myself a bigger loss?***
What if I lose my job as a trader? ***What if I keep my job? What if I get an even better job?***
What if my spouse leaves me because I'm losing? ***What if my spouse is loyal regardless of what happens?***
What if I lose my touch, my market savvy? ***What if I become an even better trader?***
What if my fear is warning me about a market turn? ***What if my fear is groundless?***

That's using positive worry as a shield to protect yourself from your negative worry. You can use positive worry as a sword to initiate a process of forward, positive thinking. Once again, you simply begin with the two magic words: "What if...?"

What if I become a very good trader?
What if I make a lot of money trading?
What if I create a methodology that makes consistent money over time?
What if I can make money trading?
What if I can make a decent living trading?
What if I can create independence and freedom through my trading?

The process is the same as with negative worry. The question directs the thought along a path. The consequences of the question need to be imagined to answer the question. These thoughts create certain emotions. Thought mixed with emotion acts like a magnet for the thought.

Worry—negative and positive—is a perfect medium for imagination. In order to keep the imagination on the side of your conscious desires, you need to reverse negative worry immediately with positive worry, and you would be well advised to initiate positive worry to fully imagine your basic purposes in trading being fulfilled.

TRADING HESITATION

"Short term comfort for long term trouble is not the trade you're looking for. The easy way is not the easy way."
—Richard Bach

"You miss 100% of the shots you don't take."
—Wayne Gretzki

" You cannot know in advance the results of any given trade...You have to think in terms of a series of probabilities."
—Mark Douglas

Many traders come to me for coaching because they can't pull the trigger on a trade. Or they can't pull it in a timely fashion. There are many factors at work here, and we'll discuss many of them, but certainly one of the primary factors in being unable to pull the trigger is the misuse of the imagination.

How on earth can you take a trade in a timely fashion if you're imagining the pain of taking a loss? How can you take a trade if it's important for you to "be right" and you're imagining being wrong?

Nancy would see the signal right away. She'd know it was a valid signal, and she'd start to shake. Her hand on the mouse could barely verify bar prices. "What if it's a loser?" she'd ask. She'd remember other trades she'd been in when she'd gotten sick to her stomach. She'd remember the times she'd taken losses. She'd freeze. If the trade turned out to be a loser, she'd feel relieved that that was one she'd missed. If the trade were a winner, she'd berate herself for missing the profit. With each passing day, she deplored herself more.

Whenever Rick would get a trading signal, he'd pause. He would look for confirmation. He'd want to do the right thing. (At that point he didn't understand that being right was taking the signal instantly.) He'd look for all the possible indications that the trade might not work. He'd check things out again. "What if I'm wrong?" would echo through his mind. Finally confirmation would come. He'd pause. He'd hesitate. He'd check everything one more time. By now the trade would be screaming confirmation. At this point Rick would either freeze and say, "Oh well, I'll get the next one." Or he'd throw himself headlong into the trade that had already left him far behind. Often just at the point he'd get in, the move would be over. To Rick, getting into the market was like trying to board a speeding train.

Both of these traders would consciously vow that next time it would be different. Next time they'd take the trade. When the next signal would come, Nancy would repeat the shaking and the inability to act. Rick would either miss it, or take it on the late side, and in any event, it would turn out to be a loser. In both cases, an unconscious pattern was being reinforced in both traders that would make it harder and harder for them to trade as time goes by. For both of them, the frustration would mount and their personal confidence would wither, as their personal discomfort would become almost unbearable.

We go towards pleasure and away from pain. Through their imaginations both these traders were associating pain to each new trade. They were associating each trade to loss—of money or of self-esteem. To take the trade, Nancy would have to imagine the trade making her money. Rick would have to imagine the trade proving his analysis correct, or else proving that he was correct in taking each trade as it comes along and ultimately confirming him in his series of judgments.

Nancy was associating massive pain to taking a trade. The pain was physical as well as financial. Until she can imagine some pleasure with an individual trade or the process of trading itself, she will continue to protect herself by not trading. Her commands to herself to take the next trade will remain powerless until she can imagine success.

For Rick, the difficulty was caused by his need to be right. The need to be right is often associated with the need to be perfect. Perfectionists are often convinced that there's a right and a wrong way to do things. And they are cursed with the need to be right. Deep inside is a sense that something awful will happen if they're "wrong." They need to convince themselves that being right is taking all the trades. Being wrong is letting the trades go by.

Rick on a deep level needs to change his belief that he must be right to a belief that trading is only probabilities, that being right is aligning a series of probabilities. He needs to assess his trades in chunks of five to ten before he considers profitability. He also needs to understand that uncertainty is the essence of trading, and he needs to get comfortable dealing with the unknowable. He's holding himself to a standard of perfection in being right about what cannot possibly be known in advance.

If you're having trouble pulling the trigger to enter a trade, no doubt you are imagining loss. You are overweighing the loss potential. You need to keep your mind focused on the potential for profit. Use positive worry to counteract your natural worry. "What if this trade is a big winner?" Picture the chart on the screen going in your direction. Imagine yourself making money on a series of trades.

One of the stumbling blocks to imagining a trade going your way is that the first act after placing the trade is to measure the risk and place a stop loss order in the market. This can get you to imagining the stop getting hit. At this point you need to think of the stop as an insurance policy protecting you from too great a loss. You never know whether this trade will be a small loser or a large profit. The place to put your focus is on the large profit.

Another reason some traders have trouble taking trades is that they don't have a verified faith in their methods. Either your methods will work over time or they won't. Check them out. If they worked in the past, set your imagination to picturing them working in the future. Remember, however, that faith is just that—faith, pure and simple. It isn't fact. Some people speak of blind faith. Blind or visionary, you have to have faith in your methods. Without faith, the traders perish.

Some traders simply haven't set their intention to actually trade. They're involved in a spectator sport—watching the market, and watching their system work in the market. This is all right, if this is all you want to do, but while it won't lose you money, it surely will never make you money either. Just watching the market day after day is really a giant waste of time and energy. Unless you do it just to pass the time of day like watching television.

If you're not taking trades, set your intention to trade that day. If you miss the first trade, leave the screen and do something else. This will tell your subconscious that you're serious about actually trading.

Another way to get your imagination working in direction of trading is to do mental rehearsal. If at the end of the trading day, you haven't taken all the trades, redo the day in your mind. Go through the day's chart and take every single trade, picking up the phone or electronically trading each signal by placing the order, putting in the stop, and managing the trade. At the end of the rehearsal, set your intention to trade tomorrow.

If trading is difficult for you to do, you have to decide that you're willing to move out of your comfort zone. You need to take deliberate, intentional moves out of the ease of never being at risk. In his book **There Are No Limits,**[2] Danny Cox, a pilot who regularly flew beyond the speed of sound talks about the experience of ejecting from a moving plane.

> "There was something one had to be keenly aware of concerning the ejection seats I used while I was in the Air Force. Basically, the pilot was strapped into a seat that was sitting on top of a 35-millimeter cannon shell. There were pluses and minuses to this arrangement. One plus was that the propulsion would lift you, in a hurry, out of any situation you felt was intolerable. A significant minus, of course, was that activating the ejection seat was a lot like suddenly being blown out into a 600-mile-per-hour wind. Not a whole lot of fun! That knowledge keeps you from activating the system for recreational purposes."
>
> "There was, however, a major problem that had to do with what some pilots did after ejecting. ...
>
> "The system worked great, until you plugged in the human factor. The designers found that some pilots, after having ejected, were clinging with a (literal) death grip to the armrest handles of the seat—the last remnant of the cockpit where, before, they'd been safe. Strictly speaking, this made no sense, because everybody knows that the seat, on its own, is not an efficient shock absorber when you strike the ground at, say, 200 miles per hour. A number of pilots rode the seat all the way down to the ground—to their deaths. All they had to do was roll forward out of the seat and the parachute would open automatically at a give altitude. They didn't. The instinct to hang on to the last vestiges of a familiar surrounding, one where they'd always been safe, was a killer."

He goes on to describe how the airforce developed a mechanism that the pilots called a "butt snapper" that literally forced the pilot out of the seat so that the parachute could unfold. At times we all need a butt snapper to get us out of our comfort zone. The moment when it's time to launch our plan, we need something that will get us moving, that will get us to release the death grip we have on our chair where we've gotten too comfortable.

Paper trading is fine. It teaches us how to work the method and it shows us that the method works or doesn't work. But paper trade too long, and you just get too comfortable. At that point you have to get out of the comfort zone and move into the arena of real life trading. You need a butt snapper. Choose a time to begin, and tell your broker, your family, your trading buddies, that this is the day you're going live.

Some people have trouble taking trades because the method doesn't match their personality. If they have a slow tempo, they shouldn't trade the one minute chart on the S&P. If they have a fast tempo, they may be uncomfortable staying the course in trading off a weekly chart. Markets differ. Time frames differ.

If you're having trouble trading S&P's go to the E-mini or go to bean oil or corn. If you can't make quick decisions to day trade, begin position trading on a close to open basis where you have all evening to analyze and prepare the morning's order. You have your own personality. There are many methods and many markets and many time frames. Choose what suits you. In any case, remember:

"Theorizing never put muscles in your arms or money in your pocket."
—Anonymous

OVERTRADING

Those who overtrade run their imaginations quite differently from those who can't trade or those who hesitate or undertrade. Those who tend to overtrade are keenly aware that you have to be in to win. They constantly imagine the probability of profit and virtually ignore the potential for loss. In this sense, if a little is good, more is better.

"He takes chances, but never leaves anything to chance."
—Jim Newton about Charles Lindbergh

Traders who overtrade may do so in terms of size or frequency. They may fail to even consider the importance of money management, let alone institute a sound money management policy. This lack of precaution and lack of balance can ultimately bring their trading to an untimely end.

Some people get a thrill out of the business of risk taking. This can work in their favor, but if it isn't balanced with caution and proper risk controls, it can be dangerous. When I was visiting Southern California for the Christmas of 1995, I noticed the cover of *Surfer Magazine* on the magazine rack in a grocery store. I was stunned by what I saw. There on the cover was a giant blue wave curling behind what appeared to be a small surfer. Across the picture were the words "The Joy of Fear."

It sounded like trading to me. After reading the March 1996 issue, I subscribed to the magazine. Let 1996 be known as the year I subscribed to *Surfer Magazine.* That year living in the Wall Street area of New York City, I always had copies of *Surfer Magazine* on my coffee table along with psychological and financial periodicals. Well, it added a bit to the mystique of my image.

The parallels of surfing to trading are uncanny in certain respects. The article "The Joy of Fear" starts with a quote from **John Berryman. *"We must travel in the direction of our fear."*** To that I would add, "we must travel in the direction of our fear and anticipate success even as we institute safety controls."

The following are the first two paragraphs of the article:

> "To come to life, some people need a giant syringe of adrenaline jabbed directly into their hearts. Others need only a 10'6" tri-fin and a ship-killing ocean to play in."
>
> "'Big-wave surfing,' Jock Sutherland once said 'is like attacking a Tyrannosaurus Rex for dinner.' And he was right. It is the ultimate pursuit of the underdog, an enormous mismatch—frail human against omnipotent ocean. But within that giant margin there are rewards. Turn your back on the black mass, do it with heart and strength, and the result is pure: one golden bullet of adrenaline to every cell in your body. And with every drop, a message: 'You've done it man. You've lived.'"

Let's change this to apply to trading:

"To come to life, some people need a giant syringe of adrenaline jabbed directly into their hearts. Others need only a futures account and a fortune-killing market to play in."

"Big time trading is like attacking a Tyrannosaurus Rex for dinner. It is the ultimate pursuit of the underdog, an enormous mismatch—frail human trader against omnipotent market. But within that giant margin there are rewards. Turn your back on the black mass, do it with heart and strength, and the result is pure: one golden bullet of adrenaline to every cell in your body. And with every drop, a message: 'You've done it man. You've lived.'"

In another article in that issue entitled "Exer Psychos," Brian Keaulane, a 34-year-old surfer is quoted saying:

> "Water is the coolest, most serene thing you can be involved with, but it's also ferocious and will kill you. To be in the water, you have to be like water. You have to know how to flow and be serene, but you still have to be strong and ferocious and have confidence. The ocean has so much emotion, and you have to become a part of it and work with it."

Once again let's change that to apply to the market:

"The market is the coolest, most serene thing you can be involved with, but it's also ferocious and will kill you. To be in the market, you have to be like the market. You have to know how to flow and be serene, but you still have to be strong and ferocious and have confidence. The market has so much emotion, and you have to become a part of it and work with it."

Surfers are a type who relish the dangerous edge and are similar to those traders who love the action and love to trade. Both need to practice their craft, be in shape, be alert, know what they're doing and exercise superb control as they work with the forces in which they play.

The year before I subscribed to *Surfer Magazine*, Mark Foo, a champion surfer, was killed while surfing. The danger is real; something top surfers had always known. When asked why they surfed the giant waves, why they would get in front of an 18-foot wave, the answer was, "we think we can make it." Exactly. Of course they do, or they wouldn't be able to do it successfully. It's the same with successful traders. They expect to win or they wouldn't keep taking the trades and staying with them and go on to win.

Let me say it again. Winners expect to win. Losers expect to lose. And both realize their expectations more often than not. We go in the direction of our dominant thoughts. We bring those thoughts into reality. We bring to pass what we concentrate upon. We become our imagination.

There's a caveat here. If you only expect to win, and apply no counterbalances, no risk restraints, you can overexpose yourself to the dangers of the market. If you're reckless in the market, if you act for the action's sake without a viable plan, if you need that adrenaline high, that taste of danger to feel alive, you need to tighten your protective shield and bring it in closer. You need to take a good hard look at the probabilities and believe them and act accordingly on them. You need a viable plan, and you need to implement that plan.

GAMBLING

Is trading gambling? What is the difference between trading and gambling? Some say that if the odds are in your favor, you're not gambling. You're playing a game of probabilities (rather than chance) that you'll ultimately win.

In the gambling industry the casino itself is not gambling, and most would agree with this. The odds are in the house's favor, and the house has strict rules for gaming that keep the odds in its favor. The house has a 2½% advantage in most games and more than that in slot machines. How can it be gambling? You never heard of a casino closing down because it got cold feet because it had a losing day.

When a trader works against the bid and the asked, slippage, and commissions, he has much more against him than the player in a game of black jack. Therefore, his methods, his money management, and his mental steadiness have got to be developed in such a way as to give him an edge if he's not to be gambling or throwing his results into the hands of chance.

Others define gambling by the instrument of play. If it's poker, cards, craps, dice, horses, and so forth, it's gambling. If it's stocks, options, or futures, it's investing or speculating.

Still others define gambling by a player's style of play. A trader presses the market when he's ahead: a gambler presses when he's behind. A gambler takes random chances. A trader prepares, studies, and waits patiently for the high probability opportunity and then acts promptly and appropriately.

Whether you call it trading or gambling, society accepts the behavior as long as you win or keep it under control. Some individuals can't stop trading or gambling until they end up in deep trouble, and they have to seek help or somebody else seeks help for them. This is called pathological gambling or continuously, massively unprofitable trading. As traders we can learn by looking at the problems and pitfalls of pathological gamblers.

Martin C. McGurrin wrote ***Pathological Gambling.***[3] In this book he distinguishes normal recreational gambling from pathological gambling. The pathological gambler displays three characteristics before gambling: a compulsion to gamble; an increasing physical and psychological tension prior to gambling; and a pronounced level of pleasure associated with the relief of tension achieved by active involvement in gambling behavior.

McGurrin describes five common characteristics of pathological gamblers. First, they vacillate between periods of extreme confidence in gambling as well as life and periods of acute self-doubt, anxiety and depression. Second, they tend to view reward and achievement through gradual, sustained effort and delayed gratification as an inferior means of financial self-support and accomplishment. Third, they typically have difficulty maintaining intimate, emotionally expressive and supportive relationships when involved in active gambling. Fourth, many pathological gamblers exhibit narcissism manifest in a grandiose sense of self-importance, hypersensitivity to criticism, fragile self-esteem and a lack of empathy for others. As a result, they use primitive defense mechanisms to guard against feelings of powerlessness and lack of self-worth. Finally, the gamblers tend to view many life events—not just gambling—as being externally controlled.

Problem gamblers tend to respond without forethought in crisis situations. They also have a relative inability to delay gratification. Problem gamblers don't discipline themselves to look for high-probability situations. They don't self-regulate. They don't utilize good risk control. They don't have good money management. And they tend to gamble with money they can't afford to lose. Sometimes they'll borrow from relatives and friends without any foreseeable means of paying it back. Sometimes they'll steal to gamble.

Problem gamblers are looking for an intensity that eludes them elsewhere in life. They go for the sense of the action, of being alive, of being a part of things. This draws them even more than the money.

In 1980 Gamblers Anonymous in Los Angeles published a list of 20 questions about gambling behavior. I have inserted the word *trading* to help you translate the questions to your own trading.

20 QUESTIONS ABOUT GAMBLING (TRADING) BEHAVIOR

1. Did you ever lose time from work due to gambling (trading)?
2. Has gambling (trading) ever made your home life unhappy?
3. Did gambling (trading) affect your reputation?
4. Have you ever felt remorse after gambling (trading)?
5. Did you ever gamble (trade) to get money with which to pay debts or otherwise solve financial difficulties?
6. Did gambling (trading) cause a decrease in your ambition or efficiency?
7. After losing, did you feel you had to return to the scene of your loss as soon as possible and win back your losses?
8. After a win, did you have a strong urge to return and win more?
9. Did you often gamble (trade) until your last dollar was gone?
10. Did you ever borrow to finance your gambling (trading)?
11. Have you ever sold anything to finance gambling (trading)?
12. Were you reluctant to use "gambling (trading) money" for normal expenditures?
13. Did gambling (trading) make you careless of the welfare of yourself and your family?
14. Did you ever gamble (trade) longer than you had planned?
15. Have you ever gambled (traded) to escape worry or trouble?
16. Have you ever committed, or considered committing, an illegal act to finance gam bling (trading)?
17. Did gambling (trading) cause you to have difficulty in sleeping?
18. Do arguments, disappointments or frustrations create within you an urge to gamble (trade)"?
19. Did you ever have an urge to celebrate any good fortune by a few hours of gambling (trading)?
20. Have you ever considered self-destruction as a result of your gambling (trading)?

Some of these questions are more suited to gambling than to trading. Also there is an assumption that the activity will produce a loss—something I would not be willing to assume about trading. The parallel is instructive.

Please note that the gamblers who created this list say that a yes answer to four or more questions is a reliable indication that you may be a problem gambler (trader) and no longer normally in control of your gambling (trading) behavior.

The important question to ask yourself as a trader is do you make money with your trading? Have you ever made money trading? How long has it been since you've been profitable? How have you funded your trading account? Remember trading needs to be supported with risk capital. Risk capital is defined as money that you can lose without effecting your life style, your future, or your personal state of well being.

Researchers in behavior modification have noted that random rewards are more effective than earned rewards in motivating behavior. For example, a dolphin will jump for an earned fish, but if every so often that dolphin is offered a jackpot of five fish, he will jump higher. Thus trading, with its random rewards, can motivate us to trade even more. It would have an inbuilt tendency to motivate us to overtrade. To gamble.

For the gambler, it's always a sure thing. The next bet is certain to win. That's how he runs his imagination. If this is what you're doing, you have to balance this with imagining the possibility of loss. You also need to be receptive to the feedback you get.

On the positive side let me mention that the origin of the word gamble, is gambol, which means to play. Without a healthy play impulse, a person tends not to be a player, tends neither to gamble nor to trade. The play impulse is what makes the whole enterprise fun.

If you're worried that you're gambling—playing games of chance that are purely that—you can stop and put some new parameters in place that will put the probabilities in your favor. You can establish written trading rules that will keep your behavior supportive of good trading results. Make sure that your trading capital is truly risk capital and is sufficient to cover probable drawdowns.

Lastly, bring the control back into yourself. Too often we live and trade in what seems to be a monumental struggle with fate. The market is a neutral arena in which you can make money if you do what needs to be done. Internal control and sensitivity to feedback may well be the difference between gambling and trading or between effective trading and problem trading.

Imagination is powerful. And because we can use our conscious mind and an act of will to direct our imagination, we have an almost magical weapon to use in support of our lives and trading. Suspect you're a gambling trader? Use your imagination to see yourself as a thoroughly prepared, disciplined, effective trader. Can't pull the trigger? Use your imagination to see yourself winning.

What do you want? What do you want to be like as a trader? What do you want to be like as a person? What do you want your life to be like? Open the floodgates of your imagination and invite yourself to dream a dream of your future.

[1] ***Awaken the Giant Within***, Anthony Robbins, Summit Books, 1991, ISBN 0-671-72734-6

[2] ***There Are No Limits,*** Danny Cox, Career Press, 1998, ISBN 1-56414-340-6

[3] ***Pathological Gambling: Conceptual, Diagnostic, and Treatment Issues,*** Martin C. McGurrin, Professional Resource Press, 1992

CHAPTER VIII

UNCOUPLING YOUR EGO

"If you think that you are God and you go into the financial markets, you are going to come out broke. The fact that I am not broke proves that I don't think I am God."
—George Soros on *Sixty Minutes*

Make no mistake about it. A trader's self concept has to be separate from his trading. Who you are as a person began before you ever thought of trading and who you will be as a person will extend beyond your trading. When personal self-worth entwines with trading, it not only damages self-esteem, it sabotages the trading.

"Authentic freedom cannot be experienced until one learns to tame the ego and move out of self-absorption."
—Wayne W. Dyer

THE INSATIABLE EGO

Don't be misled. They tell stories. They write stories. They tell how great they are. Big trades. Big numbers. Big egos. Hubris. And sooner or later, big downfalls. It goes with the territory.

Consider the outsized egos of traders who brought themselves and those associated with them to ruin. Nicholas Leeson brought down the **Barings Bank**. Victor Niederhoffer ran his fund into deficit. John Merriweather threatened the health of our banking system by betting more than fifty times his capital that his strategies were certain to work, that he could forecast with impunity the direction of various bond markets. There's a pattern here of seeming or real success for a while and then collapse for themselves and for those caught up in blindly following them.

Listen to Victor Neiderhoffer as he begins his book ***The Education of a Speculator.***[1]

> "I am an old trader, and I trade the yen in the cash market. I once had the best record among all the traders. I was rated number one in my field, and my picture was in all the newspapers. Customers crowded my doors. The attractive currency brokers talked sexy to me, told me where their customers' stops were, and where the central banks were buying and selling. The great Soros more than once called to have me trade for his own account."

> "But I got in over my head. I bought the dollar when the dollar/yen was 93. It went to 88 in just a few hours. I was eaten alive. The banks will not give me credit anymore, and many of my customers have left. I still have some customers—people who are not happy with feeding all their money to the stock market. They are afraid that it will crash as it did in 1929 and 1987. They look to me to land a big return, but without risk or drawdown. I can do it; but they don't want me to gamble, and I cannot do it without gambling. The risk creates opportunity. Still, I am humble because I have lost many times."

Victor Niederhoffer wrote this before he traded his fund into deficit. Was he truly humble? I wonder. Humble or not, the trader who wrote this clearly had not removed his ego from his trading.

In his wonderful book, ***Pit Bull***[2], Marty Schwartz tells several stories of the times he lost money because his ego got in the way. In the end he has this to say about ego:

> "I've said it before, and I'm going to say it again, because it cannot be overemphasized: ***the most important change in my trading career occurred when I learned to DIVORCE MY EGO FROM THE TRADE.*** Trading is a psychological game. Most people think that they're playing against the market, but the market doesn't care. You're really playing against yourself. You have to stop trying to will things to happen in order to prove that you're right. Listen only to what the market is telling you now. Forget what you thought it was telling you five minutes ago. The sole objective of trading is not to prove you're right, but to hear the cash register ring."

The treachery of the ego extends beyond the big traders. It effects ordinary traders, both daring and cautious, and can sabotage their trading.

Now I'm not talking about the confident trader. The trader who trusts herself. The trader who goes quietly applying her methods to the market as best she can. She's just trading. She's not busy proving or defending her self-worth.

In this chapter I will be using the word ego to represent a cognizance of self and a process of self-assessment. I am not using the word in the way that Sigmund and Anna Freud did. In the Freudian sense, the Ego defended against the desires of the Id to keep the self in alignment with the demands of the Superego. In their process the Ego developed defense mechanisms to defend against the unacceptable drives of the Id.

No. In this chapter I'm using ego in the sense of **an unstable I or a vociferous I.** Puffery, as in "Boy, what an ego!" And you know that the guy is blowing his own horn because he truly is uncertain of his self-worth, and hopes that by convincing you, it will become fact that he's hot stuff! He's a hotshot trader! In this chapter I'm also talking about the egos of the timid traders who shrink within themselves at the prospect of being wrong and the egos of those who fight the market for dear life in order not to be diminished in their own or anybody else's eyes.

Because trading is an uncertain game of probabilities filled with uncertain vagaries, an overly inflated ego or a fragile ego can easily get smashed. Defending the ego uses up unnecessary energy, distorts perception, and sooner or later, will destroy the trading. **If your self-esteem rises and falls with your trading results, you and your trading are in trouble. Self-concept has to be strong and durable and not at the mercy of the current, last, or next trade.**

We need to check our egos at the door when we start to trade. Uncertainty is central to trading. If we add the uncertainty of our own self-image into the mix of the unknowable endemic to trading, we're in for certain trouble sooner or later.

THREE TRADERS TALK ABOUT EGO

I asked Linda Raschke how she keeps her ego out of trading.

Linda: "I lost my ego a long time ago, Ruth. Or I wouldn't be around. Oh God, yes. I'm very superstitious. I believe that if you talk about it, it's a jinx. You don't talk about your performance. If you go to parties, you don't talk about trades. You don't talk about markets. To me it's something private you keep to yourself."

"Even my best friends who are traders—if anything we all cry about our losing trades, and we never talk about when we're doing well. It's like the markets are a big poker game, and you don't let on when you're doing well. You don't talk about it. It's like you kind of let it keep piling up, and you say I screwed up in the soybeans yesterday. I lost two cents here. That type of thing. You don't talk about your good trades. You never ever say to somebody, 'I bought here, and I sold here, and I did it on ten contracts.' Maybe it's the way I was on the floor. Maybe it's what I observed on the floor."

Ruth: "Good traders don't talk about it."

Linda: "You sure don't. It's considered to be—you're not a good trader if you talk about your trades. It's a loss of class. To me, if somebody talks about how good they are, it's a sign that they're not a good trader. They just don't have any experience because everybody's time comes up at some point or another. The market will put you in your place very quickly. If you think you're so much smarter than the market, it just tells me that you haven't been trading long enough."

Ruth: "Some people, because of a weak ego, feel they have to be right."

Linda: "Having to be right. That's such a cliche. It's not just a matter of the ego thing and the being right. There are some people who have the ability to say oops I'm wrong. I'm so wrong I'm going to go in the other direction..."

Ruth: "If you feel some need to always be right, you're going to be in a lot of trouble."

Linda: "I think it's more like that know-it-all personality. I think the know-it-alls are always going to get into trouble."

Ruth: "Is there anything else besides being a know-it-all that gets people into trouble?"

Linda: "Among my professional friends and colleagues, because we always tell our mistakes, our worse performances, never our good ones, it's the slight letting down of the guard in low volatility times. It's letting down the guard against those freak anomalies that can occur. The market has price behavior, the weird perverse movements that can occur, the freak standard deviation moves that take place that systems capture which are an entirely different game and a different subject. You have to understand that a system is designed to capture a statistical anomaly."

"Those types of incidents can and do and will occur with a much greater frequency than you can ever imagine and you can't anticipate the circumstances. You can't forecast a gulf war. You can't forecast a collapse in the Asian market, or the timing of it, or the way a currency is going to get squeezed or behave. You can't forecast these events. And these weird occurrences are always danger traps. They're higher volatility. They're opportunity for trades, but it's putting yourself in a position in quiet markets that can get you in trouble."

Ruth: "They're also opportunity traps."

Linda: "They're opportunity trades, but it's not putting yourself in a position in quiet markets where you have too much exposure, and that's where I see my professional friends get into trouble—that little bit of complacency where you can put on an options position, short calls or something, and then the leverage gets you into trouble."

"Leverage is like getting your fingers caught in the door and it sucks you into it. The more leverage you have on a position, the more distorted your view will be. And trust me, most professionals still do dumb things. It's because they allow themselves that one time every year to get stubborn or get too many contracts on or get too big."

"There's a fine line there between a manageable position and one that's gotten out of hand. And once it crosses that line, they get stubborn. They get too big. They have way too many contracts on, way too much leverage on, it's almost as if they have let themselves get so complacent by having a good run that it's almost asking to get knocked around to resharpen their focus."

"That's what I see. They'll sit there and work for three months and have a phenomenal quarter, and then give away half of it in one week just because it all of a sudden gets them back into the game. I think they feel like they're flipping out of the game, and so they've got to do something dumb to get back in. That's my interpretation. But it's not a matter of them being right because they know damn well they're not right and they're not going to be right. They know they made the mistake. It's like getting caught up in a hope cycle, okay? You're wrong. You know you're not right. You continue to be wrong, and it's just hoping."

"It is not given to any man to know it all. When he thinks he's the smartest man in the world, he puts himself in a class we call fools."
—Roy W. Longstreet

When I spoke with Max Ansbacher about how he kept his ego out of the trading, his answer was succinct.

Max: "I don't know. I really don't think I have a problem with that. You have to be willing to make mistakes and accept the fact that it happens a lot. But if anyone thinks they really know anything, or that they are right all the time, then they can't be in this business. It would destroy them, I think, to be wrong."

Ruth: "So anybody who thinks they need to be right..."

Max: "That they're really smart, that's not a good ego set to have."

I asked Michael McCarthy how he keeps his ego out of the trading.

Michael: "I look at it as a karma thing. If I'm a nice guy and stay humble, I'll make money. But if I start cheating people, lie to them, not be above board, it will stop working. If you're a good person, things will work out. If you're bad, you'll get yours."

Ruth: "That's your belief system. Others believe you have to cheat to win."

Michael: "Even if you win, you can't cheat and feel good about it. You know those people who seem to have trouble following them around? They get fined, have bad relationships, etc. They're professional victims with bad things following them. Nothing's following them. They're making the trouble."

Ruth: "So the thing that keeps you from letting your ego get in the way is this belief?"

Michael: "Yes, I believe if you get egotistical and are overly confident, it's over. Have you ever met a really successful person who is making money hand over fist, and they get jaded? How happy can a person like that be as compared with a humble unassuming person? I've never met an arrogant person who is happy. I've always thought it was a defense mechanism."

Ruth: "Of course it is. All the bluster and bravado and posturing is coming from an unstable person. They're trying to prop up their ego. They're overcompensating."

WHAT, THEN, IS EGO?

What is the definition of ego? The **Oxford English Dictionary (O.E.D.)** lists the following definitions:

Ego: The I, the conscious thinking subject, as opposed to the non-ego object. In every act of consciousness we distinguish a self or ego. Hence egohood, individuality.

Egotist: One who uses the word I too often. One who thinks or talks too much about himself.

Egotism: The too frequent use of the word I, hence the practice of talking about oneself and one's doings.

Egotize: To talk or write egotistically.

Egomania: Morbid egotism.

Some typical symptoms of egotizing trading would be the following:

- Not putting in stops. The ego doesn't want to be proven wrong.
- Hesitating before putting on a trade. The ego wants reassurance before it begins.
- Overtrading. The ego wants to prove itself big time.
- Getting stuck in a trade. The ego has intertwined itself with a trade and is holding on for dear life. It cannot cut out. The ego doesn't want to be wrong.

- Adding to a losing trade. The ego digs its hole deeper in a massive effort to crawl out.
- Grabbing a profit too soon. The ego wants a pat on the back.

"Do your worrying before the race—not after you have placed your bet and the horses are coming down the home stretch."

—A gambling pundit

Jim Paul tells a fascinating story of personalizing a trade in his book ***What I Learned Losing A Million Dollars***[3]. He was bullish in soybean oil and was heavily invested. The market was going up precipitously. One day in late August that year, he had made $248,000 in one day alone. It was an incredible high. A quarter of a million dollars in one day!

The following Monday he was at his desk waiting for the market to open. He was certain he would be up at least another $50,000. Not so. The market started down that day, and proceeded to continue on down. He lost an average of $20,000 to $25,000 a day for months.

At some point he started getting his clients out with small profits or small losses. But he himself stayed in the market. This was his trade. This was the *big* trade. He was going to make ten million dollars on this trade. He and his future were committed to this trade.

By the middle of October, Jim was in trouble. He was getting margin calls and borrowing from friends. By the beginning of November, he was in trouble big time. Soybean oil had gone from 37 cents a pound to 28 cents. From the high in August, Jim had lost nearly his entire net worth of $1.2 million and owed his friends an additional $400,000. Finally and mercifully, his firm pulled the plug on the trade. The firm took Jim out of the trade because he could not take himself out.

Jim committed many trading errors in this heartbreak of a trade (including scenario trading), but first and foremost, as he himself tells it, he had become the trade. He had become the position in soybean oil. The trade was mixed up with who he himself was and he couldn't extricate himself. He had egotized the trade and merged his ego with the outcome of the trade. His early profits had represented to him a personal reflection of his capability. He *became* his trade. He was going to win and win big. Nothing could stop him. Except disaster. And outside forces. His very identity was merged into the trade.

How do we separate our ego from our trading? How do we keep from personalizing a trade? How do we avoid personalizing all of our trading?

BOUNDARIES

"Good fences make good neighbors."
—Robert Frost

One way to separate your ego from your trading is to build healthy boundaries between yourself and your trading. Not only do good fences make good neighbors, good boundaries make good traders. What exactly is a boundary, and how can you use one or more?

A boundary sets limits, makes distinctions, informs you as to what is you and what is not you, makes clear the distinction between you and others, tells you where one thing ends and another begins. It distinguishes between past, present, and future. It lets you know that another's ideas, values, and feelings are not necessarily yours. A boundary is flexible and permeable. It lets information flow back and forth. It allows you to listen actively without having to take on someone else's opinions and without having to force your opinions on another person. In trading it draws a distinction between yourself and your trading, between one trade and another, between one trade and all of your trading.

Jane would see the signal to take a trade and before she could put the trade on, she'd hear a voice saying, "What if I'm wrong?" Immediately she'd feel small and diminished. The next step was simply to let the trade go by as she sat there stalled by her vulnerable ego. Jane needed a boundary between her self-esteem and the outcome of a trade. She needed a boundary between self worth and being wrong. With such a boundary she could give herself permission to not always have to be right.

John had had nineteen winning trades in a row. The tension was building and he was strung tighter than a drum when he came to see me. I congratulated him on his recent success and asked him what would be so awful if the next trade was a loser. He said, "I'd lose my self-esteem, and without self-esteem you're nothing." What an untenable state of affairs! His self-concept was riding on the results of the next trade. John needed a boundary between himself and his trading. He needed to know that his ego would be intact regardless of what happened to his trading.

A healthy boundary lets you know the difference between your business and yourself, between your trading and yourself. You are more than your business. You are more than your trading. A boundary also informs you that the results of one trade are not to be confused with the results of all of your trading. Boundaries guide you as to the difference between the past, the present, and the future.

It is essential to make distinctions in terms of time. If you experienced serious losses in the past, and you have since changed your trading strategy, your future trading will not mirror your past. Traders consciously know that, but still they often feel the terror creeping up from the past when they consider putting on a new trade. The past does not equal the future. We learn and we go on. Each day, each trade is fresh and new. The past is gone. The future is unrecorded. In such situations we need to build a boundary between the past and the present and the future. Yesterday's pain does not need to destroy tomorrow's possibilities.

We need to make clear distinctions in time when trading. We do not want to assume that what happened in the past will automatically happen today or in the future. If yesterday was an uptrend day, it does not follow that today will necessarily be the same. We need to draw distinctions so that we do not trade yesterday's market today, or, for that matter, tomorrow's market today. If we have an idea about what the future will produce in a particular market, we need to make a clear differentiation between that thought and what the market is actually doing today. As traders we need to learn from the past, be realistic in the present, and be optimistic about the future.

A boundary lets you know what are your own values and emotions and what are those of another person. You should not mistake another's emotions, good fortune, or predicament with your own. If another trader blows out after he got a divorce, it doesn't mean you will. If another trader overtrades and gets away with it, it doesn't mean you will. If your significant other thinks trading is gambling or is dangerous, it doesn't have to effect your thinking. You have studied the probabilities, and you rely upon them. If a famous guru announces that a market is on the brink of collapse, it doesn't have to become your opinion. You can build a boundary. You can give those opinions right back to them because that is where they belong.

A boundary lets you separate what you are feeling from what another is feeling. A healthy boundary lets you know the difference between your mother and yourself, your father and yourself, your children and yourself, your spouse and yourself. If your mother thinks you need a "regular job," if your father thinks "You can't play with the big boys," if your spouse thinks trading is a waste of time, you can let them have their feelings because they don't have to become yours. We are separate beings with separate needs, beliefs, values, and feelings. With a healthy boundary, we can be separate and connected, individual and together.

Boundaries can be contrasted with solid impenetrable walls, on the one hand; and with merging or having a lack of boundaries, on the other hand.

When boundaries are excessively diffuse, there is a loss of separation that can result in confusion or overidentification with another person or activity. Lack of boundaries can cause impairment of thinking and perceiving. If you can't think clearly about a trade when you're in it, you've lost your boundary. On the other hand, some traders merge with the market and become one with it as they trade "in the zone." Your results will let you know whether what you are doing is working.

Without boundaries you can lose your confidence when you experience a drawdown, instead of just taking it in the stride of trading. Without boundaries, you can confuse one losing day with a prospect of losing all your money if you fail to make distinctions between today and all the rest of your trading.

When boundaries are too rigid, they become walls. There is little transfer of ideas or emotions because they have been blocked out. It is difficult to have an emotional exchange with others and difficult to learn and grow and evolve. Walls support rigid ideas about yourself, the world, and the market. A wall is rigid and closes out information. It blocks the flow of ideas, occludes updates, and bars emotions.

If I build a wall around an idea, for example, no additional evidence or change of events will effect that idea. An illustration of this would be an Elliott Wave analyst who has been insisting since 1987 that we are perpetually on the verge of a giant bear stock market. He has built a wall between his conviction and reality.

If you build walls between yourself and other people, you cannot experience intimacy, empathy, or genuine sharing.

This is not to say that there aren't times when it's good to lose your boundaries. You want to lose your boundaries when watching a sunset, or listening to a great piece of music, or bonding with a baby, or when you are trading in the zone and you are one with the market.

Conversely, there are times when it's advisable to put up walls. There are times when outside events or emotions can be so overwhelming that walls become a necessary protection and enable a necessary separation. There are times when a wall can be particularly useful after a dreadful trading day. Take the learnings, put them someplace safe, and construct a wall if you feel like it.

There are certain cognitive and perceptual abilities necessary for developing and maintaining boundaries.

One needs ego strength, a sense of self as a separate entity with one's own values located inside oneself rather than outside oneself.

One needs to have a sense of self as a process. A dynamic relationship with time allows one to experience oneself as an ever-changing process, not as a static object. We change, we learn, we do not need—indeed we cannot—repeat what has gone before.

One needs to be able to notice both differences and samenesses. How are things, people, situations, information different as well as the same?

One needs to be able to step outside oneself and observe oneself, to be an objective observer of self and situation. (This is particularly useful in trading, and we'll be looking more completely at this later in this chapter.)

One needs to be able to identify with others. By stepping into another's shoes, one can literally shift the point of view to that of the other person for long enough to gather information.

When trading it's particularly important to maintain a boundary and to get a sense of the larger picture. One way to do this is to become aware of your peripheral vision beyond the trading screen. To do this you can wiggle your fingers back behind your head at the point where you can just barely see them. This will pull you out of tunnel vision associated with loss of boundaries, and will give you some distance between you and the screen. If you're in the zone and trading well, stay that way. Otherwise, step back so to speak.

Another way to establish boundaries is to pay attention to peripheral sounds, the sound of the computer, the traffic in the street, the birds, other voices, any music you're listening to, and so forth.

Become aware of your physical body: your back against the chair, your feet on the floor, your breathing.

Notice what is the same and what is different between this and other trades. This will put a boundary between your trades. Notice the differences and samenesses between you and your trading. This will put a boundary between you and your trading.

To create a wall make the image framed and move it into the distance. To break down the wall, bring the image closer and take away the frame.

Here is an exercise to practice building healthy boundaries. The exercise will help you build boundaries between yourself and other people. Think of a situation with another person that happens with some frequency and is damaging to your self-esteem.

Connect to your body and maintain a physical sense of yourself as you remember that situation. Watch that remembered movie through your own eyes but as you do that notice the background behind the other person, and be aware of your peripheral vision. Listen not only to both voices but to the background sounds as well. Notice what is the same and what is different between you. Ask yourself, "Whose values am I using?" "What can I learn?" If the values are your own, ask yourself, "How can I be different in the future?" Then practice reliving the experience using your own values and having made the changes.

As you go through your day be aware of when you're building walls, losing boundaries, or using and maintaining boundaries. As you develop these skills, you develop choice. The choice will improve your relationships, your trading, and your personal life. **Boundaries are your ultimate resource.**

"I looked for a helping hand—found it! At the end of my arm! And there was another one just like it at the end of the other arm."

—Jim Rohn

PERCEPTUAL POSITIONS

Another way to get some distance between yourself and your trading is to look at it from different perspectives. This is also true in your relationships with other people. In most interactions with another person there are three different and separate perceptual positions.

The **self-position** is looking through your own eyes, hearing what you hear, feeling your own feelings, holding your own beliefs, and making your own interpretations. Most of us live our lives in this position. This is the position that gives you passion. It's where the juice is. From this position we have access to some information, but not all of it.

The **observer position** is that of a neutral observer, a fair witness. This is a dissociated position. Here you watch yourself and the other person. Here you are in the role of a spectator as you listen to yourself and the other person. As an observer you'll have a third party's commentary. This gives you an impartial view, but if you stay here too long, you could end up playing the role of the cold fish.

The **other position** gives you the other person's point of view. Here you look at things through the eyes of the other, hold the other's feelings, walk and stand in the other's shoes. This position gives you the ability to identify with and through another person. Here you see the world through another person's eyes and get a sense of what they're feeling. If you live too much in this position, you could be in danger of living in the doormat position.

To explore the various perceptual positions, try this exercise. Recall a time when you had a mildly troubling face to face interaction with another person, perhaps a fight with your significant other. Quickly run the experience through your own eyes, experiencing it from your own perspective. Watch the other person as you feel your own feelings and listen to what you're saying, they're saying, and you're thinking. Look exactly out of your own eyes, not above or below them. Listen with your own ears. Feel your own feelings. If any commentary voice belongs to another person, send that voice back to them and use your own voice as your commentary voice.

Now move to the observer position. Become the fair witness. Be sure you're positioned halfway between yourself and the other person. If you're looking down on the people, position yourself at eye level. Refer to the two people by their names or he and she. Make sure that your commentary voice is separate from the two people and is the voice of a neutral observer.

Now move to the other position. Become the other person. Watch yourself from their perspective. Feel their feelings. Take on their views. Here you may not be totally accurate, but you'll get an approximation of what they're thinking and feeling. In this position, you refer to the other as I and to yourself as you.

Now move back to the observer position and gather up even more information.

Move back to the self-position and experience it once again from your own point of view. Notice how much more information you have now than before. Notice how your understanding has increased and your options multiplied.

You can uncouple your ego from your trading by periodically removing yourself to the different perceptual positions.

By going to the observer position, you can gain perspective and neutrality. Some successful traders move to the observer position when they put on a trade. If you're getting too involved in a trade, move to the observer position and look at it from that perspective. At the end of a given trade or at the end of a trading day, take a look at your trading from the fair witness position.

You can also look at your trading through the eyes of another person, for example, a trading buddy, a trading coach, or a trader you admire. What would this person say? What would they think? What, if any, advice would they give you?

LIVING BEYOND EGO

"The ego promotes turmoil because it wants to substantiate your separateness from everyone, including God. It will push you in the direction of judgment and comparison, and cause you to insist on being right and best."
—Wayne Dyer

According to Wayne Dyer in his profound book ***Manifest Your Destiny***[4], we live our adult lives in four stages of psychological and spiritual development. The first stage is the time when our primary identification is with our physical body and how it functions in our everyday world. During this stage we measure our worth and our happiness by our physical appearance and abilities. He calls this stage The Athlete.

The second stage he calls The Warrior. This is the time when we feel compelled to conquer the world to demonstrate our superiority. At this stage the ego dominates our lives. We are trying to establish our importance by differentiating ourselves from all others as separate and significant. Status and position in life are obsessions. This is the stage when we do what warriors do: conquer and claim the spoils for ourselves.

The third stage he calls The Statesman. At this stage we become aware that our purpose is to give rather than to get. While we still may be achievers and quite often athletic, our inner drive is to serve others. At this stage we move out of self-absorption, and the ego loosens its grip. By moving our attention away from ourselves and towards others, we become free.

The fourth stage he calls The Spirit. At this stage we move into our higher self. We become aware that we are an infinite, limitless, immortal, universal, and eternal energy temporarily residing in a material body. We move beyond The Athlete, The Warrior, The Statesman and move into other areas of consciousness. We become aware that this infinite energy is in all other people and things. This energy has no boundaries, no form, and no limits to its outer edges. We become part of a much larger time and world.

It is in the fourth stage that we begin to manifest all that we desire. When we begin to trust that the vital force of the universe is part of ourselves and we really are in charge of our lives and our destinies, we can let go of our ego and all the attachments to the external world of the ego. When you trust that this force is within you and you are this force, an incredible lightness and freedom will fill you, and you truly can step out of ego.

BE-IT

Ego involves separateness from all else. Let me recommend an exercise that will help you experience your oneness with the universe and release egocentricity. Go for a walk, or you can even do it inside. I prefer to do it walking down by the New York harbor. Look carefully at a tree, a plant, a cloud, a wave, or a flower or any other object such as a rock, a sidewalk, or a bench. Notice its shape and the space it occupies. Become the object and experience yourself as filling that space. Keep doing this with different forms. After a while you'll experience wonderful freedom and energy.

[1] ***The Education of a Speculator,*** Victor Niederhoffer, John Wiley & Sons, Inc, 1997.

[2] ***Pit Bull,*** Martin "Buzzy" Schwartz, Harper Business, 1998.

[3] ***What I Learned Losing A Million Dollars,*** Paul, James, Infrared Press, 1994.

[4] ***Manifest Your Destiny, The Nine Spiritual Principles for Getting Everything You Want,*** Wayne Dyer, Harper Collins Publishers, 1997.

CHAPTER IX

REPROGRAMMING THE SOFTWARE OF YOUR MIND

"The greatest revolution of our generation is the discovery that human beings, by changing the inner attitudes of their minds, can change the outer aspects of their lives."

—William James

Most of us run the programs of our mind quite unconsciously. But nevertheless we are running programs. Whether you're trading or just living your life, your mind is running certain programs. The programs effect your interpretations, your reactions, your feelings, and ultimately whether you succeed or fail.

One trader blows out a couple of times, gets a couple of new stakes, and ultimately wins big time. Another trader has a stunning loss and freezes for months, unable to pull the trigger. Another trader loses and keeps on losing and throwing good money after bad seemingly unable to learn from past mistakes. Each has somewhat similar experiences, and each processes them through different mental software. Each gets different results.

In essence, each of us has an external reality and an internal reality, an objective and a subjective view of things. As we internally map the external territory, we create the "software" programs that effect our interpretations and responses to external and internal events. The map becomes our model of the world. When we change our internal map, we can evoke seemingly magical changes in our external life.

The programs (beliefs, values, concepts, decisions, visions, self-talk, body attitudes, time orientation, and self-identity) are mostly the default programs we accepted arising from our experiences as children and adults. Our upbringing and our later experiences installed certain ways of thinking and perceiving as we reacted to people, events, situations and stimuli. Sure, we choose to run these programs, but we do it quite unconsciously. Most of us as adults have never intentionally directed our minds to consciously run a program. And yet we can.

If you're not happy and fulfilled, if you're not following good trading principles, chances are you're running one or more programs that don't serve you.

What are these programs, and how do we run them?

SENSORY FILTERS

We are all born with five sensory channels—visual, auditory, kinesthetic, olfactory, and gustatory. These channels are how we receive information, how we filter it, and how we code it for memory and for future use. We all use all of these senses, but each of us has one or more preferred or lead channels, one that we pay more attention to.

Some people are primarily visual. You can *notice* it in their words. "Did you *see* what the market did yesterday? The direction of the market is *clear*. I have trouble keeping my *focus* on the market. I *saw* it but I didn't believe it."

Some people are primarily auditory. Their words will *tell* you that hearing is their primary channel. "I *told* myself this market's going up. There was an *echo* of desperation in the market. Sometimes I can just *tune in* to the market and *hum* along with it. The market was *blaring* that it was going up but I seemed to be *deaf to* it."

Other people are primarily kinesthetic. Their words *hand* it to you. "I can *feel* what the market's doing, and I *get a grasp* on it. I get an *intuitive grip* on the market and I *go with the flow*. I usually have a *solid* understanding of the market, but that day I was in for a *bumpy ride*. The market *swallowed* my stop."

Usually the gustatory and olfactory channels are not a primary filter. "It was a *delicious* ride up, or something about the market didn't *taste* right, or I needed to *digest* the information" would be the language for gustatory perception. Whereas "I got a *whiff* that the market was going down because something didn't *smell* right" would be an olfactory perception.

What we do with these sounds and sights and feelings and even tastes and smells is one way we run our programs. How we code them in our memory and refer to them is part of our mental software. Have you ever been bothered by a recurring picture of something that happened or that you dreamed or that you fear? Have you ever heard a voice that interferes by criticizing you or perpetually warning you without good cause? Have you ever been disrupted by feelings of uneasiness or queasiness? You can take control of these sensations by moderating them.

THE QUALITIES OF SENSORY PERCEPTION

Let's start with the visual sense. We make pictures in our minds of things that have happened, are happening, and what we anticipate or fear will happen. Often these pictures flash by so quickly we're not aware of it. And yet we have made a picture and it has definitely impacted our thoughts and feelings.

For example, if you see a buy signal on your screen and—ever so quickly—you have a mental picture of the price going down and hitting your stop, you'll hesitate before putting on the trade. You may not even be aware of having seen that picture, and so you'll wonder why on earth you let that trade get away from you. Or, conversely, you're looking at the screen and in your mind's eye you see the market rising precipitously; you may buy before you get confirmation from the market and your methods. Later you'll wonder why you got so impulsive.

Sometimes you're fully aware of the pictures you're making while other times you're not. The pictures can be black and white, full color, large or small, clear or fuzzy, panoramic or framed, near or far, still or movies, flat or dimensional. Such differences effect the impact of the picture upon you. You can adjust the qualities of a picture you have to make it more or less powerful.

For example, you may have coded a memory of a botched trade you once had into a big, bright, colorful, focused, overwhelmingly large, near, panoramic movie right in front of your eyes. Such a coding would keep that memory "in the front of your mind." Take the learnings from the trade and put them someplace safe, and move the memory far away, make it dull and small and make it fuzzy. Turn it into a still framed picture, make it black and white. What a difference!

You want to have certain results from your trading. Good. Ask yourself, what would I be doing to get those results? Make a picture of yourself doing what needs to be done. Adjust the visual qualities in different ways until it feels most impactful. Snap it into place just like that and think about it from time to time. I'd be very surprised if you weren't soon doing what needs to be done.

Now let's listen to the auditory component of thoughts and memories. We hear ourselves talking to ourselves. We also hear others talking to us. In our memories we may hear the music that was playing in the background, the sound of the wind in the trees, the rain on the window, the shouts on the trading floor, or words said to us.

One trader I worked with heard a voice just before she'd go to put on a trade saying, "What if I'm wrong?" Strangely enough, it wasn't her own voice but rather the voice of a man. We knew that the probabilities of her methods were that she'd be right. We also knew that being right was taking all the trades and letting the chips fall where they may. I had her practice moving the man's voice way out into the distance and bringing back her own voice saying, "What if I'm right? What if this trade is a big winner?"

When dealing with the auditory component of a memory or a thought, you can change the qualities of sound and listen to which is more or less impactful. You can change the loudness or pitch or tempo or location of the sound. You can alter the duration, frequency, rhythm, or even change the sounds themselves to something else. You can also change the way you language an idea.

If you have a critical voice while you trade, try just moving the location of the voice. Sometimes this alone is enough to alter its impact. Other times it might be important to change the words themselves. If you're saying things like: "Why don't you get a real job? You could blow out! You can't do this! This market is impossible!" Then it would no doubt be important to change your self-talk. Half the time one isn't even aware of what one is saying to oneself. Monitor your self-talk to make sure it supports you in your trading.

With the kinesthetic modality, we're talking about primary physical sensations: heat or cold, sense of touch, pressure, movement, contraction, expansion, a tingling, a tightness in the chest, butterflies in the stomach, rate of breathing, heartbeat, tension or relaxation of facial, neck, shoulder muscles and so forth. All these sensations are communicating to you while you trade and will get lodged in your body as a memory. If your hand shakes on the mouse, if you feel like you're getting punched in the stomach, if you feel like you're floating, you're receiving a kinesthetic communication just as graphic and powerful as pictures and sounds.

You can increase or decrease the intensity or rate and tempo of these sensations. For example, imagine yourself trading with feelings of alert calmness. Your mind is alert and your body is calm. Your breathing is slow and rhythmic. Your shoulders are relaxed. Your posture confident. Do these things even as you think of the trading.

SEPARATING AND COMBINING SENSORY CHANNELS

Take a memory of something that happened, in trading or elsewhere; and review it simply from the visual standpoint. Notice what you were seeing. You'll see an image or a cluster of images. Pay attention to the colors, the changing light, the movement, and so forth.

Maybe you were walking on a beach and you see the birds against the blue sky, the white clouds floating, the light dancing on the water like diamonds, the dark blue-green waves rolling in rhythmically, the foam of the white caps, heat waves rising from the sand, and a woman with a brown pony tail in a red bikini running down the beach towards you.

Now take that same original memory and listen only to the sounds. What was being said? Do you hear the sounds on the street, the hum of the computer, a radio or TV playing, the sound of your own breathing, the voice of your broker? Listen carefully.

Take the beach example. You hear the waves rolling in, children playing in the distance, the seagulls crying, the wind in your ears, your footsteps on the sand, and your own voice saying "good morning" as the girl runs by and you hear her feet hitting the sand and her rhythmic breathing as she says "hi."

Now concentrate on the feelings of that same first memory. Are you sitting? Do you feel the back of the chair and your feet on the floor? What are you touching? How is your breathing? What are you touching? Are you relaxed or tense? Where is your center of gravity?

Going back to the beach example, you feel the hard wet sand beneath your feet as the cool waves wash over them. You feel your body moving gracefully and rhythmically as you walk along, your arms swinging. There's a gentle breeze and you feel it blow through your hair. You feel the hot sun. You feel your heartbeat speed up as the girl approaches.

If you want to change a memory, you can go back over it and change the qualities of perception. Start with what you're seeing. You can turn it from a movie to a still or vice versa, look at it from a different angle, bring it closer or move it away. These are your images. It's your show. Changing different aspects of your mental image gives you a freedom of choice. How you perceive something changes the impact it has on you.

Next change the qualities of what you're hearing. Turn up the volume. Turn it down. Change the pitch, the rhythm, the location of the sounds. Add some music if you want. Change the words. All this adds even more choice about what the memory says to you.

Lastly change the kinesthetic qualities of your physical sensations. If you're burning hot, cool it down. If you're feeling panicky, change it to excitement. Alter your breathing. Add a smile. Turn up the intensity of the feelings. Turn them down. Smooth the tempo you feel, or speed it up. Once again you have choice and you change the impact it has on you.

By changing the qualities of perception in all three dimensions, you've altered the effect the memory will have on you. You've taken control of a memory program that you've been running. If it's a positive memory, you'll want to alter the qualities of perception to make it more powerful. If it's a negative memory, you'll want to change the qualities of perception to make it less impressive.

Now do it with a future memory. For example, take the next trading day. Create it the way you'd like it to go. Begin with the visual, move to the auditory, and end with the kinesthetic. You might just be surprised at how that changes the trading.

TIME ORIENTATION

"Time then exists as a conceptual reality, an understanding of the relationship between events—and not anything actual or literal beyond our nervous system."
—L. Michael Hall

Think about it. The past really doesn't actually or literally exist except in our minds. Those things that happened in the past have truly passed away. Those events no longer continue. What does remain is our own memory or interpretation or distortion or deletion of what has gone before. Past events only exist in our mind.

The same is true of the future. As a reality the future only exists in our mind. We can't touch it, smell it, taste it. The events and experiences that will occur on a coming day in the future only exist in our minds.

That leaves us with the present. The present does exist, and we are free to do in the present what we choose. We can buy, sell, or sit on the sidelines. We can love, we can hate. We can speak or remain silent. And soon the present moves into the past and it is forever gone except for the consequences. We are left with a new present and can only act in that present. There are no "if only I'd" possibilities. It's gone. However, there is a new present, and we can act in that present.

So now we're long, and the market is going up or down, and once again we can buy more, sell, or sit on our hands and do nothing. We've loved and we're glad, or we wish we hadn't. We spoke or remained silent, and now we can speak again or remain silent, but we can't undo the consequences of the past. We can, however, change our memory of the past.

"Let anyone try to attend to the present moment of time and one of the most baffling experiences occurs. Where is it, this present? It has melted in our grasp, fled ere we could touch it, gone in the instant of becoming."
—William James

We live in the now, in the present; and yet we can time travel to the other time zones—to the past, or to the future. In order to live in the psychological present in a healthy and balanced way, we can integrate the past and the future even as we live in the present. We can live fully in the present even as we integrate the resources we find or create in the past or the future.

Some people are so past oriented, they lose the present and destroy the possibilities for the future. They get stuck in the past, allowing a negative event or trauma to dominate the present. Others keep replaying an idealized or romanticized past and constantly find the present coming up short.

Some people are so future oriented, they neglect the possibilities of the present. They can be so enamored of the future they fail to notice what could go wrong, or they can be overwhelmed by all that needs to be done. Or they can be so fearful of the future, they live their now in dread.

It's important to have a healthy balanced psychological present. Sure, we learn from the past and we plan for the future, but if you're too much in another time zone, you may find yourself mentally and emotionally unavailable to people, experiences, and present events and thoughts. You could be preoccupied, distracted and unfocused on what is happening right now—and we know that is where you need to trade.

By being balanced in the psychological present, you are not only able to experience immediacy in activities and relationships, you are also able to architect a desired future.

How we code our past or future has a great deal to do with how it impacts our present.

CODING TIME

"It's never too late to have a happy childhood."
—Richard Bandler

Each of us have different ways of coding time. Take your finger and point in space to your past. Now point to your future. Point to your present.

Now think of something you do everyday like taking a shower, brushing your teeth, feeding the dog, or driving to work. Make a picture of yourself doing that a week ago. A month ago. A year ago. Five years ago. Ten years ago. Even longer ago. Now make a picture of yourself doing this tomorrow. A month from now. A year from now. Five years from now. Ten years from now. Many, many years from now.

Notice where you placed the pictures in the past and in the future. Notice quality differences in the pictures between near and far times, between past and future. The pictures of your past and future should have been placed in the same direction you pointed when you pointed to your past and future.

You have just shown yourself how you code time. This is your time line. Time lines vary from person to person. For many people the past is behind them, their present goes through them, and their future is in front of them. These people tend to live in time. They can get lost in current activities and fail to be on time for scheduled events. Other people find their past to their left, their present a few feet in front of them, and their future straight ahead and to their right. These people tend to live through time. They like to plan and execute the plan on time.

If you placed your past right in front of you, you may have trouble being available in the now, and you may have difficulty planning for your future. You may get stuck in the past or find yourself condemned to keep repeating the gestalts of the past. Try moving your past over to your left or behind you, and notice how that feels. You can always move it back if you want to.

John is a floor trader who is now quite successful, and yet when he began trading he was always worried about whether he'd make enough money to cover expenses and whether he'd make enough money to keep his backer. Even after he was very profitable and well past his old situation, he'd get into the same old feelings of being on the brink of disaster after a couple of controlled losses. I asked him to point to his past, present, and future. His past was right in front of him, his present was inside him, and his future was off to the right. I had him take his hand and move his past over to his left. "Wow!" he said, "That's a tremendous relief!" Now when he's had a couple of losses, he simply slows down, and begins to look for new opportunities.

PUTTING IT TOGETHER

Think of a past event that gets in the way of trading effectively. Make a picture of it. Adjust the qualities of the picture to make it less impactful. If it's big and bright, make it dull and small. If it's right there in your face, move it away. If it's a movie, make it still, and so forth. Put it in the appropriate place on your past time line.

Make a picture of how you'd like to be and trade in a similar situation in the future. Give it the qualities of your future pictures. Place that in the appropriate place on your future time line.

TIME LINING

Think of a behavior or attitude you have in your trading or in your life that doesn't serve you. Perhaps you become fearful while you trade and this causes you to hesitate too long before putting on a trade or causes you to jump out of a trade too soon. What is the root cause of this problem, the first event which, when disconnected, will cause the problem to disappear? When was the first time you felt this emotion?

Allow your unconscious mind to float up above your time line, and go back to the past, and go back to the event itself and drop down into it and as you reexperience this event and notice the feelings, pay attention to any learnings that you would like to preserve. Put the learnings someplace safe.

Now drift up again over your time line, and as you look at that event down there, consider what resources—what knowledge, what beliefs, what skills, what attributes you now have that would have helped you way back then. Now, as you think of those resources, and remember times when they were available to you, make a fist with your dominant hand. Allow those positive memories to flood you. As you focus on them, rev up your representations visually, auditorily, and kinesthetically. Let them become even stronger as you stack the memories one on the other. Good. Now just let the thoughts go, and open your fist.

Now drop back down to just before that event, and from this position—before it ever occurred, before you ever felt those crippling emotions—look through the event to the present time. Notice how the emotion is drained from the event. You haven't even felt it yet. Notice how that same negative emotion is drained from your life.

Now, gathering up your resources as you remake that fist with your dominant hand, move forward into the event noticing the difference it makes having these resources available to you. Relive the event with these resources. Having these resources available to you changes the impact of the events and how you behave in them. Now, moving forward reexperience subsequent events with these same resources. Notice what a difference it makes as you relive old experiences in a new way with your powerful resources. Going all the way into the present and moving forward into the future notice how this new approach radiates forward and makes a delightful difference.

THE INTERNAL MAP

Now, what have we done? Have we really altered history? Of course not. We've simply altered the internal map you have of the history—the meanings, the significance, and the repeatability you have been giving to an event or a cluster of ideas in the past.

There are at least two realities. There is the reality of what actually occurs or has occurred in the outside world, and there is the reality of the internal mental map—representations and interpretations—you make as you go along. This internal model of the world becomes your personal operating system, the principles from which you observe, interpret, and act.

As traders we need to be particularly alert to this duality of internal mental experience and external direct experience. Our own internal interpretations of us as participants in the market and our interpretations of what has occurred or is occurring in the market may be quite different from events in the external world. You need to ask yourself whether or not your mapping of events is serving you well.

If you map the market as a dangerous place, your response to market behavior will be quite different than if you perceive the market to be a neutral arena in which you can make money. If you portray the market as chaotic and confusing, your response will reflect that; whereas if you interpret the market as a field that reveals itself in relatively predictable or probable ways, your behavior will reflect that. If you delineate yourself as somebody who can respond reliably to market action, you will behave in the market—the external world—in certain ways. On the other hand, if you internally characterize yourself as somebody who repeatedly falters or blunders, your actions will echo that interpretation.

We make interpretations and then interpret those interpretations on higher and higher levels. These frames of reference control our thinking and thus our trading and our actions. The higher the frame of reference, the more the control.

Let's look at a possible set of interpretations

- "The market's going up."
- "My indicators say it's time to buy."
- "What if it turns around and goes the other way?"
- "I'll probably get stopped out and lose another chunk of money."
- "If I keep this up, I'll lose all my trading capital."
- "These markets can't be traded."
- "What's the difference. Nothing matters anyway."
- "I'm worthless."

These interpretations formed a hierarchy of frames of reference. The higher the frame of reference, the more the control. The "I'm worthless." frame had it's impact on every interpretation below it. Any interpretation from the third one on could have been enough to stop or at least impact the trading. However, as you get to the thoughts behind the thoughts, you can see how the interpretations were guided. At any time during the sequence, many of the frames were outside the conscious focus, but at work nonetheless.

Taking it back the other way, let's change the "I'm worthless" to "I'm worthy." Notice the difference in thinking at the lower levels.

- "I'm worthy."
- "What I do makes a difference. It matters. I matter."
- "Markets can be traded profitably."
- "I can win back my losses."
- "I could make a lot of money on this trade."
- "What if this is a big winner?"
- "My indicators say it's time to buy."
- "The market's going up."

These self and world concepts are frequently held unconsciously in the back of the mind. Our conscious thoughts are being molded by them without our awareness. It does, however, make a difference between a successful trader and a losing trader. When you're having thoughts that sabotage your trading, step back and ask yourself what is the thought behind that thought? And what is the thought behind that thought? You'll get to the place where you know you need to do some belief change work.

LANGUAGING

In addition to representing our time line with pictures, we language our time. All along your time line, you've been telling stories. You've been telling stories about today and tomorrow and certainly about yesterday.

Your story is your story, and while it has many twists and turns, it has recurring themes. The characters may change. The events and setting may change. And yet, there is a familiarity to the stories. You could say the stories are caused by fate, by karma, by a character flaw, by a character strength, or by simple random occurrence. In truth, there is one common denominator to all the chapters or stories, and that is the teller of the stories. You are the narrator of your story. More importantly, you are the author of your story.

True, your parents and siblings and teachers and culture and government did certain things. But you gave the happenings meaning and significance and built your life accordingly. Two boys are raised by the same cruel, no good, violent, criminal father who ends up in jail. One grows up to be just like Dad. The other becomes a pillar of the community and has a powerful, positive impact on other youth growing up. One says, "What chance did I have? I'm just like my no good, son-of-a-bitch father." The other says, "What choice did I have? My father showed me all the ways not to go." One went script, the other counterscript. Each lived his own story.

What is your story? Take a look at how you code your past linquistically. Finish the following sentence beginnings.

The theme of my life has been a story of ... (Some suggestions: overcoming hardship, struggle, triumph, victimhood, revenge, learning, disappointment, rejection, success, failure, relationships, love, bad luck, ease, popularity, creativity, stress).

____

____

____

____

The theme of my trading has been a story of...

____

____

The plot of my life has been a story of ... (Some suggestions: a tragedy, a comedy, a soap opera, a drama, a fairy tale, a flat repetitive tale, Superman/woman, Horatio Alger, rags to riches, riches to rags, poor little rich boy/girl, The American Dream, etc.)

____

____

The plot of my trading has been a story of...

____

____

Up until now in the story of my life, I have thought, believed, acted ... (Some suggestions: Look for beliefs and concepts that have internally motivated certain decisions and choices you have made.)

____

____

Up until now in the story of my trading, I have thought, believed, acted...

____

____

RESTORYING

It's never too late to relanguage your explanations of time. We can put new twists on old stories and tell brand new stories for the future. Looking at the story that you've lived up until now, you can ask certain questions. Who or what storied you with that story? What would have been a better theme for your life? Are there any subplots you're missing? How well has that narrative served you? Would you recommend to somebody else that they live that story? Are there any counter examples to this story?

Looking at the past, notice other aspects that you might have missed. You can sort for another aspect of your life and trading. Up until now the story of my life has also been a story of...

____

____

Up until now the story of my trading has also been a story of...

____

If I had it to do over, I would make the story of my life a story about...

If I had it to do over, I would make the story of my trading a story about...

Looking to the future, you can begin to tell a whole new story. From this day on, I will increasingly become a person who...

From this day forward, I will increasingly become a trader who...

As this person who increasingly is becoming more ________, you can write a whole new story. As this new person, what will your story be? Fill it with sparkling moments. Tell it with new counter examples to your old problem laden story. Develop a new theme, a new approach, a new plot. Just for fun, write up a new story. From now on the story of my life is a story of...

From now on the story of my trading is a story of...

Step into your story and live it with rich sensory detail. What do you see? What do you hear? What are you feeling? Enrich it with concrete detail. And when you're fully into this new story, clasp your hands and say, "My Story." Now imagine going into the future and living your story. When you need to be reminded to live this story, just clasp your hands and say, "My Story."

HYPNOSIS

One of the best ways I know of to change the software of your mind is through hypnosis. Hypnosis was approved by the **American Medical Association** in 1958. It has been proven effective in pain management, academic achievement, athletic improvement, alleviating addictions, changing habits, and many other areas of self-improvement. I use hypnosis with traders to help them trade in the same state of excellence that Olympic athletes use for competition.

Hypnosis bypasses the critical mind and establishes selective thinking. Done well, hypnosis utilizes high quality suggestion both direct and indirect. When done with skill and wisdom, hypnosis can have a powerful and beneficial effect.

We go naturally into a trance every ninety minutes: you'll be driving along thinking about things, and all of a sudden you're where you wanted to go, and you say how did I get here? You were in a trance. Or you're at your desk at work on something, and all of a sudden you catch yourself staring out the window dreaming about something else and you snap back to get to work. You were in a trance.

Just before you fall asleep at night and when you first wake up in the morning, you are in a hypnotic state. This is a very good time to give yourself positive suggestions. Many people do just the opposite. "I'll probably have another sleepless night. I can never sleep when I'm worried about something." Or, first thing in the morning, "I just dread today. That deal is probably going to fall through." They're hypnotizing themselves to bring about what they don't want.

Traders frequently trade in a trance. That is why the things you say and the things you imagine while you're trading have such power over you. Imagining the worst that could happen and indulging in negative self-talk during trading is as foolish as going to a hypnotist and asking them to give you suggestions to fail at your trading. If you're in a trance when you're trading, you can use that trance to imagine yourself trading gracefully and to give yourself positive suggestions.

In addition to using half hour hypnosis sessions and half-hour self-hypnosis tapes, I coach traders to use a simple technique for giving themselves suggestions that will improve their trading and their self esteem. The technique only takes a few minutes, yet it can alter attitudes that aren't serving the trading well, and it can enhance and amplify ideas that are supportive of effective trading. Each week I give the traders I coach a new affirmation that addresses current and key aspects of their trading. They use the affirmation within this technique with excellent results.

Before you start to do the technique, you need to have a positively worded affirmation that will address the issue you are concerned about. It has to be positively worded because the subconscious mind drops out any negative and accepts the reverse of what you intended. For example, if you say, "Don't overtrade," the unconscious mind will hear "Overtrade."

Let's say you have a verified system that makes money, but you're not following the system. I would give you the affirmation: *"Now I consistently trade my system because my system makes money over time."* (Because is one of those magical persuasive words that slides right into the mind with conviction).

Be sure to have your affirmation thought out and prepared before you begin your self-hypnosis. If you start to look for an appropriate affirmation once you're in hypnosis, you'll pull yourself right out of trance as you go to your conscious mind. The conscious mind is wonderful. Use it first before you put yourself into trance and then just let things play themselves out.

Here is the technique:

SELF HYPNOSIS

1. Look up and fix your gaze on a specific place on the ceiling above your head.

2. Take three deep breaths and relax even more on each exhale.

3. On the fourth deep breath, allow your eyes to close down as you exhale and go loose and limp all over.

4. Relax the little muscles around your eyes to the point where they wouldn't open even if you tried.

5. Test your eyes to make sure they won't open. (Eyes won't open if you're really relaxed.) And let yourself go deeper within.

6. Say your prepared affirmation to yourself.

7. Visualize yourself doing your affirmation. Indulge yourself in a little daydream of success.

8. Let in the feelings associated with this. Allow yourself to feel really good about it.

9. Anchor the feeling with a specific physical gesture such as making a fist or clasping your hands or touching your thumb to a particular finger and as you make this gesture, also anchor the feeling with a cue word such as "Trust," "Winner," "Go," "Trader," or "Success."

10. Open your eyes.

Then, when you're in the middle of trading, all you need to do to evoke the power of the trance is to repeat that gesture and that word, and the same feelings will come back to you. This is your kinesthetic and auditory anchor for the content of the trance.

There are many other ways to put yourself into a trance, but this way is quick and reliable.

A PATIENT DETECTIVE

As you work with these methods for changing your mental software, be patient. After all, it took you a lifetime to get your mind to operate the way it habitually does. If one process doesn't work very well for you, try another process. Don't be afraid to use repetition. Repetition is how you've created your current thought processes. It may well take several repetitions of each technique on different aspects of your thinking to make a difference.

Act the role of detective. What must I be thinking, believing, saying, picturing, and so forth to be doing/feeling this? How am I creating this? Once you have found the how, then use these exercises to reverse the how to something that serves you well.

CHAPTER X

THE PHYSIOLOGY OF EXCELLENCE

A physiology of excellence is your short cut to mental balance and readiness for effective trading.

There are three primary ways to change your mental and emotional state: focus, beliefs, and physiology. The changing of any one of these will alter your state.

First, let's consider focus. What you focus on effects your current reality. It's what you are experiencing at that time. If you focus on your past, that's what dominates your reality. That reality will be further effected by whether your attention is on pleasant or unpleasant memories. If your focus is primariliy on the future, that is what colors your reality. If you focus on potential disasters, you will be fearful; whereas, if you focus on your goals, you will be hopeful. When you focus on the present and sort for what's pleasant and good, that becomes your current reality. Conversely, when you focus on the present and sort for what's missing or what's unfair or unpleasant, that becomes your current reality. By changing your focus, you change your state.

The second way to change your mental and emotional state is to change your beliefs. What you believe effects the meaning you give to your experience. What you believe effects what you're willing to do or not do. A change in belief is very impactful on many levels of your experience. The difficulty lies, however, in identifying limiting beliefs and then changing them to more empowering beliefs. It can be done, but it takes some doing.

The third way to change your state is by changing your physiology. It's simple, it's immediate, and it's effective. Facial expression, posture, movement, gesture, breath-

ing and voice tonality and tempo can all be considered physiology. Your physiology profoundly effects your thinking, your emotions, and your behavior. Your physiology is a powerful communicator to yourself and to your external world. It impacts your personal self image as well as the image you project to the world.

Floor traders realize this. If you're slumped over, slamming tickets against your arm, kicking, and frowning, you're not only going to be in an unresourceful state for handling whatever's going on, you're setting yourself up for others to take advantage of you. If you stand straight, breathe deeply, look alert, and maybe even smile a little, you'll be much more able to do what needs to be done and maybe even get a little cooperation while you do it.

If you walk around smiling, you're communicating to yourself that there's something to smile about. Not only that, but other people will smile back at you. And you'll be confirmed that there's something to smile about. **Remember your physiology is a powerful message both internally and externally. That message feeds back to you through your feelings and through the responses of others to that message and creates more of the same.**

What's commonly realized is that physiology reflects emotions. We cry when we're sad. We laugh at something funny. We frown when we're puzzled. We hang our heads when we're shy or ashamed. We slump when we're depressed. What isn't so commonly realized is that our physiology actually changes our emotions. Facial expression and posture and breathing and gestures and voice tone and tempo will alter your internal state.

Do an experiment. As you read this, slump your shoulders forward and sink over your rib cage and bend at the waist while you drop your head down so that your chin almost touches your chest. Lower your eyes and frown a little bit. Breathe shallowly or hold your breath. It's hard to get positive or excited about anything while you sit like this. How easy it would be to get depressed if you stayed like this. Now add to this the two other ways to change internal state. Focus on the worst part of your trading. Remember all the times you lost money by doing something stupid. Imagine losing money in the future by trading poorly. Now say to yourself, "I'll never be able to trade effectively." Pretty awful, isn't it?

Stop. Sit straight up even as you read this. Hold the book up so your head is straight and your eyes looking forward. Lift up your rib cage. Center your weight in the chair. Put your feet flat on the floor. Smile. Breathe deeply for a while. Notice how things seem to improve. Now add focus and beliefs. Remember the times when you made money trading by following good trading practices. Imagine yourself trading even better in the future. Now say to yourself, "I can make money trading." What a difference!

Manic depressives have been helped in their depressed state by being given the prescription to smile for 30 minutes each day. As you read this, smile and notice the difference a simple smile makes. There are 80 muscles in the face that move blood to the brain, and smiling increases this blood supply. Smiling also alters your oxygen levels and stimulates the neural transmitters.

Such a little thing. So easy to do. Smile. The simple act of smiling changes your physiology and emotional state. We've already noted how smiling causes others to smile in return and builds a self-fulfilling cycle of pleasantness. The reverse is also true. Frowning or grimacing creates negative emotions and evokes them from others as well.

When you go to the mirror in the morning, smile at yourself and wish yourself a good day even as you take a few deep breaths of fresh air. You might even find it usesful to keep a mirror near your trading station to check your expressions from time to time. Since state of mind is so vital to how you trade, keep in mind that facial expression not only reflects what you're feeling, it produces and augments feelings. Try keeping an open expression of acceptance for whatever the market gives you. This will create a mind set that you can handle whatever happens. And you can if you've got a plan.

In ***Anatomy of an Illness,*** Norman Cousins writes how he healed himself from a long and debilitating illness by laughing his way to recovery. He used laughter to mobilize his will to live and to prosper. Many viewed his recovery as miraculous.

Laughter heals. This gives us a reason to laugh at our trading predicaments and mistakes. It's much better to laugh if after a long run, you take a profit; and it still goes on without you than to get all frantic for missing out as if there's never going to be another opportunity or another opportunity to ride a trade to the end. Laughter enables you to accept your foibles even while you learn from your mistakes and correct them the next time around. Laughter also clears your physiolgy and helps you get ready for the next trade.

I never realized how much I laughed during a trading day until I had broken several ribs in an automobile accident. When you have a broken rib, it's powerfully painful to laugh. I did the best I could then not to laugh at occurences, but my assistant was laughing and before long I was too.

How do you sit while you trade? Are you scrunched up, tied up, tipped over to one side? Are you leaning back (laid back)? Are you sitting on the edge of your chair? Do you need to lean forward to see the screen? Are you in a defensive posture with your arms folded? Or is your center of gravity balanced straight in the chair?

When a trade starts to go for you or against you, what are you doing with your body? Are you holding your breath? Are you tensing up your muscles? Frowning? Is your heart beating fast? Are you getting hot or cold? What exactly are you doing?

What would you be doing if you were in a calm, alert, aware, and self trusting state of mind? Try doing that as you trade. I know. You're tense and concerned. It doesn't matter. Arrange your physiology *as if* you were calm, alert, aware, and self trusting. Breathe that way. Sit that way. Use that facial expression. Relax your shoulders and your arms. And when you talk to yourself, use a tempo that matches calm, alert, aware, and self trusting.

I have often advised traders who hesitate in taking a trade to stand up when they see the signal. This tells them it's time to take action. Standing tells them that they can rise to the occasion, that they can stand on their own two feet.

In a later chapter, we'll be talking about the arrangement of your trading office and your trading station to enhance optimal physiology for trading.

Physiological manipulation is an effective tool for controlling the brain. As a trader, it's important that you be aware of how much it effects you and utilize this simple way of changing state through changing physiology. It's not just some extraneous thing that's happening, it's an important part of a cybernetic loop that becomes your trading.

Each of us has a physiology of excellence—a physiology that is associated with resourcefulness and flexibility. This physiology may change with context, and it can also be pulled across context. For example, think of an activity where you feel strong confidence. Get into that experience and access those feelings. Sit, stand, gesture, talk, and breathe as you would in that experience. Memorize the physiology and practice it. Now think of trading even as you utilize this physiology. When you get into a stressful situation in trading, you can get up and move away from your trading station for a moment. Assume your physiology of excellence and return to the trading.

You can also consciously model the physiology of a person you admire and would like to emulate. In the past you no doubt unconsiously modeled the physiology of a parent, teacher, or other role model. That physiology may or may not have been a positive force in your life. Strangely enough, people in general imitate the defects of others much more readily than they imitate their strengths.

We all have unconsious postural patterns, some of which do not assist us in the best use of ourselves. You can begin by becoming aware of your body and it's tensions, your posture and gestures. Then straighten up, hold your head up, lift up your rib cage, center your body. If you're feeling good, you'll feel even better. If you're feeling "down," things will look "up." It's very much like that song about standing tall in a storm, or the poem about reaching for the stars. You can also copy the movements and stance of somebody whom you admire and who uses his or her body effectively.

OPTIMAL STATE OF HEALTH FOR OPTIMAL TRADING

Trading, like any activity, is best done from a state of vibrant good health. What constitutes good health? Good health is more than the just absence of disease. It's also the presence of a radiant energy, a vitality of healthy feelings.

A physically healthy person is well nourished, well exercised, well rested, undrugged, and well supported by optimistic, confident, and balanced thinking.

Well nourished means eating moderate amounts of fresh foods: chicken, fish, fruits, vegetables, and whole grains. It also means taking food supplements because food today is frequently deficient in minerals and vitamins. Research and discover what vitamins, minerals, and herbs you need and which are of the highest quality, because not all food supplements are created with equal potency or deliverability. Well nourished also means drinking lots of good clean water.

Well exercised means daily vigorous exercise-aerobic and anaerobic—for a minimum of one half hour, preferably longer.

Well rested means getting whatever amount of sleep your body wants. If you live on the West Coast and get up early to trade, you have to go to bed early. If you trade currencies, you can't trade them all day and all night as well. If you have trouble sleeping, you need consultation and training in how to run your mind so you can sleep restfully through the night. As a professional hypnotist, I have been amazed at the number of people who have come to me in serious difficulty because they hadn't been able to get to sleep, stay asleep through the night, or wake up in the morning.

Undrugged means no damaging drugs, no cigarettes, no excessive alcohol, no cocaine, no marijuana, no heroin and so forth. It also means avoiding prescription mind altering drugs. Just because a doctor gave it to you doesn't mean it's good for you. And while we're on the subject of drugs, don't ever fool yourself into thinking you trade better when you're stoned, or drunk, or tranquilized. You may get lucky but you won't stay lucky.

"To wish to be well is a part of becoming well."
—Seneca

"Our prayers should be for a sound mind in a healthy body."
—Juvenal

Vibrant health is supported by healthy expectations. If you're healthy, expect to stay healthy and become even more invigoratingly healthy. If you're sick or injured, expect to get better.

Anticipate living a long and productive life. If a parent or sibling died at a particular age, say 40, look forward to living to 90 and beyond. You are not doomed to replicate their demise. Expect to flourish, bursting with health even as you age. Getting older chronologically doesn't have to mean breaking down or decaying unless that's the vision you hold and the way you talk to yourself and others.

The immune system is typically referred to as an army. Doctors, medical texts, and the media frequently use metaphors of war when referring to the immune system. I object to the use of the war metaphor with the immune system just as strongly as I reject the war metaphor as being beneficial to trading. War is debilitating over time. In war you use your resources recklessly and you're at tremendous risk of being injured or dying. A few months of looking at your body (or your trading) as a war zone will needlessly exhaust you.

I prefer to use the metaphor of learning for the immune system. The immune system is learning 24 hours a day and it never forgets anything. That's why you never have the same cold twice. The immune system of a sixty year old is forty years smarter than the immune system of a twenty year old. Your immune system is continually becoming more intelligent, more capable, more evolved, and more resilient. Thinking of it this way enables you to create pictures of a healthy, long future.

If you view your body as a learning organization that is getting smarter all the time, you will implant in the mind-body a bias toward increasing health. Conversely, if you view your body as a machine that is disintegrating and becoming antiquated, you will create a mind-body bias toward decreasing health. Hey, you want to hang around and watch your children and grandchildren and great grandchildren—and your money—grow.

"Health and cheerfulness mutually beget each other."
—Joseph Addison

Forgiveness is also important for health. Harboring resentment and anger debilitates the body as well as the spirit. Many people report that when they let go of bitterness and long standing resentments, a great weight is lifted off them and they feel years younger. It's also important to release feelings of self-anger and guilt.

Equally important to health is to be aware of your own values and what's really important to you, and to live in accordance with those values. If you're living your life to appease somebody else's values, sooner or later you'll create illness within yourself. You want to honor your own values and do what's important to you. It's your life. Make it a joyful and healthy one.

The following are a series of exercises that use both body and mind to achieve an optimal state for trading—or anything else for that matter.

THE EXERCISES

QUIETING REFLEX

This is an exercise designed by Charles Stroebel, MD. He created the exercise to help people control stress and lower blood pressure. I have modified it, so that traders will associate a relaxed physical and calm mental state with their trading. The exercise only takes six seconds each time you do it.

- Sparkle smile. (This releases the tension around your eyes.) As you...
- Breathe deeply all the way to the bottom of your feet.
- Exhale. As you...
- Say "Mind alert. Body calm." As you...
- Relax your jaw, tongue, and shoulders.

Do this exercise each time you enter your trading area, each time you enter a trade or exit a trade, each time you change activities during the trading day, each time you leave your trading area, and whenever you even think about trading.

RELAXATION RESPONSE

This is a meditative exercise developed by Herbert Benson, MD that I have somewhat modified for use by traders.

Conditions necessary for the elicitation of the relaxation response:

- A quiet environment-as free as possible from outside distraction.
- A comfortable position—sitting is best (lying down may encourage sleep).
- A "mental device"—a sound or word silently repeated. The purpose of this is to break the train of distracting thoughts and give yourself an internal focal point.
- A passive attitude—this is the key element. People need to be free of concern about how well they are doing—when distracting thoughts occur, calmly return to the repetition of the sound.

Here is how you do the "Relaxation Response:"

- Sit quietly in a comfortable position. Ideally your feet should be flat on the floor, one hand overlapping the other in your lap.
- Close your eyes, take two or three really deep breaths, exhaling slowly.

- Relax your muscles as completely as possible begining from the top all the way to the bottom. Head to toe.

- Breathe easily and naturally. Repeat a single word to yourself as you breathe in and again as you breathe out. Dr. Benson suggests the word "One." You could also repeat a word such as "Peace," "Calm," "Health," "Clear," "Light," "Wise," or "Love." Or you could say "I am" as you inhale and one of the words such as "Peace" as you exhale.

- When you notice that you are daydreaming, calmly return to repeating your mantra the single word of your choice. Maintain a "let it happen attitude."

- Continue for 10 to 20 minutes—you may peek at your watch but don't use an alarm. When you finish, sit quietly for a couple of minutes, first with your eyes closed then with them opened. Wait a few minutes before you stand up.

Practice the technique once or twice daily for no more than 20 minutes per session. Digestion interferes with the elicitation of the relaxation response, so wait a while after eating before practicing. Many traders have told me that meditation has helped them overcome trading hangups.

RHYTHMIC BREATHING

(ORIENTAL BREATH CONTROL)

This ancient exercise was translated by the hypnotist Ormond McGill, PhD, and I have simplified and modified it for use by traders. Rhythmic breathing is the base of the exercise and then various mental exercises are used with it to create energy, transfer thought, heal self and others, as well as transform emotions, and acquire desired mental qualities.

"All is in vibration." says Ormond McGill. As you do this exercise you can become aware of the motion of the universe and of your own body rhythm and pulsation. The main principle is to acquire the mental idea of rhythm. You can think of the measured count of music or the rhythmic step of soldiers: left, right, left, right: one, two, three, four; one, two, three, four conveys the idea. Except that this is timed to the beat of your heart.

First ascertain your normal heart beat by taking your pulse. Then count 1,2,3,4,5,6; 1,2,3,4,5,6 getting the heart beat firmly in your mind. A bit of practice will fix the rhythem in your mind so you can reproduce it in your breathing.

The formula for rhythmic breathing requires that the inhalation and exhalation be of equal duration while the breath retention and the pause between breaths be one-half the number of the inhalation and exhalation.

- Sit erect in an easy posture with your hands on your lap.
- Inhale slowly a "complete breath" for six pulse units (pulse beats and/or heart beats).
- Retain the breath in the lungs for three pulse units (counting three pulse beats).
- Exhale slowly through the nostrils for a period of six pulse beats.
- Count three pulse beats between breaths.
- Repeat the rhythmic breathing cycle (steps 2 through 5) over and over, getting a definite rhythm into the breathing. Practice until you can sense the rhythm of the vibratory motion throughout your whole body. You will begin to experience the "power" rising within you.

Once you've developed the rhythmic breathing to the point where you can do it automatically without conscious thinking and counting, you can add the mental processes.

Recharging Yourself With Vital Force

Anytime during the trading day that you feel your vital energy is at low ebb, you can use rhythmic breathing to restore and enhance energy. Sit erect in a chair with your fingers interlocked and your feet crossed. This closes the body circuit and prevents any energy from escaping through the extremities. Breathe rhythmically until you feel the effects of the recharging.

Acquiring Mental Qualities

Sit erect and breathe rhythmically as you visualize the qualities you desire to cultivate. Imagine yourself in possesion of these qualities and create a daydream of yourself acting with these qualities. Perhaps you want to see yourself entering and exiting trades with profound trust and courage. Perhaps you want to imagine yourself taking profits and losses as no big deal, calmly working the process with confidence. As you do this demand that your mind develop these qualities. Keep breathing rhythmically as you hold firmly the vision of yourself feeling and acting with these qualities. The rhythmic breathing assists the mind in forming new combinations, and you will find yourself growing up to your ideal.

Anchoring

Emotional states and memories get anchored (connected) to certain physical, auditory, visual, olfactory or gustatory phenomena. Once associated, the simple stimulus will automatically evoke a certain response. Since this chapter is on physiology, we'll be utilizing kinesthetic anchors.

Remember Pavlov's dogs that salivated when they heard a bell ring even though there was no meat? They had made an association between meat and the ringing of a bell. Once the association was made, the simple ringing of the bell without the meat was sufficient to cause salivation. The stimulus and response were automatic. An auditory anchor had been created.

When you see a Christmas tree or a Santa Claus, whatever associations you have to Christmas will come to mind. Some people will respond with warm excitement; others with a muffled sadness; a few with simple boredom. It's the same visual anchors with different associations or memories.

For me, a crisp, cool, wind flecked with snow or a sultry breeze on my face can evoke memories and feelings quite automatically. I've made an association to the kinesthetic stimulus. The smell of balsam always evokes pleasant feelings and memories of camp.

Have you ever had a bad trading day, shake it off, rebuild your trading readiness, and still find yourself sinking into despair the next day as soon as you sit down in front of your computer? Yesterday's feelings of despair could be associated with the feel of the chair (kinesthetic anchor) or the sight of the screen (visual anchor). I would suggest changing the chair or putting a pillow on the chair to change the kinesthetic anchor and putting some colorful stickers around the screen to change the visual association. Sit with a different posture. Wear yellow glasses. Play different music in case there's an auditory anchor. Change the stimulus.

Kinesthetic anchoring is easy to do. When you've done something right, when you're feeling great, you can make a unique physical gesture or touch at the height of the emotion and you'll be able to recall that feeling later by repeating the gesture or touch.You can also create an anchor by using the memory of the joyful or successful experience. Remember the experience and when you're really into it, fire off the gesture or touch.

The gesture or touch needs to be specific so that it can be duplicated. You can make a fist or touch your thumb to one of your finger tips or pull your earlobe. Or you can create a sliding anchor by running your hand across your shoulder or down your arm or leg.

You can also kinesthetically anchor other people by using a specific touch at the height of their emotion. Later when you want to evoke that emotion, simply repeat the touch.

Kinesthetic Self Anchoring

- Think of a resource that will help you with your trading, such as courage, confidence, detachment, strength, calmness—whatever you want.
- Identify a time, a specific situation, where you had this resource strongly.
- Remember that experience as though you were living it now. See what you saw. Hear what you heard. Feel what you felt.

- When you're really into this, make a specific gesture such as making a fist and hold it for 10 seconds while you relive the experience of the resource.
- Release the anchor (the fist or whatever). Look around and take a deep breath.
- Repeat steps 3 and 4 several times.
- Release the anchor and think of something else for a while.
- Use your anchor and hold it for 10 seconds. Notice how the feelings associated with your resource come flooding back.
- You have now anchored your resource. When you're trading and you need this resource, use your anchor.

MULTI-DIMENSIONAL INTERVENTIONS HOLOGRAPHIC RESOURCING

This process was developed by Stephen Nicholas based on a hologram. The features of a hologram are the three dimensionality of the image and the phenomena where each part of the holographic plate contains the whole image "caught" in the structure of the interference pattern.

- Identify three resources that you would like to bring into your trading. Some possible resources could be courage, confidence, discipline, perception, detachment, alertness, resilience, trust, faith, focus, or conviction. You choose what you want in your trading.
- For each of the three resources, identify a time when you experienced effectively using that resource. Also identify what is important to you about each of the resources. Select a separate visual metaphor to represent each of the resources.
- Write the name of each resource on a piece of paper and place them about 10 steps apart on the floor so they make a triangle.
- In sequence, step unto each of these pieces of paper and reexperience a time when you utilized the resource. Step off the paper and visualize the metaphor.
- Step unto one of the resources once again experiencing it and slowly then begin to walk towards another of the resources. Notice what it's like to be moving away from one of the resources and moving towards the other. Do this slowly in about ten incremental steps.
- When you reach the next resource get fully into the experience of that resource. When you're ready then begin the journey back to the first resource, moving slowly away from the second resource and back to the first resource.
- When you get back to the first resource, imagine yourself trading with this resource.
- Step off the first resource and step outside the triangle and go to halfway point between the first and second resource and notice the connection between the two.
- Step on the third resource and experience it, and select the first or the second resource as the next point in your journey. When you get there, imagine yourself trading with that resource, and when you're ready, go back to the third resource, and imagine yourself

trading with that resource. When you've done that once again step off the resource and go halfway between the third resource and the resource you traveled to and notice the connection.

- Repeat step 9 between the two resources which have not yet been connected.
- Circle round all three resources, walking, skipping, running, even as you imagine yourself trading with these resources firmly in place.
- Step into the center of the triangle and feel the connection between each of these three resources and the top of your head. Imagine yourself trading with all three of the resources. Choose a metaphor to represent this new totality.
- Trade with these resources.

NEW PHYSIOLOGY FOR TRADING BRINGING FRACTALS TO BEAR

This exercise helps you to bring a new physiology to bear on your mental state when trading. First you identify the physiology you have when you're in a less than optimal trading state. Then you decide what state of mind you'd like to trade in. You identify a gesture that represents to you that state of mind. You begin to do the gesture and then do it in fractals all through your body. (A fractal is a smaller part of a whole that can get smaller and smaller into units. Imagine a triangle being subdivided into many triangles.) You then transfer the new gesture in fractals to the trading environment.

- Place a piece of paper on the floor to represent your trading. Step unto the paper and get into the experience of trading. Now assume the physiology of trading when it's less than optimal. Exagerate that physiology.
- Step off the paper and decide what state of mind you'd like to trade in. Select a gesture that represents that state of mind. Practice the gesture. Then imagine yourself doing the gesture with each part of your body-your forehead, eyebrows, mouth, shoulders, little fingers, waist, hips, knees, toes, and so forth. Do this for a while as you think about the state of mind you're representing.
- Step back on the piece of paper that represents your trading. Assume the first posture of the less than optimal. Exagerate it as you think about trading. Now shift to the new posture and gesture with the fractals even as you think about trading.
- Just before you begin trading, do the fractal dance!

CHAPTER XI

YOUR OFFICE

"Your space is your kingdom. How you arrange that space and what is included in it determine whether energy flows freely around you."
—Angel Thompson

Environment is all-important. It's the context in which you operate. Your office deserves thought and care and upkeep so that you can trade most effectively.

If your office is a spot on a trading floor, you can skip this chapter unless you have a home office as well. The important thing for you to do is to anchor a physiology of excellence to your spot on the floor. Two exercises to do in connection with the geography of your trading place are The Quieting Reflex and New Physiology for Trading outlined in the prior chapter, "The Physiology of Excellence." These are also good exercises to anchor an upbeat state of mind to your home office.

Your office is best thought of as a sacred space for your work. Dedicate this space to your personal excellence and well being. Make sure it facilitates your work. Secure it so that it's free of intrusive noise and interruptions. Make it a place of calm beauty that satisfies **your** inner being.

All this may sound rather pretentious or overstated, but in fact it is not. Your office is the locus of your source of wealth. It's where you spend the majority of your time. It's a large part of your world.

Creating a sacred space for your work is a high order. Where do we begin? Let's begin with the basics.

CLEAN OUT THE CLUTTER

Clutter is stuck energy. You need to make room for clear, clean, moving energy. What is outside of you is inside of you, and what's inside of you is outside of you. Wow. Take a look.

"Never underestimate the effect of clutter on your life. Whenever I meet people who tell me they are stuck, I know that if I visit their homes I will almost always find lots of clutter. Clutter accumulates when energy stagnates."
— Karen Kingston

When you clear out clutter, you release fresh, new energy in your body. By getting rid of everything that has no significance for yourself or your business, you free yourself and restore yourself. You create space for energy to move. You open up creative possibilities in the present when you get rid of meaningless stuff. You create room for new wealth.

It's interesting to observe that cultures with few material possessions are often more spiritually intact than cultures that accumulate lots of material things. Cultures that own lots of material things often lose their spiritual focus completely.

What is clutter? Necessary research materials or findings are not clutter. Anything that truly facilitates your business is not clutter. Clutter is anything that you are keeping that serves no current or future purpose. In cleaning out clutter, don't ask yourself, "Will this be of use some day?" Ask yourself instead, "Of what value is this to me?" Or, "What does this do for my business?"

I am told that businesses worldwide use over fifteen million miles of paper every day. That's a lot of paper. The challenge is to throw out all the paper that is no longer useful and to appropriately file the rest.

Where do you begin? Each day, after you get stuff, throw out what's no longer necessary and file the rest. As for past clutter, begin by cleaning out one drawer a day. Clean out one file at a time. Get stuff off the floor.

Clear off your desk each time you shift activities. When I trade, I have nothing but that day's trading materials on my desk. When I write, I have nothing but the relevant materials to that article or that chapter on my desk.

Get rid of everything that serves no purpose in your life. You'll walk taller, feel younger and lighter, and be freer.

SCREEN AND PHONE PLACEMENT

Surprisingly enough, where you place your trading screens can impact your trading effectiveness. One reason for this is that screen placement can effect your body posture which in turn can effect your emotional state. The other, and more powerful and astonishing reason, is that the position of your eyes has a direct relationship to your perceptual and mental strategies.

The easiest way to find your best screen position is to simply experiment putting them in different places and trading with that placement for a few days. The most important screen is the one from which you get your trading signal. However, the placement of all screens has something to do with optimum performance.

Make certain the screen is the right distance for your vision that you do not have to pull back or squint or lean forward to see. Make sure you do not have to sit on the edge of your chair or lean way back to put the screen into focus. Such physiology would give your mind clues that you were "on edge" or "laid back" or pulling away from the trading.

Also, make sure that your screens are located in such a way that your physiology is that of excellence. You should be sitting up straight with your head up and your body not slumped over or twisted in any way. As we've demonstrated before, your body speaks directly to your mind.

In addition to your general physiology, your screen placement effects the position of your gaze. Strangely enough, the position of your eyes dictates the sensory cues you receive. Some people begin their thoughts by making mental pictures. (It happens so quickly they may not be aware of it.) Others begin by talking to themselves or by hearing something. Still other people begin their mental processes with a feeling. These are the sensory cues for a mental strategy.

Once I visited the currency trading room of a major bank, and was surprised to observe that every single trader—and there were many of them—had his screen down on the desk and to his right. To get market information each trader had to look down to his right. This would put ninety per cent of the traders into a feeling or kinesthetic state. Some would trade well from their feelings. Others would not.

We talked about primary representational systems in chapter nine, "Reprogramming the Software of Your Mind" and noted that each person has a primary representational system for accessing information through a particular sensory channel. Generally that would be visual (internal and external pictures), auditory (internal and external sounds and words), or kinesthetic (internal emotions and physical feelings).

We all use a combination of the sensory channels in various sequences for thoughts and decisions. However, we all have one primary mode in which we generally begin our thought and in which we are most receptive and effective.

Strangely enough, you actually look different directions to access different representational systems. To access internal visual representations, you look up and to the right or left or straight ahead defocused. To access internal auditory representations, you look level to your right or to your left as though you were looking at your right or left ear. To enter a kinesthetic or feeling state, you look down and to your right. This is true for ninety percent of people; the other ten-percent would look down and to their left.

It is said that the eyes are the windows to the soul. They truly are the windows to thought processes. You can notice these phenomena by watching the eyes of people talking on television—those that are really talking and thinking and not just reading prepared thoughts from a teleprompter. Those who look up are accessing visual cues. Those who look down are accessing cues from a feeling state. Those who look towards their ears are listening to a voice inside.

When you look up, you facilitate a visual state. When you look down and to your right, you facilitate an emotional state. When you look level right or left, you facilitate an auditory state.

What does this mean for screen placement? Well, you probably want to spend most of your time looking in the direction of the eye accessing cues of your primary representational system. If you are a visual person, and your screen is situated down and to your right, you will no doubt find it an awkward placement. If you are a kinesthetic person or you go into a feeling state to make a trading decision, you just won't function at your best if your screen is above your head.

Let me give you an example from outside the trading area to show you how important screen placement is for optimal functioning. The screens that are used to test candidates taking the Series 7 and Series 3 Brokers' Examinations are placed directly in front of the candidates. Candidates who are kinesthetic and have studied for the exam looking down, have a terrible time trying to access information while looking up or straight forward, particularly under a stressful situation. They are in a visual-accessing mode while they try to access the information stored in a kinesthetic way. It doesn't work for them. I instruct them to read the question and multiple choices and then look down and let the answer materialize in their mind.

Since you can place your trading screens wherever you choose, it's a good idea to give it some thought and experimentation, and position them where you feel you best function. If you're experiencing a lot of fear while trading, for goodness sake, get your screens up higher.

If you're fearful while placing the order, try placing your phone some place other than down and to your right. Try placing it down to your left, and since this is the auditory digital (talking to yourself) accessing cue, prepare something encouraging to say to yourself such as, "What if this trade is a big winner?"

That brings us to the left and right part of accessing cues. You need to decide whether to put screens and phones, not only high, low or level, but whether to put them straight ahead or to the right or left. The right and left relate to whether you are remembering or constructing (creating).

Ninety percent of the population looks to their left to remember and to their right to create, left to right, past to future, just the way you write. Ten percent is organized to do it the other way, and these ten percent are usually left handed, although not always.

If you ask your lover where she was last night, you might notice whether she looks to her left to remember or to her right to construct.

Let's put it all together. Imagine you are looking at the face of a large clock in front of you and that your sensory cues are aligned with the ninety percent majority. You look up to 12:00 for olfactory cues, at 1:00 for visual constructing, at 3:00 for auditory constructing, at 5:00 to enter a feeling state, at 6:00 for gustatory cues, at 7:00 for auditory digital (talking to yourself), at 9:00 for auditory remembering, and at 11:00 for visual remembering. Remember you look to your left to remember and to your right to create or construct, the same way you read.

How do you determine what your primary representational system is? Remember we all use all of the representational systems, but we each have a preferred or lead system. There are several ways to tell. The verbs, adjectives and adverbs you use to describe your experience will give you a clue as to how you perceive and represent your reality. We talked about sensory filters in chapter nine, "Reprogramming the Software of Your Mind."

Listen to your words as you talk. A **visual** person will use words like these: I see what you're saying. That looks good to me. It's not clear to me. I went blank. Get a new perspective. Can you picture that? Show me. Focus your ideas.

An **auditory** person will say things like this: I hear you. That rings a bell. That sounds good to me. Something tells me loud and clear it's a great idea. That clicks with me. I'm out of tune with the market. Listen to me. Talk to me. Let me sing your praises.

A **kinesthetic** person will talk like this: Grasp the idea. Get a handle on it. That feels right to me. Get in touch with yourself. A solid understanding. I'm up against the wall. Get a grip. I have a feeling you're right. Hand me the facts. Let me place the facts before you.

Speech tempo can also help you find your primary representational system. Visual people speak very quickly. A picture is worth a thousand words. Often their voices are high pitched, and can be piercing. An auditory person will savor their words and sounds and is likely to have a sonorous voice. A kinesthetic person will speak very slowly and will also process information more slowly.

In making a trading decision, unless it's completely mechanical, you will probably use all three representational systems. Perhaps you will feel that something is alerting you to take action (kinesthetic—eyes down to your right). You might look at a chart (external visual—eyes on the chart) and compare it with a visual memory (internal visual—eyes up to your left). You could then say to yourself that this is good opportunity (auditory digital—eyes down to your left).

Perhaps you will see something externally first (visual—eyes on the chart), then remember a similar pattern (visual—eyes up to the left), then talk to yourself (auditory digital—eyes down to your left), and finally get a feeling (kinesthetic—eyes down to the right).

Maybe you will remember a chart pattern (eyes up and to the left), feel (eyes down to the right), and then internally hear something about trading (eyes level to your left). Or you hear something externally (eyes level), look at the numbers (eyes on the numbers), and feel something (eyes down to the right).

To discover what your decision making trading strategy is, you can mentally get back into a time when you made an effective trading decision and relive the steps. What—and in what order—did you see, hear, or feel, internally and externally? Compare this with other times when you made an effective decision and look for the similarities of process.

When you identify your most effective strategy for making a trading decision, you can rehearse it mentally. Just as an athlete goes over and over the flawless performance of his craft, you can do the same with your decision strategy.

Once you have elicited your primary representational mode and your best strategy for making a trading decision, look again at your screen and phone placement. Is your most looked at screen in a position that would equate to the eye accessing position of your primary representational system? From where are your first and confirming signals coming? Are the screens in the appropriate places? When and where in the process are you remembering or constructing? Are the screens to your right or to your left?

Do you tend to overtrade or undertrade? Where, then, would be the best place to put your phone or the screen from which you do your electronic trading? If fear makes you undertrade, get the order placement vehicle out of the lower right quadrant. If excitement makes you overtrade, do the same thing.

There is no absolute right or wrong way to place screens as long as it allows your physiology to be one of excellence. If you can make your decision process easier and more comfortable looking in the direction of your natural strategies, it's well worth a little trial and error to find it. Play around with your current screen set-up to find the arrangement that works best for you.

ELECTROMAGNETIC CONSIDERATIONS

Humans are electromagnetic biochemical beings. As such, we are extremely sensitive to electromagnetic fields (EMFs). Furthermore, we create our own fields. The **World Health Organization** states that "the human body emits electromagnetic fields at frequencies of up to 300 GHz."[1]

We can experience electromagnetic stress when we are bombarded with artificial electromagnetic fields generated by various electrical equipment. Excessive amounts over extended time penetrate and alter our cellular processes and can lead to a loss of vital life force and can even weaken an immune system.

You need to be aware of electromagnetic fields in your office. Electric lights, electric cooling and heating mechanisms all generate strong EMFs. Keep them at a distance.

Color televisions emit large EMFs and can maintain their charge for several days even after being unplugged from the wall. The larger the screen, the greater the EMFs. You want to keep an average sized screen at least six to ten feet away from your body. And turn it off when it's not adding anything necessary.

Computers, a central part of most traders' activity, create many health hazards. When you sit in front of your computer screen, you are being bombarded by many different emissions, such as visible light, ultraviolet light, VLF (Very Low Frequency) electromagnetic radiation, ELF (Extremely Low Frequency) electromagnetic radiation, and sometimes soft x-rays.

To help alleviate the harmful effects, you can use radiation screens, wear natural fibers such as cotton, have plants near the computer equipment, and, of course, turn computers off when you're not using them.

Something else you can do is to switch to a laptop with a liquid crystal display screen, which is less harmful than the cathode ray tube of conventional computer screens. One caveat about the laptop is don't put it on your lap or you will actually soak up more radiation than you would working with a conventional monitor.

Cellular phones should only be used when conventional phones are not available. Cellular phones work on microwave frequencies, and the radiation emitted by these phones is absorbed directly into the head of the user. There are reports that regular use can cause headaches, migraines, ear and eye problems, and the possibility of brain tumors.

If you use beepers or pagers, it's better to keep them off your person. If you have to wear one, shift the place you wear it from time to time.

AIR CLEANSING

In addition to electromagnetic dangers, there are the dangers of chemical pollutants found in carpets, adhesives, plastics, synthetic fibers, household cleaners, and decorating materials such as paints and wallpaper. Many carpets, flame resistant fabrics, and wall coverings such as plywood and wood varnishes and so forth have been treated with formaldehyde and give off fumes for years. All this can be dangerous in enclosed areas with limited ventilation.

Plants help to cleanse the air. **NASA** looked for ways to cleanse the air of space capsules, and discovered several types of houseplants that have the ability to cleanse pollutants from the air including formaldehyde. These plants are peace lilies (Spathiphyllum Wallisii), peperomias, goosefoot plants (Syngonium Podophyllum), dwarf banana plants, golden pothos (Scindapsus Aureus), Chinese evergreens (Aglaonema), Spider plants (Chlorophytum Elatum), and Mother-in-law's tongue (Sansevieria Trifasciata Laurentii).

These plants not only filter the air but they increase oxygen and improve humidity and negative ionization. In addition, they're beautiful. They provide a touch of nature that offers peace and calm.

LIGHTING

Lighting can effect our moods and our health. I think of light as a nutrient like air or water. Natural daylight is the best lighting of all. The next best is full spectrum lighting. The worst is fluorescent lighting. Fluorescent tubes actually emit the same type of radiation as cathode ray tube computer monitors. If you use fluorescent lighting, you're getting a double dose. In addition fluorescent tubes give off toxins such as phosphor used to coat the inside of the tubes and mercury vapor found inside the tubes.

SOUNDS

What are you listening to when you trade or when you're working? Are you listening to a squawk box; and if you are, does this improve your trading? Are you listening to **CNBC** or any other television programming, and does this make your trading any better? Is any of this stuff relevant to your method of trading? Are you listening to other traders shouting? This could give you clues. Or are you listening, as I too frequently am, to garbage trucks, sirens, and jack hammers? If you're lucky, you're hearing sounds of nature—wind in the trees, birds singing, water lapping, waves crashing, or rain on the roof.

What you listen to effects your energy, your relaxation, and your ability to learn and to think.

The Bulgarians developed a system of superlearning that reputedly had students learning as rapidly as 1,000 and more foreign language words in a day. In Berlitz language schools 200 words after several days or 30 hours of immersion training is considered successful. Unfortunately, forgetting the words after rapid high-pressure learning is also frequent. With the Bulgarian approach, 500 words a day was just "Mach 1." In 1966 a group learned 1,000 words in a day, and in 1974 a rate of 1800 words in a day was recorded. By 1977 Dr. Lazanov, who pioneered superlearning, reported some people capable of learning 3,000 words in a day.

Dr. Lazanov began his research at the Institute of Suggestology. His work on superlearning began by studying people who had proven paranormal capabilities like clairvoyance and telepathy. He learned how people can enhance and access their natural powers.

It's a fascinating study and not fully relevant to trading; but briefly, superlearning is accomplished first by building self-confidence and removing fear and stress. Then using music with 60 beats per minute in 4/4th time, which would be found in the slower portions of classical Baroque music, a teacher reads the words in ten second intervals while the students breathe rhythmically to the recitation and repeat the words to themselves. If you'd like to learn more about this, read the book **Superlearning** by Ostrander, Schroeder, and Ostrander.[2]

Baroque music—music by sixteenth to eighteenth century composers such as Bach, Vivaldi, Telemann, Corelli, and Handel—assists people with learning whether or not they like it. In the slow movements, the music has a very slow base beating 60 beats per minute like a slow human pulse.

The music used in superlearning has nothing to do with personal choice or taste in music. It's a specific music with sonic patterns with a specific purpose. It relaxes the body and energizes the mind. Even plants are reputed to grow better with Baroque music.

If the squawk box or TV add nothing to your trading, why not replace it with Baroque music?

"Some sounds are as good as two cups of coffee. Gregorian chants are a fantastic energy source. I work with them as background music and sleep only three or four hours each night."

—Dr. Alfred Tomatis[3]

Sounds so good, I decided to put on some Gregorian chants as I write this. Dr. Alfred Tomatis is a renowned French ear specialist. He was called in to help solve a problem in a remote Benedictine monastery in France. A young abbot had ordered the monks to do "less chanting, more practical work." Shortly after these new reforms were instituted, the monks grew torpid. They were sleeping longer and were still exhausted. A physician called in put them on a conventional diet, but their condition only grew worse. Seventy of the ninety monks were sitting in their cells doing nothing, withdrawn and depressed.

Dr. Tomatis reintroduced their lengthy chanting schedule, and the monastery once again rang with the sound of their voices. Soon they were feeling better, sleeping less, and working more.

According to Dr. Tomatis, your ear is your primary organ of consciousness. It's made not only for hearing but also to use sound to charge the electric potential of the brain. The cortex then distributes the resulting charge through the rest of your body. The central grey nuclei in the cortex act like small electrical batteries to generate the electricity for the brain to produce the electrical brainwaves you see in an EEG. For Dr. Tomatis, ear force equals brain force. He sees the ear as the means to restore your cosmic vitality. For him the ear/brain link is a cybernetic system meant to invigorate the entire organism both physically and psychologically.

In order to get the beneficial effects of the sound, however, you have to be able to hear it. It's the high frequencies that recharge the brain, and unless you're trained to hear them, you don't. Dr. Tomatis found that by varying the high and low frequency sounds, you give the middle ear a gymnastic workout so that it reopens it's high frequency hearing power. Then the sound can be transformed into energy in the ear. The auditory nerves then can do two things: one nerve branch can energize the brain cortex, and the vestibular nerve can determine posture and muscle tone throughout the body. Mind and body, that unique partnership can be energized through appropriate sound.

No wonder Johnny can't trade. He's listening to the wrong sounds. Are you frantic during the trading? Try listening to slow, Baroque music. Are you exhausted at the end of the trading day? Try listening to Gregorian chants.

FENG SHUI

Feng Shui (pronounced fung shway) is an ancient Chinese art of enhancing and harmonizing the flow of energy in your surroundings. It is a practice built on the idea that the auspicious placement of buildings, paths, doors, furniture, plants, mirrors, and other objects can ensure a good life. By providently locating and orienting your office and home and establishing its interior design to allow cosmic energy or chi to flow freely, you can promote success and happiness.

Well, I don't know. It's a bit of a stretch for me. I do believe that beauty and design and taste are all important to well being. One just feels better in a tasteful and lovely surrounding. It lifts the spirits and supports the psyche on an unconscious level.

Beauty of self, surrounding, sound, and creations is a very high value to me. It dictates my actions. However, I must admit, I rarely have a client who lists beauty as one of his (definitely)/hers (occasionally) top ten values.

But we were talking about feng shui. Maybe I better go put the Gregorian Chants back on. Feng Shui is a complicated language of symbology. And there is documented testimony of its power. It began 3,000 years ago in China as people were deciding the most auspicious place to bury their dead so that they could get their blessings.

Today it's about living consciously on the earth and enjoying the highest quality of life force. It is the art of balancing, harmonizing, and enhancing the flow of natural energy.

"I think of my home as a magical manifesting machine, the interface between myself and the universe."

—Karen Kingston
Creating Sacred Space With Feng Shui[4]

"For centuries, the Chinese have known that when you are willing to change the outside, inner change is already beginning to occur. Change your surroundings and you change your life."

—Angel Thompson
Feng Shui, *How To Achieve The Most Harmonious Arrangement Of Your Home And Office*[5]

Basically, Feng Shui is about the five elements: wood, fire, earth, metal, and water. Each element represents a season, a time, a direction such as North or South, certain qualities, and certain virtues. Particular colors, materials, and shapes can evoke each element.

Wood is the element of spring when wood sends out new green shoots to reach for the light. The energy is similar to the energy of dawn when the sun rises in the East, which is the direction of Wood. The qualities of wood are creation, nourishment, upward growth, and primal anger. Its virtues are love of humanity, benevolence, balance between roots and branches, family and career, and flexible thinking. If you're having trouble being flexible trading, find some wood or green object and place it with intention near your trading station. Wood is represented by green and by all types of wood as well as natural fibers, vegetables, fruits, flowers, and plants. Its shapes are tall, columnar, rectangular, and oblong.

Fire is the element of summer and is represented by the sun at noon when it's hot and bright. The summer is a season of full growth and promise, and because the sun travels through the South, that is the direction of this element. Flames give fire its red color and triangular, pointed shapes. Fire is the element of life and light. Its qualities are intelligence, spirit, human and animal life. Its virtues are wisdom, reason, and etiquette. Its color is any hue or shade of red. It is represented by animal products, including leather and wool, shiny fabrics that reflect light, and anything that generates light or heat. To represent the fullness of your trading, use an object to represent fire such as something red or triangular in shape or anything that generates light and heat—a light, for example. Place it with intention near your trading station.

Earth is the element of Indian Summer. This season placed between summer and fall represents a period of calm and stability when the hours of darkness equal the hours of light. Earth has no direction according to the Chinese because it is the center of our lives, but sometimes it takes on the direction of the Southwest. The energy of Earth is reliable, dependable, calm and centering. Earth's color is earth tones or yellow, probably after the Chinese yellow soil. Its time is the middle of the afternoon after the morning has peaked. Its shapes are square, boxlike, or flat. With too much earth we become too stable, unchanging. With too little we may have trouble attracting money or resources.

Its materials are anything that comes from the earth—bricks, clay pots, sand, marble, rocks, and crystals. I keep two beautiful clay pots on either side of my computer to attract wealth. I placed them there with that intention, and whether Feng Shui works or not, they are definitely visual anchors representing abundance to me.

Metal is the element of fall, a season to match the fading light of the sun in the west, which is its direction. Metal is produced by contraction and reduction of earth. Coins were minted out of silver and gold, so round, coinlike shapes represent metal. Metal represents sharp thinking, intense focus, and the ability to make a decision. Its qualities are reversal and withdrawal, and its virtues are morality, ethics, and precise thinking. Its color is white, gray, and silver, and its materials are any metal as well as mirrors coated with silver or aluminum. Because Earth and Metal sequence each other, together they produce wealth and financial success and are considered fortunate. Be sure to place some metal objects next to your earth objects with the intention of creating wealth. Hey, it could just be scissors or a stapler. I have a little mirror that reflects back the space of my room as well as a large, deep, peaceful night ocean painting thus giving me Water as well.

Water is the element of winter. It concludes the cycle. It's dark and deep like water. In winter there is little sun shining in the North, which is the direction of water. Water is life; nothing can live without water. Water represents communication, the transmission of ideas, wisdom, and social interaction. Water's color is black and its time is midnight. Its materials are glass and water. Its shapes are curved and wavelike. Without enough water a person could be isolated or lonely or have dull vision and lack of clarity. Just to be sure you have clarity, add some water, perhaps a glass vase with water and flowers.

According to the Chinese, there are good and bad energies. What you want are the healthful chi flowing freely, and you want to reflect back any bad chi or energy. Feng Shui is based on the principle of creating harmony and ease in your home and office so you can create it in your life.

The thought is to have flowing curves and patterns rather than geometric angles. As there are no straight lines in nature, the Chinese believe that sharp corners and pointed objects produce disruption and disharmony. They believe these angles emanate invisible rays.

There's a wonderful example in Hong Kong where the people take Feng Shui quite seriously. Some even say that because Hong Kong follows Feng Shui principles in ninety percent of its properties, and has created great wealth and prosperity, the effectiveness of Feng Shui has been documented. The Bank of China built a seventy-story building with sharp angles. The architect allegedly designed the building to send arrow like killing chi at its competitors. Neighborhood business reportedly sued the bank because of its killing chi. In the meantime they all hung mirrors in their windows to reflect back the killing energy. So, of course, the bank got its karma back.

The idea is to avoid having sharp angles and straight arrows and lines pointing at you. This includes the sharp angles of furniture and beams on your ceiling.

Mirrors reflect energy in and out. They are used so frequently in Feng Shui that they are called the aspirin of Feng Shui. Any size will do. Remember they work symbolically. However, large mirrors, if feasible and called for, will reflect more light and energy and can reflect that which you choose to multiply. For goodness sake, don't use a large mirror to reflect what you don't want or what isn't pleasing.

Feng Shui gives a lot of advice about desk placement in offices. Don't put valued employees near the door: they'll leave. Don't you sit near the door: you'll be fired. Don't have separations between you and your employees: you won't get the best from them. Don't sit with your back to the room or back to the door. Anything can get you in the back, and you won't be engaged.

The problem with this is that who wants the back of the computer to be facing the room—there's even more pollution and ugliness rendered. The solution is to put a mirror where you can see what's behind you. Even a small mirror will do the trick. I did exactly this, and it opened up my horizons surprisingly.

The bagua is a Feng Shui grid derived from the I Ching. It's an eight-sided grid that can be laid over the plans of your home or office to show which areas of your surroundings represent which areas of your life. Each of the eight areas represents an area of your life. Each area has its own energy field and each represents a distinct and separate activity of your life.

There are baguas within baguas within baguas. For example, your land has a bagua and your building has a bagua. Each room has it's own bagua, and even your desk and your bed have a bagua. The bagua of each building, apartment, and room is determined by the front door, so the speak, the most used door. Your desk entry is where you pull up your chair.

North is always north on the bagua, however, you twist it around so that any direction aligns with the direction of the entry door. Now comes the point of confusion. In the five books I read, each seems to determine the direction of the entry door differently. One says follow your nose and look out the door because that is where the energy is coming from. I decided to buy that one. You may want to research more. Thus, if you look south when you look out the front door, that is where you line up the bagua. If I'm sitting on the west side of my desk looking east, when I turn away from my desk and look back, I'm looking west. Then that is how I line up the bagua to determine which portion represents which.

These are the directions and the representations of the energy of the various aspects of your life as well as the element they represent.

DIRECTION	AREA OF LIFE	ELEMENT
East	Health	Wood
Southeast	Money	Wood
South	Fame	Fire
Southwest	Love	Earth
West	Family	Metal
Northwest	Travel and Friends	Metal
North	Business	Water
Northeast	Knowledge	Earth

It all gets very complex. If you're interested, go to the library or a bookstore and pick up several books on it. There are two important things to remember. One, if things are going well, don't worry about it. In other words, if it ain't broke, don't fix it. Two, don't make it a major focus in your thoughts. Just let it be a calm, quiet, supporting factor in your office.

PRIVACY

If you trade on a trading floor, you're not going to have much privacy. And you probably don't want or need it. However, you do need to insulate yourself from unwanted opinions or criticism. Keep in mind, an opinion isn't worth much. It's much more important to listen, watch, and feel the markets. Watch how the markets react to the news. Just do the best you can using good trading principles, and forgive yourself your mistakes even as you learn from them.

If you have a home office, you need to work out an arrangement with your family, so that you won't be unduly interrupted during trading or research. When you make the agreements, however, make sure the schedule includes quality time with your family. If you can't get the necessary cooperation, it's probably best to get an office away from home.

I heard of one writer who would get up each morning. He'd breakfast, shower, shave, and dress fully in shirt, suit, and tie. He'd bid his family farewell and walk once around the block only to reenter the house and go to his home office. When he was through for the day, he'd put on his coat, walk around the block again, and enter the home saying, "Hello, I'm home!"

FINALLY

Well, this has been a lot of talk about your office. In the final analysis, all that's important is that you have a space, no matter how large or small, that supports you practically, mentally, physically, and spiritually—quietly and in the background—so that you can be the most you can be as a trader and enjoy being there during the process.

Maybe you'll make just one or two changes, but they will be the right ones for you. I must say my arguments for cleaning clutter were so persuasive to me, I'm still cleaning and feeling lighter with every load out. The small mirror I put on my desk and to my right reflects the rest of my large wonderful space, and I am no longer face to the computer, face to the wall when I look to my right to choose my next words. My earthen vases restore my connection to Earth and lend confidence about the success of this book and of my trading. The Baroque music and Gregorian chants focus and energize me. Maybe tomorrow I'll add some more changes, and that will be even better.

Why don't you begin comfortably and easily with one or two changes? Let me suggest a priority. Ditch the clutter, and then add something beautiful that pleases you.

[1] EHC 137: **Electromagnetic Fields,** WHO, Geneva, 1993

[2] **Superlearning,** Sheila Ostrander and Lynn Schroeder with Nancy Ostrander, Delacorte Press/Confucian Press, Inc., 1979, IBSN: 0-385-28952-9

[3] **Supermemory, The Revolution,** Sheila Ostrander and Lynn Schroeder, Carroll & Graf Publishers, Inc., 1991, ISBN: 0-88184-691-0

[4] **Creating Sacred Space With Feng Shui,** Karen Kingston, Broadway Books, 1997, ISBN: 0-553-06916-0

[5] **Feng Shui, How To Achieve The Most Harmonious Arrangement Of Your Home And Office,** Angel Thompson, St. Martin's Griffin, 1996, ISBN: 0-312-14333-8

CHAPTER XII

THE CONFIDENT TRADER

The confident trader is confident because he has found out what works; he's verified that it works; and he trusts himself to do what works. History and experience have proven that his confidence is well placed.

The confident trader is not overconfident. That's foolish and dangerous. The confident trader is not underconfident. That's ignoring the probabilities and the proven research.

The confident trader trades in trust. She trusts herself and her methods and the general process of trading. The **Oxford English Dictionary** defines trust as confidence in or reliance on some quality or attribute of a person or thing, or the truth of a statement. It goes on to define trust as the confident expectation of something.

Now trust is not fact. The future never is fact. Facts only exist in the present and past. The confident trader acts in the present with faith about the future. The confident trader has faith that the process will work over time. Therefore, she can easily, gracefully, and courageously accept the raging uncertainties of the market.

If you don't trust your methods, don't use them. Find something you can trust. If you don't trust yourself to apply your methods to the market, you'll need to find a coach who can work with you to get you to the point where you will automatically do what needs to be done.

DRAWDOWNS

The confident trader understands that drawdowns or periods of loss are temporary. Because they are temporary, it's no big deal. An unconfident trader, on the contrary, becomes fearful and unsettled because he is worried that the drawdown will continue and severely damage the account. He's worried that he might be out of business soon.

The confident trader, on the other hand, takes the drawdown in stride because it's no big deal. Maybe she'll step back for a few days, but it's pretty much business as usual. I spoke with Linda Bradford Raschke about this.

Ruth: "How do you handle a drawdown?"

Linda: "I don't really think about it. It depends on if it's a drawdown that's a slow grind, or if it's something like a price shock—a severe price move against you. Let's see, the last time I can remember getting dinged by a real sharp price move was when I had a cotton position on. It was a good position, a good trade because the pattern was there, the probabilities were there. I was doing what I should be doing, that type of thing. The market unfortunately gapped down two and one half points the next morning and dropped down the limit immediately; and of course, it was the last day of the quarter. You sort of get a sixth sense of here we go. It's Murphy's Law. I shrug it off to that. Or I say it just figures: I can't believe this is happening again. You know, this can happen about three times a year, but five times a year is getting a little absurd! You know, you do that."

Ruth: "And if it's a slow grind, what do you do?"

Linda: "If it's a slow grind and nothing's really clicking, if the markets are sort of sloppy and maybe you're trying to force it a little bit, maybe you're overstaying your welcome because they are so sloppy, you're not getting that satisfaction of having any good trades; so you do tend to hold things a little bit longer. That would usually be when I would step back and quit trading for a day or two. I'll still sit there and monitor and watch them; but I'll just wind things down, and get very, very small, and then start fresh again. I'll do a few meaningless, harmless trades. I'll try to pick a dollar out of gold or something innocuous like that, a few cents out of sugar—and then something manages to catch back up again."

"I have found if you're in a drawdown, if you're in a difficult position, or something's not working for you, you're not going to turn it around by having positions on. You have to make sure you get out of everything. Not just the losers, because your perspective is off. You have to get your clear mind and your clear perspective and get your objectivity back. And you're only going to do that if you wipe the slate clean. That's a hard thing for me to do, but I know by now it's not going to get better until you do that. And so you just have to do that."

Other traders, primarily mechanical systems traders, find it necessary to trade consistently through a drawdown. I spoke with Michael McCarthy about this.

> Ruth: "You have said you get through your drawdowns by continuing to keep going. You get through your periods of expansion and success by staying humble."
>
> Michael: "Drawdowns excite me though."
>
> Ruth: "How do they excite you?"
>
> Michael: "Because when they happen, I know that they're short lived and that I'm going to make a lot of money afterwards. My drawdowns only last maybe a month. Look at the trades. It's only maybe three or four trades and then it's over. That doesn't tell you about the magnitude of it. I'm sure over time I'll probably have a 15% drawdown one time. The period preceding a drawdown and the period following a drawdown are good money makers."
>
> Ruth: "Good. That's your belief—that it will be over soon."
>
> Michael: "Yes, unfortunately, that's when the complaints from clients come. And I try to explain my position, and they see me as unsympathetic. And I see them as illogical and emotional. I try to keep my clients out of their own way a lot of times. The clients that trust me the most do the best. They don't open and close their accounts at the worst times or question my every move. They let me do my thing—it's in their best interests."

CONSISTENCY

Confidence breeds consistency. And consistency breeds confidence, especially if the consistency is well founded and well researched. I asked Michael McCarthy what put him in that small percentage of traders who constantly make money.

> Michael: "I'm consistent. The best trades have always come when it looks like the world is coming to an end."
>
> Ruth: "What makes you consistent?"
>
> Michael: "Being emotionally cold does it. I never worry about losing a lot of money."
>
> Ruth: "How much of this is because you trust your research?"

Michael: "All of it. You know, if you do your homework, you're confident about what you're talking about. But if you don't know what you're talking about, you're not confident because you know that it's not well researched. But there's a lot of confidence when you know your stuff inside and out."

Ruth: "You have tremendous faith in having done the homework, and that's what makes the difference for you. It's the quality of your research and your faith in it. Would you say that's true?"

Michael: "Yes."

Ruth: "What would you say to the person who because of a certain discomfort in trading finds it hard to be consistent?"

Michael: "Well, if that's the way you are, you'll have to find a situation that will put you in a good frame. Let's say you have a good trading system, but you're an emotional nightmare. Well, it means you get the system out of your hands and give it to a money manger. For some people, that's really the best thing for them to do. For other people, don't trade if you're a hopeless nerveball."

"For some people, trading can have the negative effects of gambling. And if that happens to you and you just can't get rid of that, maybe you shouldn't be trading. Maybe you should go invest in real estate. Maybe you should put your money under the mattress, and that's okay. You must be comfortable or you won't do it consistently."

"If you quit, you want to weigh the fact that, okay, now you're not playing. Now you're not making 30%. You don't feel like a man because of this or whatever. Then you compare that to the fact that you're not making yourself an emotional basketcase. Well, maybe, net/net that's better. Maybe, then, it's not. Well, okay, go out and make money and go be a nervous wreck, if that's what comes to be."

"If you're not comfortable, either your system's bad, your money manager's bad, or nothing's bad. It just doesn't fit you. If something is making you uncomfortable, you need to change it until you find something comfortable."

"You may go from dropping your trading system to another system that fits you better. Maybe it means dropping trading and giving it to a money manager. If that's not comfortable, just go out and buy T-Bills. Then you sleep. Maybe that's better."

"I have people who do better with their own business. It could be something obscure like plumbing. They make more money. They have confidence in it because they understand it. A lot of people don't trade because they don't understand it, and that's smart. You know yourself and your limitations. That's something to be proud of.

TRADING RULES OR GUIDELINES

Some traders have absolute rigid rules that they trade by. Others have a loose set of guidelines. The confident trader, knowing what works for her, will generally adhere to the rules. It's a matter of probabilities, and the probabilities need to be engineered in a consistent fashion. Michael McCarthy and Linda Raschke both approach this subject differently.

Ruth: "What are some of the trading rules you live by?"

Linda: "I don't have any hard and fast rules. I've seen some traders have their twenty commandments. I really have it down to a process, kind of go through the routines. I would say the one thing that I follow pretty much now, because I can afford to, is that I trade with less leverage than I did in the eighties. I have more money and I can afford to do that. When you're not using a whole lot of leverage, it's much harder to get in trouble."

Michael McCarthy, being a different kind of trader, approaches rules as commandments.

Ruth: "What trading rules do you live by?"

Michael: "Well, I don't want to be trite and say things like follow your system. Everybody writes that and no one listens. I would say you write down your commandments, whatever they are. Follow your system. Take all the trades. Whatever good behavior things you write down you want to have. Be very honest about it. And don't show it to anybody, because if you show it to anybody, you're probably not going to put down what you really need to do. If there's a weakness in you, put that down, that you're not supposed to do this. I would make all the commandments positive statements. I follow my system. I enjoy taking every trade. I'm happy to be on the right side of the market. All affirmations. With every trade you do, make sure you don't violate your list. It may not always be 'right' to follow the commandments—but it's **always** wrong to ignore them."

"And when you do, when you are on the wrong side of your commandment list, **immediately** get on the right side of it **no matter what**. Because it's sort of like a drug addict who has just started using again. Or like an alcoholic who has just had another drink. Don't sit there, and after a sip of beer, say, 'Oh my God, I'm an active alcoholic again.' It all just keeps on going and soon you've had a keg of beer. Don't do that. Stop drinking. Fine. You've had one sip. Don't say you're an alcoholic again and beat yourself up. Just say, 'I'm back on the wagon again. I'm looking forward, and I'm not going to look back.' I don't believe in negative motivations for long term success. You are supposed to enjoy your life along the way. That's another book, however."

"Never look back. That should be on everyone's commandment list. Don't say this trade has to be a winner because my last three were so bad. You can't put conditions on the market because of something that happened on your personal side."

"Let anything that happened in the past be there without guilt. Look forward. There's no point in ever allowing yourself to have a bad emotion. It's so unproductive. There's no benefit with bringing negativity into anything. Sometimes you can, but not with this. I think you need to keep things positive and good."

"As far as trading rules, just make sure that everything is comfortable and confident."

Ruth: "And stay on the side of your commandments, and if you slip, just go right back. I've pointed this out to smokers. If you have one cigarette, it doesn't mean you have to go back to it. If you had a tray of glasses, and you dropped a glass, it doesn't mean you have to tip over the whole tray."

Michael: "Yes, there's no advantage in continuing bad behavior."

BETTER AND BETTER

The confident trader is extremely optimistic about the future of his trading. He's realistic about the past and the present, and expectantly optimistic about the future. We've talked extensively about optimism in previous chapters because it has a lot to do with a trader being able to assume risk without undue trepidation. To trade successfully a trader needs to be optimistic about future trading. It could be a cautious optimism, but it's optimism none the less.

The confident trader turns past failures into feedback. The feedback enables her to learn from mistakes and correct them. She operates from the philosophy that mistakes are all right as long as she fixes them. She does whatever it takes to fix the mistakes, whether it's research, developing new skills, or turning to others for guidance and help. She's not afraid to ask for help. She's confident. Her self-esteem is not at stake.

I believe it's important to be psychologically upwardly mobile. A trader—or anybody for that matter—needs to be continually growing from a personal point of view.

What used to be called self help is now called personal growth. The shift in words depicts the shift in attitude. The focus is now on making something good even better, rather than on simply fixing something that's weak or damaged.

The Japanese have a philosophy in business and relationships that it is important to be continually and gradually improving. It is based on the value of constant and never ending improvement. Their word for it is kaizen. They will speak of the kaizen of the economy, the kaizen of the production line, the kaizen of the relationship. By making small improvements daily, the Japanese understand that they can create remarkable successes that most people wouldn't dare to envision.

I coach my clients to assume a value of the rock bottom importance of continually improving the quality of their lives and their trading. By seeking constant and never ending improvement, they never need to fear slipping backwards. They learn to live and trade in the space between where they are and where they want to be. In so doing they expand their comfort zone and they enlarge their view of the future. They develop a mental toughness, a resilience, and a radiantly positive expectancy. Ask them how they're doing and they might well answer, "Better and better." Because they are.

Nature has an aphorism: "Grow or die." If every single day you work on improving some aspect of your life or yourself, you never need to worry about maintaining your current life style or relationships because you are focusing on improving them. If every single day you strengthen your thought processes and your self-trust, you will brighten your future and increase your optimism.

SERENITY PRAYER

There are, of course, certain things that can't be changed or improved: snow, sleet, drawdowns, limit moves, unfavorable news, bad fills, and the general treachery of certain market days. When this happens you need to adopt the wisdom of the well-known Twelve-Step prayer.

"God, grant me the serenity to accept the things I cannot change, the courage to change the things I can, and the wisdom to know the difference."